The Byzantine Dark Ages

DEBATES IN ARCHAEOLOGY

Series editor: Richard Hodges

Against Cultural Property, John Carman
The Anthropology of Hunter Gatherers, Vicki Cummings
Archaeologies of Conflict, John Carman
Archaeology: The Conceptual Challenge, Timothy Insoll
Archaeology and International Development in Africa, Colin Breen and Daniel Rhodes
Archaeology and State Theory, Bruce Routledge
Archaeology and Text, John Moreland
Archaeology and the Pan-European Romanesque, Tadhg O'Keeffe
Beyond Celts, Germans and Scythians, Peter S. Wells
Building Colonialism, Daniel T. Rhodes
Combat Archaeology, John Schofield
Debating the Archaeological Heritage, Robin Skeates
Early European Castles, Oliver H. Creighton
Early Islamic Syria, Alan Walmsley
Gerasa and the Decapolis, David Kennedy
Image and Response in Early Europe, Peter S. Wells
Indo-Roman Trade, Roberta Tomber
Loot, Legitimacy and Ownership, Colin Renfrew
Lost Civilization, James L. Boone
The Origins of the Civilization of Angkor, Charles F. W. Higham
The Origins of the English, Catherine Hills
The Remembered Land, Jim Leary
Rethinking Wetland Archaeology, Robert Van de Noort and Aidan O'Sullivan

Roman Reflections, Klavs Randsborg
The Roman Countryside, Stephen Dyson
Shaky Ground, Elizabeth Marlowe
Shipwreck Archaeology of the Holy Land, Sean Kingsley
Social Evolution, Mark Pluciennik
State Formation in Early China, Li Liu and Xingcan Chen
Towns and Trade in the Age of Charlemagne, Richard Hodges
Vessels of Influence: China and the Birth of Porcelain in Medieval and Early Modern Japan, Nicole Coolidge Rousmaniere
Villa to Village, Riccardo Francovich and Richard Hodges

The Byzantine Dark Ages

Michael J. Decker

Bloomsbury Academic
An imprint of Bloomsbury Publishing Plc

B L O O M S B U R Y
LONDON • OXFORD • NEW YORK • NEW DELHI • SYDNEY

Bloomsbury Academic
An imprint of Bloomsbury Publishing Plc

50 Bedford Square	1385 Broadway
London	New York
WC1B 3DP	NY 10018
UK	USA

www.bloomsbury.com

BLOOMSBURY and the Diana logo are trademarks of Bloomsbury Publishing Plc

First published 2016

© Michael J. Decker, 2016

Michael J. Decker has asserted his right under the Copyright, Designs and Patents Act, 1988, to be identified as Author of this work.

All rights reserved. No part of this publication may be reproduced or transmitted in any form or by any means, electronic or mechanical, including photocopying, recording, or any information storage or retrieval system, without prior permission in writing from the publishers.

No responsibility for loss caused to any individual or organization acting on or refraining from action as a result of the material in this publication can be accepted by Bloomsbury or the author.

British Library Cataloguing-in-Publication Data
A catalogue record for this book is available from the British Library.

ISBN: HB: 978-1-47253-604-4
PB: 978-1-47253-603-7
ePDF: 978-1-47253-606-8
ePub: 978-1-47253-605-1

Library of Congress Cataloging-in-Publication Data
A catalog record for this book is available from the Library of Congress.

Series: Debates in Archaeology

Typeset by RefineCatch Limited, Bungay, Suffolk

Contents

List of Illustrations   viii

Introduction: Dark Ages   1
1   Historical Overview   7
2   Material Evidence and Meaning   43
3   Cities   81
4   The Dark Age Countryside   123
5   The Dark Age Economy   155
6   New Directions   187

Bibliography   195

Index   237

List of Illustrations

Maps

1	Byzantine Empire of the sixth century	8
2	Byzantine Empire in the eighth century	22
3	Shipwrecks of the medieval period	182

Figures

1	Constantinople	10
2	ARS form 107	45
3	Constantinopolitan Glazed Ware Pottery II	56
4	'Coptic' style copper bowl from ninth-century Amorium	75
5	Plan of Nicopolis	89
6	Butrint: City and Vrina Plain in Late Antiquity	94
7	Early medieval Butrint	97
8	Roman central Corinth (plan of Roman Corinth)	99
9	Corinth in Late Antiquity	101
10	Central Corinth c. 1100	107
11	Plan of Amorium	110
12	Plan of Amorium baths	111
13	Plan of Hierapolis	115
14	Cappadocia, tuff cones and gardens	147
15	Complete LR 13 type amphora	177
16	LR 13 type amphora from Kos	178
17	Günsenin type 1 amphora	180

Introduction: Dark Ages

Transformation vs. decline

Why write a book, especially a book on Byzantium, with 'Dark Ages' in the title? Freighted as it is with the cargo that is partly teleological and partly the product of humanist repulsion of barbarism and Christianity (whatever those are), the term 'dark ages' is both judgemental and scintillating. The Dark Ages live on in popular culture as the stereotype of the medieval world (which usually means the medieval world apart from Byzantium, which is rarely mentioned). The history of the label has been unwound by several scholars, among them Theodor Mommsen (1942), who attributed the term to the Renaissance (or late medieval) scholar Petrarch (d. 1374). And Lucie Varga was clear in tracing the history of the expression that it was pejorative and intended to contrast the 'enlightened' eras of the Roman Empire and the Renaissance humanists and their successors with the intervening centuries of barbarism. As Janet Nelson notes, the term Dark Ages is laden with materialist, religious, and humanist cargo and is thus understandably shunned and deemed inappropriate as a marker of periodization. This is especially true outside of the Anglo-Saxon academy (under whose umbrella I place UK scholars as well as many in North America, Scandinavia, Australia, and New Zealand) where the term rarely appears. In fact, recent magisterial works on the Mediterranean that tilt towards Italy and the west for the most part eschew the Dark Age label, preferring instead 'early medieval' to signify the period of roughly 500–1000, give or take a century on either side.

Periodization remains a contested arena in Byzantine studies. Does one adopt the viewpoint of the French school, with its 'proto-Byzantine' age that ends with the accession of Heraclius (610–641) or the 'early', 'middle', and 'late' conceptualizations of other schools of thought, each with their own starting and ending points? Confusingly, 'early Byzantium' is often synonymous with 'Late Antiquity'. 'Early Byzantium' usually corresponds to the period from the founding of the capital in 324, or perhaps as early as 284 with the start of the reign of Diocletian, until the Arab conquest of the 630s and 640s. A more positivistic conceptualization as common among many students of Late Antiquity would proscribe the Dark Ages and instead consider the end of Late Antiquity as occurring around 750; this may work in the Caliphate where the year marks the rise of the 'Black Banners' of the 'Abbasids and the fall of the Umayyads, but the same year found Byzantium gripped by economic recession, war, and religious controversy. The reign of Basil II (976–1022) is typically taken to mark the apogee of the medieval empire and the pivot of the 'Middle Period' of Byzantine history, which most consider as terminating with the fall of Constantinople in the Fourth Crusade in 1204, while the Late Byzantine period usually encompasses 1204–1453. There is scholarly recognition that the society of Heraclius or the Isaurian emperors (711–802) is of a markedly different order than that of Justinian I (527–565) or Basil II (976–1025). Greek supplanted Latin in the army, bureaucracy, and legal culture. Monumental building all but ceased. The empire lost the bulk of its territory to foreign powers. Urban patterns fundamentally changed over most of the Byzantine world. Most striking for historians, the output of written documents plummeted. It seemed therefore appropriate to George Ostrogorsky in his survey which remains essential reading for the training of Byzantinists the world over, that 'Dark Ages' be applied (Ostrogorsky 1969: 87) to the epoch immediately following the reign of Heraclius. While the 'Iconoclast' era has sometimes served as a proxy and perhaps more interesting label, 'Dark Ages' may still apply to Byzantine history and material culture. Archaeologists such as Timothy Gregory (1993), Florin Curta (2005), and Eric Ivison (2007) have found the Dark Ages a useful category at the same time they reject its pejorative connotations. In any case, discussion of the appropriateness of 'Dark Ages' – which I often use synonymously with early medieval – could go on for many pages; suffice it to say my defence of my title will proceed over the remainder of this work.

Whose Byzantium?

Writing a book about the material culture of Byzantium requires little justification. Although recent years have seen a galaxy of impressive works on the late antique and early medieval Mediterranean world that view the Roman world and its successors in broad context and over the *longue durée*, few have placed Byzantium at the centre of inquiry. Is Byzantium best seen as nested within a larger Mediterranean, Eurasian or world cultural matrix, or is it best viewed on its own, in isolation, as an object of 'Byzantine studies'? The question is of course too great to be answered here, but in the present work I attempt to look more distinctly within, and outward from, the territories of the early medieval empire. There are good reasons for doing so, even though the reputation and knowledge of Byzantium has arguably suffered from its being placed in a silo of its own. After all, historians who examine the medieval world through the lens of broad, comparative trends will point to elements within the Germanic-led successor kingdoms of the west – most notably Merovingian Gaul, the Ostrogothic Kingdom of Theodoric, and the Carolingian Empire – of the continuation and adaptation of Roman institutions and ideas and the sophistication of western structures (Wickham 2005). In such discussions, the role of Byzantium is either sidelined or ignored. Even in economic studies, where older scholarship afforded greater latitude for the role of the eastern Romans in European trade, the recent trend has been to view the Caliphate as the dominant presence, even on the northern shores of the Mediterranean (McCormick 2001). Perhaps, as Cameron (2014) has suggested, these approaches are partly to escape charges within the academy of scholarly Eurocentrism (odd if one considers these works still place Europe at the centre of their studies) or the parochialism that has plagued archaeology and history since nationalist thinkers gave rise to both professions as practised today. Certainly, scholars practising this pan-Mediterranean, or even pan-European (if Europe excludes the lands of Poland, Hungary, and east to the Urals) (Wickham 2005) perspective have achieved remarkable things. There is, to my knowledge, no parallel within Byzantine studies that seeks to integrate the empire within wider Eurasian history.

Where, and to whom, does Byzantium belong in these discussions? The question is increasingly relevant as the Turkish state and its citizens take an ever more active role as custodians of their cultural heritage. A new generation of Turkish-born and -trained historians and archaeologists is investigating and writing new histories and archaeologies for consumption in Turkey and the world over. This is laudable but comes with a great weight of responsibility; nationalism, religion, and other cultural forces are ever in tension with scientific endeavour and academic integrity.

Byzantium remains uniquely international – belonging to no one country, no one culture, no one discipline. Despite its millennium-long existence, written sources are scarce for many places, times, and subjects of inquiry. As Byzantine studies evolve, archaeologists will offer the most new data of any discipline and hopefully shed a great deal of light on the empire and its inhabitants. A generation of scholars who have grown up out of the shadow of the Cold War (though hardly free of the perils of nationalist tensions) need to contribute to this project as vigorously and as objectively as possible. The good news for them is, as we shall see in the pages that follow, there is a great deal of work to be done. Many new discoveries and roads to exciting and likely fundamentally altering interpretations lie ahead. To spark such debate is one of the great challenges of this book.

Indeed, if most scholars accept that the East Roman Empire was politically in retreat and psychologically demoralized after its initial battering at the hands of the armies of the Arab-led takeover of the Levant, the extent to which society was altered is a matter of crisp debate. Did the Byzantine economy contract to such an extent that money became a rarely seen thing in the provinces? Did the cities shrink so much that only a handful remained, like the remnants of burned-out stars in a once-thriving constellation? Did long-distance trade slow from a rush to a trickle as the Mediterranean was ripped from the grasp of New Rome? These are some of the topics touched upon in the chapters that follow. Of course, as with any area of inquiry our questions are conditioned as much by what we know as what we do not, and the Dark Ages puts this fact under an even harsher light.

In undertaking this study, I have endeavoured to limit my discussion to evidence and debates pertinent to the seventh through the tenth centuries, or roughly 600–900 AD. Inevitably, given the dearth of evidence which researchers of the early modern and modern period often find difficult to grasp, there are times when comparative evidence is drawn upon to plausibly fill in the gaps or raise possibilities. In the end, undertaking this work has opened my eyes to the great challenges of making firm statements about this demanding and exciting period, and I am grateful to my colleagues who have done the hard work of amassing primary data and those who have undertaken (often magisterial) syntheses. Most of the case studies I have selected come from the areas that formed the core of the state, namely Asia Minor and the Balkans, though I have drawn contemporary or near-contemporary material from neighbouring areas. Transliteration is notoriously difficult, and in this I have generally followed the conventions of the *Oxford Dictionary of Byzantium* for Greek unless the English people or places are so well-used (e.g. Heraclius rather than Heraklios or Justinian rather than Iustinianus or Iustinianos).

Finally, this series is about debates in archaeology and material culture. I have tried to flesh out the opposing and sometimes multivariate positions on specific issues. When sharp distinctions are lacking, I have endeavoured to amplify some of the problematic areas with my own analyses, which, it is hoped, will further advance the discussion.

1

Historical Overview

There is no precise date for the start of the Dark Ages of Byzantium but there is a broad consensus that institutions and state structures were under severe strain by the second half of the sixth century AD. Society and elite culture also witnessed marked metamorphoses; if the number of works of surviving authors is any indication, literacy was declining. In 529, Justinian closed the Neoplatonic *Akademia* in Athens, the last haven of polytheist philosophy and an emblem of the Hellenic tradition (Cameron 1969). The emperor Justinian ruled for nearly four decades (527–565), although his period of influence was even longer, since he was likely a major administrative force during the reign of his uncle, the illiterate former guardsman, Justin I (518–527). Together these reigns comprised nearly half a century, a span that makes Justinian one of the longest serving political figures in history.

His reign was one of paradox. Many regions experienced shock and upheaval while others enjoyed peace and peak prosperity. Costly wars with Persia (525–530; 540–562), the Nika rebellion of 532 – which left much of the grand capital in ashes – the expansion of the empire by conquest in Italy, North Africa and Spain, and the arrival of the bubonic plague in 542, all proved costly both in material and social terms. Massive earthquakes levelled Antioch in 526 (Procopius II.14.6) and struck the city again in 528 and 531. Larger regional quakes followed in central and northern Syria in 531–534 and others struck the Levant in 551, severely damaging the coastal cities. Earthquakes buffeted cities throughout Cilicia, Syria, and Mesopotamia in the years 565–570 (Sbeinati et al. 2005: 355–59) (Map 1).

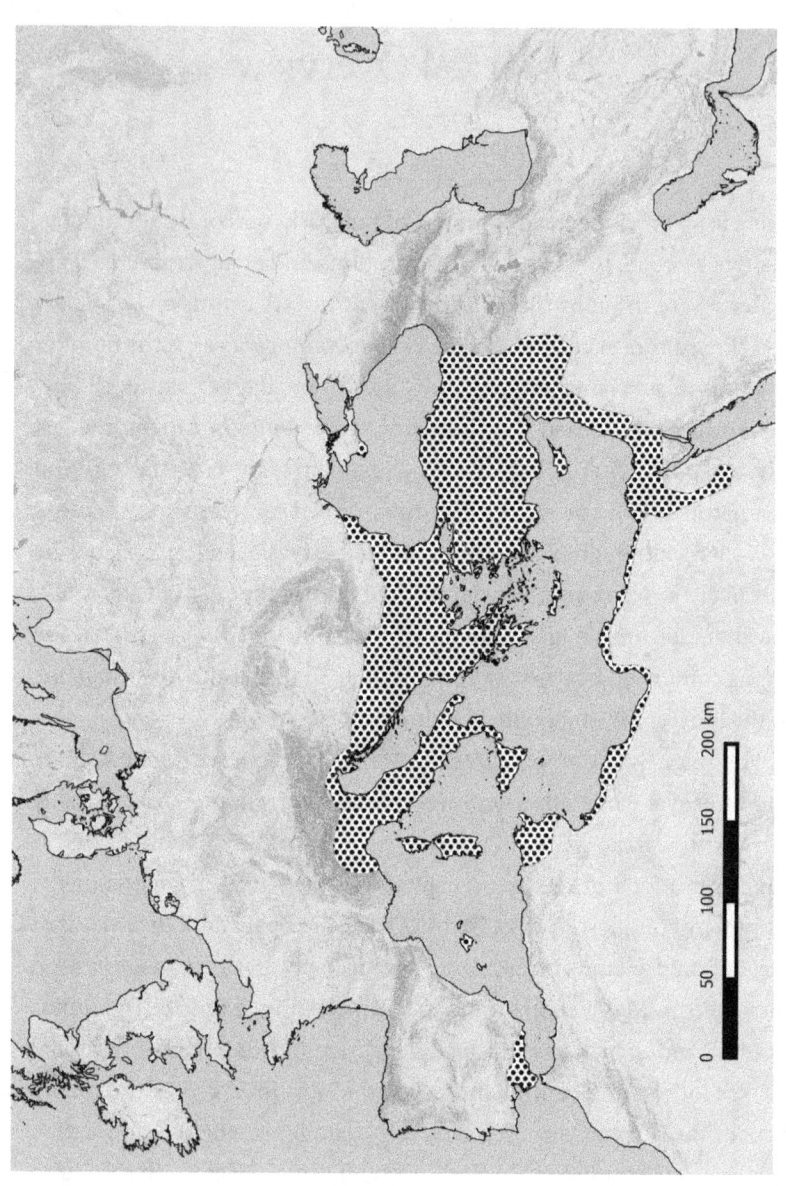

Map 1 Empire of the sixth century (Michael J. Decker).

The wars begun under Justinian lasted more than three-quarters of a century. When the year 600 arrived, the empire was in a morass. In Italy, the Lombards, Germanic invaders and former allies of the empire, occupied much of the northern and central peninsula. Ravenna, Rome, and the southern coastlands were maintained only barely. Corsica, Sardinia, and Sicily remained in imperial hands, but the remoteness of the former two islands makes the likelihood of sustained and deep Byzantine influence there unlikely. Sicily was more populous, wealthy, and connected to the fortunes of the empire and the bishops of Rome. Moreover, the island was both a productive granary and strategic hub that linked the imperial capital Constantinople (Fig. 1) with Italy and Africa and the imperial authorities clearly viewed it as a place of importance.

In the Balkans, the fall of Sirmium (modern Sremska Mitrovica in Serbia) to the Avars in 582 was emblematic of the troubles facing the empire. In facing aggressive and far-flung enemies, the maintenance of the classic lines of defence – in this case the Danube and its watershed – taxed an already weakened army and its support network. Following peace with Persia, the emperor Maurice (580–602) went on the offensive against the Avars and made considerable inroads against them. But the fall of Maurice to a military coup proved fatal to Constantinople's Balkan strategy as internal strife and the renewal of hostilities with Persia greeted the usurper, emperor Phokas (602–610). Although their views on the particulars often differed, scholars have conventionally considered it axiomatic that the end of the sixth and start of the seventh centuries witnessed the expansion of the Slavs into the southern Balkans (Charanis 1952; Setton 1952; Weinberg 1974). Now the whole subject is a contested area, in large part due to the gradual separation of scholarship from certain nationalist concerns (Curta 2010). The question of Slav settlement in the southern Balkans is hotly debated. Invasions attested in the textual sources by 'Sclavenes' and viewed as pillars of the argument for widespread Slav

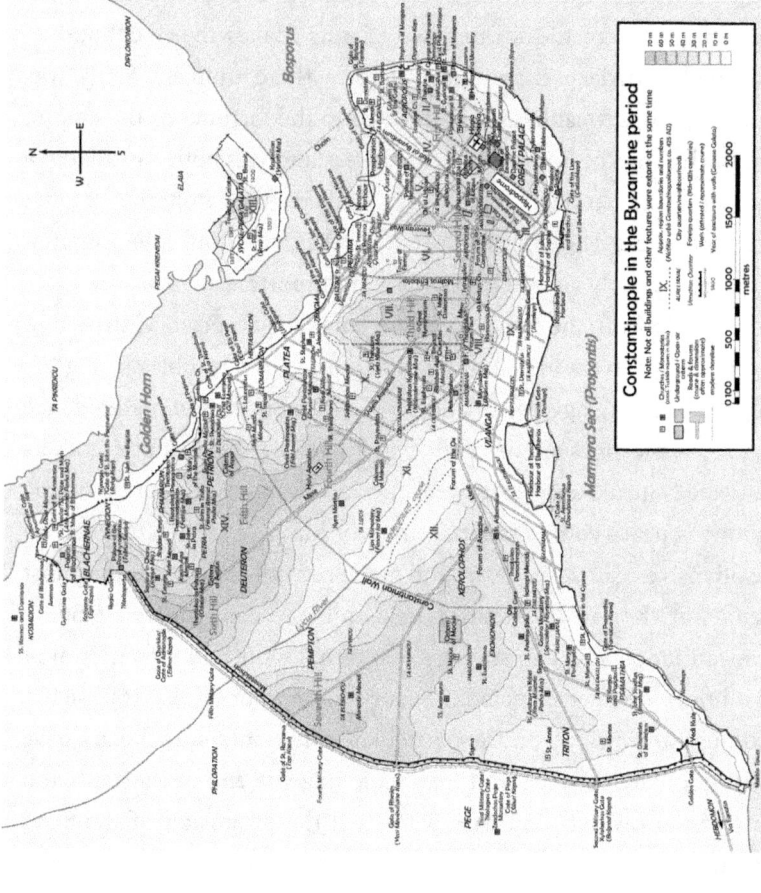

Fig. 1 Constantinople (C. Plakidas, Creative Commons).

colonization may in fact be witnesses to Avar attacks (Curta 2011: 16–17). Two general schools of thought can be described as 'invasion' versus 'infiltration', with the 'invasion' school seeming to predominate in the literature for the moment (Garvie-Lok 2010). Substantial reappraisal of the archaeological material will continue to render problematic previously accepted, simplistic models, as we seek to understand complex problems like the origins and spread of Slavic culture.

The bubonic plague and other epidemic diseases struck significant portions of the empire at fairly regular intervals. The best known of these, the 'Justinianic Plague' of 542, is but one of many; other infectious outbreaks are recorded in 557–560, 573–574, 590–591, and 597–599. At least eight epidemics struck the citizens of the empire in the seventh century and a similar number probably in the eighth century: Stathakopoulos (2004), who has collected and commented on these events, concluded his work with the year 750. Obviously these disease outbreaks have potentially serious demographic implications but scholarship on the plague remains rather stunted and tends for the most part to rehash discussion of textual sources (Sarris 2002; Little 2007), with the result that scholars rather simplistically approach these outbreaks as either deeply disruptive or unimportant moments exaggerated by contemporary authors for various reasons. Archaeological science will help us to nuance this rudimentary approach. Indeed, the reconstruction of fragmentary DNA from *Yersinia pestis* in Germany is a clear step forward in the otherwise staid debate surrounding the Justinianic Plague (Wagner et al. 2014).

Other serious environmental disturbances are also notable, but their effects are ultimately unknown. The 'dust-veil' event of 536–537, in which the rays of the sun were partially blocked and the moon appeared dim, was accompanied by stunted growth rate among plants. The dust-veil event is recorded in both texts and tree rings examined via dendroarchaeology. Horizontal cuts across the bole of trees reveals annual growth rings; when periods of climatic stress occur, little or no new growth is added. These sources apparently indicate global disruptions to plant growth, although the precise implications are unknown (Koder 1996; Stathakopoulos 2004: 265–68). Alongside the textual evidence for the atmospheric phenomenon or phenomena that caused the dust-veil event, other environmental indicators support the view that the sixth century was at the leading edge of long-term changes in climate (discussed in more detail in Chapter 4). Historians especially are uncomfortable with ascribing historical causality to events beyond human control and even some archaeologists are hesitant when assessing the role of environment in their area of study. Scholars seem to view endeavours to integrate climate and other environmental studies as leading to determinist conclusions in which human agency is rewritten and anthropogenic-centred histories and archaeologies morph into environmentally focused discourses. Studies like those of Jared Diamond (1997, 2005), who is neither an archaeologist nor a historian but rather a trained ornithologist and bioscientist who has expertise across disciplines, is emblematic both of the sorts of polymath (less charitably called generalists) more likely to take on such macroscopic views.

In Byzantine studies, most neo-determinists are popular writers like Keys (1999), whose work is carefully researched but provocative, and William Rosen (2007), whose well-written text follows many of the core tenets of Keys' earlier work. Some Byzantinists have been open to debating the roles of these episodes, but for reasons considered above, natural phenomena are rarely considered as decisive in the historical process. Archaeologists, on the other hand, seem generally more open to reckoning the influence of natural phenomena on human affairs (Hirschfeld 2004), but a few historians such as McCormick (2003, 2012; McCormick et al. 2007) have also attempted to integrate these elements into their narratives or engaged seriously with them.

There is no single study that examines in holistic fashion the different subsets of environmental, social, economic, and political factors that expressed themselves in the life of the empire. Such a work has yet to appear due to the specialization required to attain a deep understanding of any one of these areas. But, traditionally, most scholars have viewed each one of these spaces as having endured significant turbulence in the sixth to tenth centuries. Most talked about, and in many ways the easiest to access, is political conflict, in which late antique and early medieval authors took considerable interest as political history dominated classical historical production. The authors of our texts learned and were shaped by these classical exemplars as well as the Bible and the writings of the church fathers. Late antique and early medieval historians were themselves elites whose class was frequently at the centre of government maelstroms and it was thus doubly natural for them to take a great deal of interest in high-level politics. However, the influence of wars and other political tumult on daily life for the majority of the inhabitants of the empire remains hazy. Archaeologists must still fight the tendency to attribute nearly every charred layer on every excavated site to the nefarious handiwork of barbarians, and understandably so. The empire warred incessantly throughout the sixth century and even more feverishly in the seventh; texts are replete with notices of violent encounters between the empire and aliens. The seventh century opened with the rebellion of the North African exarch Heraclius the Elder (d. 610), whose sons Heraclius the Younger and Niketas wreaked havoc in the Mediterranean and Egypt and hamstrung the war effort of the emperor Phokas (602–610). When, in 610, the younger Heraclius swept to power in the wake of the civil war, the empire was foundering militarily; his reign (610–641) proved pivotal. In 613 near Antioch, the new emperor suffered a defeat harsh enough to keep him out of the field in the east for almost a decade. In that time, the Persians under the Sasanian dynasty occupied the whole of the Roman east, including the most populous and richest cities: Edessa, Antioch, Damascus, Jerusalem, Caesarea, and Alexandria, all fell to the enemy. One of the great questions for Byzantine scholars is the sway of this long phase of warfare on life in the cities and countryside; for the first time since the third century, the Near East was under Persian control. To scholars like Tchalenko (1953–1958) and Foss (1977), the Persian War and occupation was a turning point in the history of the eastern lands of the empire. Others, such as Avni (2010, 2014), have questioned the validity of this interpretation. We will discuss in Chapter 3 the material evidence pertinent to the fate of cities and problems of the scholarly approaches to urban change.

Only in 622 did Heraclius manage to rebuild the army and take the offensive. The reliance of the emperor on an advance of church silver, confiscations, and forced loans demonstrates how desperate were the straits of the empire in these difficult years (Kaegi 2010). Fiscal crisis is indicated by a decrease in bullion stocks and instruments to remedy massive shortages caused by the loss of the eastern provinces. However, the surge of currency issued under Heraclius, undoubtedly the result of heavy military spending, meant that the empire was heavily monetized. The issue of the silver hexagram coin weighing 6 *grammata* is telling. The hexagram often featured on its obverse a cross potent on a globe above three steps with the legend 'God help the Romans'. Saturated with imperial and Christian symbolism and pregnant with angst, the new silver coin encapsulates difficult years for the emperor. The new currency is a loud proclamation of a world under the rule of God and an overt attempted act of propitiation to the divinity. It is also a clear example of the potential of material objects to offer a deeper understanding of a specific moment in history. With imperial finances shored up in large part by drastic pay cuts and the introduction of silver coins for salaries (Treadgold 1997:

290), Heraclius was able to recruit new troops to replace his losses as well as enter into an expensive but ultimately decisive alliance with the Western Turk khaganate (Howard-Johnston 1999). In 626 the defenders of Constantinople successfully foiled Persian attempts to cross the Bosphorus and join an Avar–Slav force outside the city walls. The Avars and Persians were forced to retire as Heraclius campaigned deep into the Sasanian Empire. By 628 a series of Roman victories shook the Sasanian Empire root and branch; the venerable enemy of Byzantium collapsed into civil war. The Sasanian Empire would die within two decades, cut asunder by the sword of the armies of nascent Islam.

The 'Byzantine' period sometimes begins with the accession of Heraclius, although others, such as Treadgold (1997) believe the reign of Diocletian (284–305), in which the empire was divided into territorial halves governed by co-emperors, marks a watershed from which a new historical turn can be detected. The reign of Heraclius certainly marked a defining moment. Greek replaced Latin as the administrative language. The pace of the production of literary and historical texts went over a cliff – not a single contemporary witness of the Arab invasions survives in Greek from within the empire. Indeed, there is no known historian who wrote a full narrative account of events of the second half of the seventh century (Treadgold 2013). As astounding as was Roman success against Persia after the disastrous start of the reign, the stupendous failure of Heraclius against the armies of the Prophet's successors is equally perplexing.

Since the professionalization of historical inquiry in the nineteenth century, scholars have debated the cause of the decline of Roman power in the east. Many have decided in favour of exhaustion on the part of the two great states of late antique southwest Asia, as Byzantium and Persia reeled under repeated blows dealt across decades of vicious warfare (Tchalenko 1953–1958; Foss 1977). Others (Kennedy 1985, 2007; Liebeschuetz and Kennedy 1988; Liebeschuetz 2001) have looked to earlier and varied root causes for the decline that contributed to the breakdown of imperial authority and local governance before a previously disparate and politically fractured group of Arab tribesmen. Among the losses were the great patriarchal sees of Alexandria, Antioch, and Jerusalem, jewels in the crown of the empire whose severance was unimaginable, especially after their recent delivery from the hands of the heathen Persians. In material terms, the fall of Alexandria was like losing a right arm, for that city was the greatest centre of learning in the Mediterranean and no mere economic hub, but also the spiritual head of Egypt, the most populous region in the empire. The loss of Egypt was incalculable – even if the population after the Justinianic Plague is reckoned at the low figure of three million estimated by Kaegi (1998: 34) as opposed to the nearly five million of Sarris (2006: 10). As much as a quarter of the population of the entire Greek East lived along the banks of the Nile whose floodplains were the major source of surplus grain that fed most of the imperial court, bureaucracy, and army. Syria was likewise thickly populated and sustained several large, prosperous cities. Although probably diminished in the turmoil of the mid-sixth century and later, some of these settlements remained places of some import. The assumption that many elites fled the great cities amidst the pandemonium of the Persian and Arab invasions is far from certain and requires vigorous research. Nonetheless, the massive loss of manpower, skilled workers, and bureaucrats along with food and tax revenues of the heavily urbanized east could not be replaced. Instead, the empire shrank back to its borders during the bleak years of the Persian War, with the Taurus Mountains marking the limits of a porous frontier zone with a broad swathe of territory contested between Constantinople and the caliphates in Damascus, Samarra, and Baghdad.

In the Balkans, the situation appears equally bleak. Settlement numbers and area seem to have contracted in many regions by the second half of the seventh century at the latest (Bintliff 2013), and entire regions were completely depopulated (Curta 2013b). The evidence of coin hoards indicates a decline in military and other economic activity: following the presumed withdrawal of the army from the southern Balkans to fight in the east by the second decade of the seventh century at the latest, there is a striking cessation in coin hoard finds. A sharp decline in pottery imports, the apparent termination of major building projects, and the abandonment of many known sixth-century cemeteries by the first quarter of the seventh century are telling indicators of serious demographic and economic recession (Curta 2011: 62–65). Whereas for Asia Minor the focus of scholars has been on the continuity or fracture of public life expressed via the material remains of cities, the concentration in the Balkans has been rather on the 'ethnicity' of people. The most rancorous part of the narrative again has nationalist roots – the question of Slav settlement within the region. In large part due to our basic need for narrative, scholarly discourse has fallen prey to a need to interpret evidence in light of national stories. Another reason for the concern of 'peoples' or 'tribes' and the like is that scholarship remains dominated by a culture-historical approach in which written documents are privileged over archaeological evidence, and this is nowhere more true than of the eastern 'European Everyman', the Slavs (Curta 2009). The nature of the Slavs and their role in the shaping of the early medieval social, cultural, and political landscape of the peninsula naturally remains especially contentious in countries where modern Slavic languages are spoken. Given the role of historical discourse within the performance of modern ethnicity, this is not a great surprise. The Greeks, on the other hand, would see things rather differently and through a lens no less coloured by nationalism; according to traditional thinking of some in the Greek academy, the alien Slavs washed against the breakwaters of Hellenism but did not even scarify its façade.

Although the early encounters between Romans and Muslims have been understood as an unbroken string of triumph for the 'Community of Believers' of proto-Islam (Donner 2012), the empire was not entirely impotent. Constans II (641–668) in particular aimed to project power along the borderlands of the empire and in his ancestral Armenia. He personally led an expedition there in 652, but the Byzantines could not hold in the east under the determined onslaught of the forces of the dogged governor of Syria, Mu'awiya b. Abi Sufyan (661–680). In 657 Constans II took advantage of the First Fitna (civil war) of 656–661 and again campaigned along the eastern marchlands in an attempted show of force along the contested border; this foray re-established Byzantine overlordship in Armenia (Treadgold 1997: 314). The empire continued to bleed, however, with Anatolia and Africa suffering nearly annual incursions by Muslim raiders. In Byzantine Italy, the northern imperial enclave of the Exarchate of Ravenna strained under pressure from a tribal confederation led by the Germanic Lombards who had settled in Italy; the city finally fell to them in 751.

With Roman power flagging throughout the Mediterranean, the caliphate expansive, and the movements of armies and refugees commonplace, it is small wonder that scholars have taken a particularly dim view of the second half of the seventh century. In 663 Constans landed in southern Italy and then tried to brace resistance in the Byzantine west against the encroaching caliphal forces. The emperor took up residence in Syracuse on Sicily, where he was rumoured to be contemplating establishing the imperial capital. The emperor's stay proved fatal: in 668 as Constans bathed, an attendant bashed in his skull. Constans' son Constantine IV (668–685) faced two major rebellions simultaneously as well as Mu'awiya's invasion in support of one of them. Mu'awiya ordered a series of expeditions into Anatolia and his troops blockaded the capital in an effort to conquer the empire. The written sources tell us of many cities sacked and occupied by the Arabs on their way to the capital, including the important centres of Amorium, Chalcedon, and Cyzicus (Treadgold 1997: 371–72). It was probably around the time of Constans that the system of themes was developed. Each theme was a super-province that hosted one of the old mobile field-army groups prior to the onslaught of the Arabs. Soldiers who survived the early confrontations with the Arabs were enrolled in these new units and settled throughout the territories. The regions in which these soldiers were billeted assumed the name of the army corps that they hosted. Some scholars believe that, in order to find the land and means to support these units, former state lands were at least partially distributed to the troops (Treadgold 1983; Hendy 1985), although others disagree (Haldon 1993).

Following the evacuation of the Balkans by Roman troops around 620, it is likely that the Byzantine hold on northern Greece was tenuous. While the Arabs advanced in the east, the second city of the empire, Thessaloniki, endured a terrifying siege at the hands of hostile Slavs but was aided by allied Slavic groups. From the *Miracles of St. Demetrios*, our source for these events, Macedonia seems to have been home to both hostile Slavic elements and those in the service of the empire (Lemerle 1979–1981; Curta 2011: 108–9). The state's grip on the south of Greece and that imperial authority was largely restricted to the coastlands and administrative centres, especially Corinth and Athens. Both of these had apparently been reduced in size since the fourth or fifth centuries, although the available evidence does not allow us to draw firm conclusions (see below Chapter 3). In any case, sometime in the seventh century most of the Peloponnese lay beyond the authority of Constantinople, whatever the identity of its inhabitants. By the end of the century, the newly established Bulgar polity cast a shadow over the northern Balkans and threatened imperial interests there.

Politically, the situation in Asia Minor improved towards the end of the reign of Constantine IV (668–685): internal dissension forced the caliphate to pay tribute to the empire and allowed Constantinople to recover somewhat. The precarious situation of the caliph 'Abd al-Malik (685–705), whose authority barely exceeded the boundaries of Syria due to insurrections throughout the Muslim empire, emboldened Justinian II (685–695, 705–711). The empire rode, Mazeppa-like, on the back of the unbridled ambitions of an emperor who sought to reclaim his place as dominant ruler in the Mediterranean. Although his reign started well, the tenure of Justinian II was marked by onerous tax burdens in support of his overweening military aspirations. In the 690s the caliphate resumed the offensive in the wake of the disastrous showing by the Byzantines at the battle of Sebastopolis, and soon after the leaders of a palace coup deposed and mutilated Justinian. The anarchy and paralysis that followed the overthrow of the emperor accelerated the loss of territory in Africa, the Caucasus, and Cilicia. The poor performance of his lacklustre successors allowed the indefatigable Justinian II a second accession to the throne in 705 with the assistance of the Khazar Khanate. The unpopular emperor could not maintain his position, however, and was overthrown and executed in 711; amidst the anarchy that followed Justinian's demise, the caliphate solidified its rule in Cilicia and opened the route to Constantinople. The alarming Muslim advance included the capture of Sardis and Pergamum. By 717 the armies of the caliph had readied the death blow to the empire and launched their historic siege of Constantinople. The assault collapsed in the face of determined Byzantine resistance led by the usurper Leo III (717–741). Although he survived the massive challenge from the caliphate, a decade later Leo faced rebellion in the naval themes and an Arab invasion that sacked Gangra in Paphlagonia (modern Çankırı 140 km north of Ankara) and besieged Nicaea, just 90 km south of Constantinople. The Iconoclast version of Christianity embraced by Leo III, which rejected religious figural imagery, deepened divisions in an already demoralized society. While the house that Leo established, the so-called Isaurian dynasty, held the line in Anatolia, it fared less well abroad and internal resistance effervesced.

The reign of Constantine V (741–775) opened with bitter civil war and, a decade later in 751, the Exarchate of Ravenna fell to the Lombards. The borders of the empire had contracted to nothing more than strips of land around settlements that previously lay at the heart of a thriving civilization (Map 2). The loss of Byzantium's outpost in northern Italy had fateful consequences for imperial influence on the European stage: in a few short decades, the Carolingian Franks established themselves on the shores of the Adriatic and the settlements of the Venetian lagoon, then vassals of Constantinople, began a slow crawl from the marshes to Mediterranean dominance. In Anatolia, local Byzantine commanders battled annual Arab raids and refined guerrilla tactics by which they survived the worst. By the mid eighth century, Muslim invasions were merely deleterious instead of critically threatening. Victories over the Bulgars in the 760s and the settlement of refugees fleeing the Bulgar khanate helped the fortunes of the empire in ways that we can only guess. Against these successes can be marked Arab raids and devastation of cities in Pisidia in central Anatolia in the 770s. By the 780s, however, imperial troops advanced in the east as the recently established 'Abbasid dynasty had yet to consolidate its hold over its territories.

The advent of the ninth century witnessed the end of the Isaurian dynasty – its last member, the Machiavellian Irene, was overthrown in a palace coup in 802. Her replacement was Nicephorus I, the *logothete* (head of the treasury), who implemented several critical reforms that made him deeply unpopular and caused few to mourn his death in an ambush by the Bulgar khan Krum in 811. Also mortally wounded in the campaign was Nicephorus' son and heir, Stauracius (d. 812). The Bulgar crisis led to the deposition of the indolent emperor Michael I (811–813) by one of his commanders, who assumed the throne as Leo V (813–820). Leo followed his usurpation with a victory over the

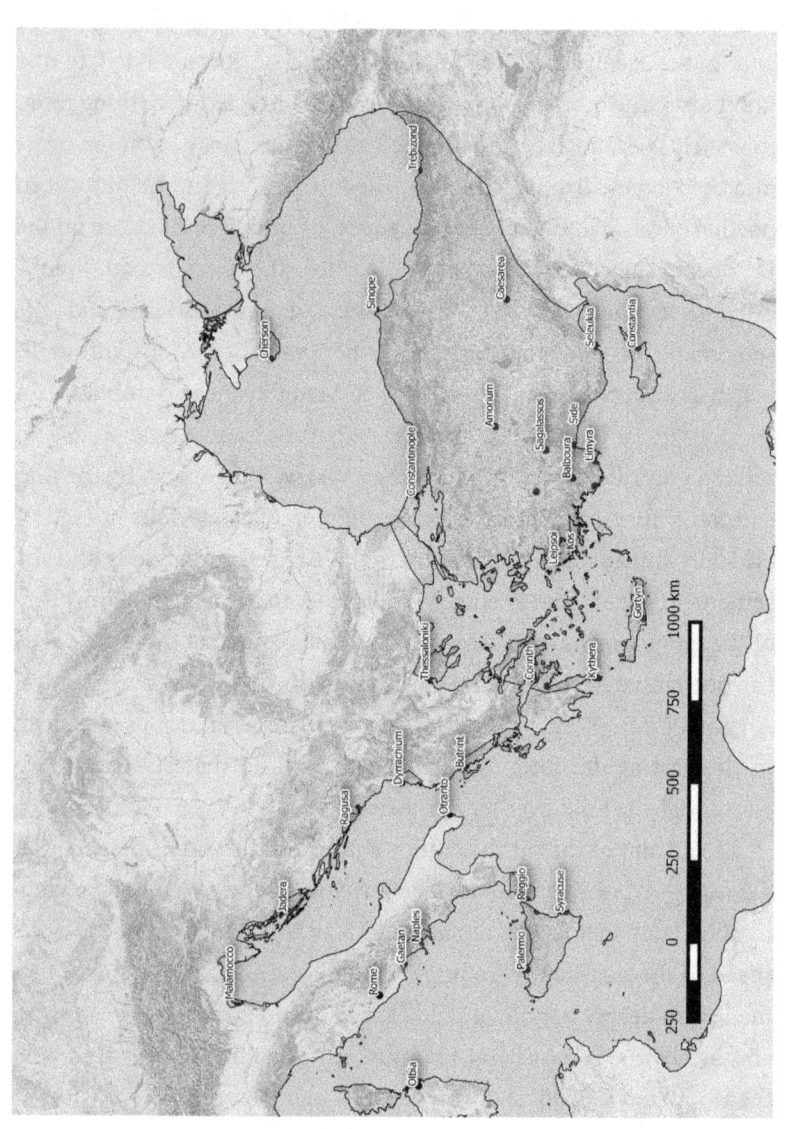

Map 2 Empire in the eighth century (Michael J. Decker).

Bulgars near Mesembria (modern Nesebar in Bulgaria) that settled the Bulgar question for decades. For those interested in the nature of life in the Dark Ages, the roller coaster political fortune of the empire is revealing. For the citizens of the empire there was little respite from invasion – even those who did not face invasion directly shouldered the omnipresent burden of the tax collector and military recruiter whose duties were to feed the coffers and army respectively. We have to be cautious: the political events recorded in sources written by elites, whose interest lay in the affairs of other elites, are perhaps not the best reflections of conditions in the empire as a whole. Nonetheless, the lack of textual sources is in many ways a great impediment to us, particularly in the realms of economic and social matters. With almost no contemporary histories, we rely on a handful of saints' lives, inscriptions, and documents such as ecclesiastical texts. The canons of the Council in Trullo (Quinisext Council) held in Constantinople in 692, for example, offer evidence of widespread disruptions: barbarian attack had forced many bishops to flee their sees and generally eroded the authority of the church (Di Berardino 2006). Given the dearth of written sources, archaeological evidence must replace text in the canon of sources regarding many questions of interest to students of Byzantium. In many instances, the data collected from survey and excavation are the only sources of information we have for a great many places in the empire from the seventh to ninth centuries. Fortunately, archaeologists will continue to provide new data (though not all of equal quality, certainly) on which we can enlarge the scope and scale of our inquiries.

Michael, known to history as Michael II (820–829), murdered his friend and benefactor Leo V at Christmas Mass in 820. Although he established the Amorian dynasty, Michael II was himself a ruler of ordinary abilities. After surviving a civil war, the emperor proved unable to stop a group of Muslim freebooters from seizing Crete and establishing an emirate there. The conquest of Crete was a grave blow to imperial prestige and the island's size and position in the centre of the Aegean allowed Muslim raiders to threaten the heart of the empire and harass shipping throughout the east. Sicily, also invaded, was successfully defended at the end of Michael's reign. Theophilus (829–842), Michael's son and successor, is widely considered the luminary of the Amorian dynasty. Although Theophilus suffered reverses in Sicily and in Asia Minor, his fine gold coinage and building programmes attest a turn in the economic fortunes of the state. Theophilus' son Michael III (842–867), the last of the Amorians, appears to have ruled over an empire that had regained its footing as a major power in Eastern Europe, while the battle of Lalakaon in 863, a Byzantine victory, symbolized the end of the sustained Arab threat to the Byzantine heartland of Anatolia. Over the next century and a quarter, Byzantine forces steadily extended the eastern boundaries of the empire. Importantly, it is not just the military sphere on which scholars base their conclusions about the improvement in the vital signs of the empire but rather an increase in literary production, the coin supply, and an apparent overall rise in the population and economic activity that appears to have far exceeded eighth-century levels (Treadgold 1997).

Just as there is no consensus on the precise moment that announces the Dark Ages, so agreeing on where to mark its end is also predictably difficult. In this book, I will focus on the years 600–900, a chronological limit to which the evidence does not allow complete adherence: occasionally material on either side of these boundaries must be discussed, either to provide context or comparative perspective. As for the selection of the start date, there is little enough to be said against it. At the start of the seventh century, Byzantium embarked on a turbulent century of political, social, and economic upheaval. As noted below, the material markers of the changes in society, while incompletely known and understood, are dramatic. The end date is a bit more difficult to pin down. The year 900 makes a convenient cut-off point for a study whose core foci are debates within the seventh to ninth centuries. Other good terminal dates could also be suggested, notably the start of the Macedonian dynasty founded by the regicide Basil I in 867; the Macedonians would dominate the middle centuries of Byzantium and oversee the peak of its territorial expansion. Declaring an end to the 'Dark Ages' with the accession of Basil is thus not unreasonable, but there are indicators that demographic and economic activities were intensifying already in prior decades. Assigning an end to a study of the Dark Ages at mid-century would certainly be sensible but the nature of the evidence, much of which is only loosely dated, is better suited to rounding things off at the turn of the tenth century.

The growth of the literate population of the empire during the tenth century is reflected in the higher standard of learning and renewed interest in classical texts and classicizing forms of expression (Treadgold 2013). The end of Iconoclasm and the stabilization of the Islamic and Bulgarian frontiers brought fresh air to the sails of a ship of state so often adrift. This largely prosperous course continued from Basil I (867–886) until 1071.

The Macedonian dynasty (867–1056) coincided with the peak political and economic power of Byzantium. Over its two centuries, societal transformations that had been evolving since the end of late antiquity finally coalesced into stable forms. Eleventh-century Byzantine culture looked quite different from the late antique world of the contemporaries of Heraclius and, in so far as we can discern, considerably unlike the intellectual and tangible environment of the Dark Ages. The trend during the tenth century appears one of expansion both inwardly, in the mental space of Byzantine elites, in writing, and self-expression, but also outwardly, with the cultural colonization of the Balkans and Russia via diplomacy, missionizing, trade, and military conquest in the east. The growth of Byzantium's population, economy, learning, and political influence coincided with developments in many western regions, namely the swathe of central Europe ruled by the Ottonian dynasty. By the ninth century, the anchor points of European political supremacy were firmly in the north and west astride new exchange networks hardwired into these rising kingdoms whose descendants would dominate European history for centuries to come (Hodges and Whitehouse 1983; McCormick 2001). Environmental shifts also help to etch a sensible chronological boundary. Western Europe of the tenth century experienced a warming trend. Greenland had been warming since 900, and by mid century most of Europe's population experienced the moderating temperatures of the so-called Medieval Warm Period (Fagan 2008). We still know relatively little about the extent to which Byzantium was affected by these general climate trends.

Thus far we have only skirted the fringes of the problem of evidence, which is touched upon in Chapter 2. Since aspects of archaeological evidence will also be examined throughout other chapters, I will forego a lengthy discussion of these for the moment and restrict myself rather to issues of the written sources. Textual scarcity is apparent for the period AD 600–900. While the sixth century is, by ancient standards, well known, thanks to the classicizing historians Procopius of Caesarea, Agathias, Menander Protector, and Theophylact Simocatta, to say nothing of annalistic and chronicle sources like John of Antioch, the seventh century is barren by comparison. The latter century produced no historical narrative that covered the crucial turn of those years. Even if he is 'bombastic, chronologically unsound and neglectful of western events' (Baldwin 1991), Theophylact is nonetheless to be preferred to the alternative: the incomplete scraps of his successor chroniclers with which we are left after Theophylact broke off his history with the end of the reign of Maurice. It is unfortunate that Theophylact never acted on apparent plans to write his history chronicling the reign of Phokas (Whitby and Whitby 1986).

Those historical works that follow Theophylact include the so-called Paschal Chronicle and the presumed history of Trajan the Patrician (Treadgold 2013: 10), now lost, but which apparently continued the Paschal Chronicle down to the coronation of Constantine V, son of Leo III, in 720 (Treadgold 2013: 15). A subsequent unknown author, suspected to be the patriarch Tarasius, recorded events down through 750. The principal surviving compiler of the Dark Ages, Theophanes the Confessor (d. 817–818), relied heavily on these sources as well as that of the patriarch Nicephorus, whose defective chronicle, which began with the reign of Phokas in 602 and ended with the wedding of Leo IV and Irene in 769, relied on the anonymous continuator of Trajan the Patrician (Treagold 2013: 30).

Although his work remains the major source for the era in question, Theophanes' (d. 817) *Chronicle* is not a primary source (Mango and Scott 1997); he apparently finished a work largely the result of the efforts of George Syncellus (d. *c*. 813), who covered events from *c*. 781 to 813. For these, and much earlier information as well, George depended on the Syriac historian Theophilus of Edessa (Hoyland 2011; Treadgold 2013: 42–45). As inadequate as Theophanes is as a source, he is to be preferred to his successors. As Treadgold (2013: 78) notes: 'Today only one mediocre formal history and two minor chronicles survive complete from the hundred-odd years after 820'; this extreme dearth hampers our understanding of the decades with which our study ends. Although there has been no exhaustive attempt to survey the Latin, Arabic, Syriac, Armenian, Georgian or other foreign sources to help flesh out our lean understanding of the circumstances of the Dark Ages, these would be unlikely to radically expand our knowledge. By far the richest trove of written sources, the body of Arabic histories and literary texts (El-Cheikh 2004), has not to date yielded changes in the basic accepted facts of Byzantine history. The scarcity of texts, especially good narrative histories, is alone sufficient to consider these centuries the 'Dark Ages' in the most neutral possible sense; the seventh to ninth centuries are mostly impervious to the attention of the scholars who make use of these documents.

Research on Dark Age Byzantium

Scholarly interest in the Byzantine Dark Ages has been limited. Unlike the western Mediterranean and Northern Europe, where the leading-edge work of Henri Pirenne (1937), although appearing posthumously, had a considerable impact on historical inquiry, especially in economic history but particularly in archaeology, Byzantium has long suffered from a general lack of economic interest among historians. Bury's *Cambridge Medieval History* (1913), covering the fall of the Levant and the expansion of Islam to the West, contains no serious discussion of trade or economy – in keeping with the interests of the day, it is strictly political narrative. In 1917, the German economist and reformer Lujo Brentano wrote an economic history of the empire focusing on political economy; despite its relatively rapid translation into Russian (Brentano and Plotnikov 1924), it did not have wide influence. While Macri (1925) wrote an economic history of the Macedonian period – despite its brevity the first monograph to focus intensively on the economic history of one period of Byzantium – he relied on textual data for his analysis. It is telling that the eminent Swiss-born Austrian historian Ernst Stein found as the outlet for his own early economic study of Byzantium a short-lived journal whose focus was Ottoman history (Stein 1923–1925). Not much later the Russian-born Yugoslav Byzantinist George Ostrogorsky (1929) published a piece that signalled his interest in the Byzantine economy and material culture from a historian's perspective. The interest of Ostrogorsky endured; in many ways, he is the first historian to foreground economic history into the wider narrative of Byzantine history.

Despite these initial forays, examinations of financial and material matters, students of Byzantium only sporadically took up the challenge. Given the obsessions of the day – authoritarianism and Marxist or fascist command economies – it is hardly surprising that nearly all of the above-mentioned studies deal with political economy and view the Byzantine state throughout its existence as a closed, centrally administered economy. Such an economic system could be read as backwards or as a primitive model for modern states to improve upon, but the fundamental authoritarian bent and lack of commercial culture in Byzantium was not really questioned.

Since economic expressions of materiality are often deemed the most accessible and the Dark Ages have traditionally been thought to represent a nadir of the European economy, an examination of production, consumption, and trade remains important today. Study of the Byzantine economy, like most scholarship on the empire, lagged behind that on the western medieval world. In a major work of leading British Byzantinist Norman Baynes, Andréadès (1948) penned the chapter on economic life, a flawed effort that still considered Gibbon's *Decline and Fall of the Roman Empire* (1776) an authoritative secondary source. Andréadès (1924) had earlier argued with Stein over the scale of the Byzantine economy, as expressed in the imperial budget, and was thus one of the only Anglophone scholars to take an interest in the subject.

The first volume of the first edition of *The Cambridge Economic History: The agrarian life of the Middle Ages* appeared during the epochal upheaval of the Second World War (Clapham and Power 1941). In this seminal work, Ostrogorsky mapped out his vision of the Dark Age (a term that he did not employ) landscape of the empire, with the dominant motifs being the sweeping administrative reforms of Heraclius, the collapse of the wealthy landowner in the chaos of the seventh century, an infusion of immigrant labour, and the see-saw struggle between the crown and the grasping rich over the land and the bodies that worked it (Ostrogorsky 1941). Although many of Ostrogorsky's major points are in need of modification or thorough revision, little has occurred to date (Lemerle 1979; Kaplan 1992). Bold and compelling as it was in its day, Ostrogorsky's work, like that of his fellow contributors, is emblematic of the *Zeitgeist* of the 1930s and 1940s. One subsection in the book is entitled 'German land-hunger: German assaults on the Empire' (Koebner 1941: 19), forcing one to wonder if the chapter dealt with AD 41 or 1941.

Telling, too, is that the historian selected to write the chapter of the updated *Cambridge Economic History* in 1952 was Steven Runciman (1952), the polymath and doyen of British Byzantinists, but hardly an economic historian as we would recognize it today, or an archaeologist. Runciman, far from engaging critically with the 'Pirenne Thesis', as it had become known, accepted it without analysis: 'But transport along the Mediterranean now tended to be by land, along the North African coast, as the Arabs did not control the sea' sums up the trade and transport situation after the fall of the Roman East to the armies of proto-Islam, after a mere paragraph of discussion (Runciman 1952).

Unsurprisingly, nearly all of these early studies rely almost exclusively on textual sources. The archaeology of the Roman East was virtually non-existent. While the American discoveries of Byzantine materials at Corinth found some audience (Kourelis 2007), the more striking excavations of the Great Palace of the emperors in Constantinople (Istanbul), first by the French (1921–1925) and then the Walker Trust and the University of St. Andrews (Talbot Rice 1947–1958; Bardill 1999), did not catapult Byzantium into the mainstream of scholarship or public perception. Pottery studies and the close dating of features were little known arts and seldom, if ever, applied in the archaeology of Byzantium, or anywhere else for that matter. The continued occupation and massive post Second World War expansion of Istanbul has limited excavation. Embarrassingly, we continue to be utterly dependent on a handful of texts and published studies from which to form our impression of one of the most important cities in world history.

It is probably not a drastic overstatement to say that for decades art and architecture were the only two subjects in which Byzantine archaeologists took much interest. Dogged by its poor reputation and the cultural bias of western academics, Byzantine archaeology suffered a dimmer fate than its history. There was no Byzantine archaeological pioneer of the stature of A.A. Vasiliev or Georg Ostrogorsky of the world of the historians. Historians, fortunately, can work without destroying their data – the same cannot be said for archaeologists. Archaeology, growing as it did out of the antiquarian and romantic movements of the eighteenth and nineteenth centuries, was one of the last realms of inquiry to be professionalized. The work was (and is) dirty and often tedious. Many archaeologists no doubt desired the need to make spectacular, attention-grabbing finds in the mode of Schliemann at Troy, rather than undertake a painstaking scientific work. Worse, many 'archaeologists' were nothing more than amateur treasure hunters like Luigi Palma di Cesnola, sometime US consul and avid looter (Cesnola 1877). In addition to these difficulties, which gave 'professional' archaeology a slow start in Europe, was the worm of nationalism that further rotted the apple.

Archaeology in the nineteenth century was mostly about the great historic civilizations prized within the Enlightenment and Romantic world, especially Greece, Rome and, after the Napoleonic expedition to the Nile, ancient Egypt. There was no room at the table of chauvinist scholars for a decadent civilization: Byzantium was medieval and Christian. In the eyes of humanist scholars, the hybridity of Byzantium repulsed; it was too familiar to exoticize and too 'Oriental' to deem 'western'. It did not help matters that most of the former territory of the empire lay under the control of one of the oldest and most odious political rivals to European cultural hegemony: the despised Ottoman Turks.

Archaeologists like Schliemann (1874, 1884) at Troy and Benndorf at Ephesus (Benndorf 1898) met the standards and interests of their day; digs likes these and the first years of American work at Corinth, the Austrian and the early University of Pennsylvania Museum work at Gordion (Sams 1994) were not scientific excavations, although they would become more so as they evolved. Projects like these were hardly interested in medieval material. Context and environment, the stuff of daily life, were not priorities. Their participants wore their interests on their sleeves and their interests lay in the classical world or, more broadly, the past as detailed in classical literature and the Bible. Byzantium was 'post-interesting' (the way in which more than one archaeologist in the Middle East have described the period to me). As the magnificent public centres of Ephesus came to light, the overburden of medieval and modern layers were simply dug through, only rarely mentioned, and almost always left unrecorded. This scene was repeated throughout all of the major classical cities of the east put under the spade. It has begun to change only quite recently, meaning a great deal has been lost. This is not to decry the methods or their practitioners, which would be akin to asking a medieval king to consider building an airfield. We remain in the early days of institutionalized, 'scientific' approaches in many disciplines, and the creation of a culture and shared values and standards among academics takes quite a long time to develop and will be perpetually redefined as we go. It was, and sadly remains for some, inconceivable to require archaeologists specializing in earlier periods to meticulously record, study, and publish the medieval material that they encounter.

In the 1950s, as anthropology began to dominate archaeology and introduced new theories and methods, the professionalization of archaeologists accelerated. This was especially the case throughout

Western Europe and the USA, where scholars were less hidebound by nationalist concerns, although still trapped within their historical narratives and national mythologies. One of the earliest excavations to take somewhat seriously the medieval levels was Corinth, where the American School had been excavating since 1896. The publications of hundreds of medieval objects by Davidson (1952) and medieval architecture by Scranton (1957) are commendable and were watershed moments in the world of Anglo-Saxon Mediterranean archaeology. Robinson's excavations, which began in 1959, provided some of the first systematically studied ceramics and small-finds from the Byzantine period in Greece. Nonetheless, Byzantium proved somewhat impervious to broader movements within archaeology, in large part because of the array of nation-states atop the former lands of the empire in which the study of the civilization was (and is) enmeshed. Many of the most promising regions for research, such as Bulgaria, Romania, and Serbia, suffered decades of Soviet domination. Archaeologists in these countries therefore remained rather isolated from western ideas and standards or otherwise resistant to them, and were often too poor to support multidisciplinary archaeological research as excavations became increasingly involved and expensive. Under such competing outlooks, some of them tied to scholars with specific religious or ethnic agendas, an international school of Byzantine archaeology with a recognizable intellectual or physical heart did not materialize. This has seriously undermined inquiry in all aspects of material culture, the economy among them.

In the decades following the release of the Corinth publications, materials were excavated from medieval layers at sites in the eastern Mediterranean, such as Emporio on Chios (Ballance 1989), Nichoria in Messenia (McDonald et al. 1983), and Samos (Isler 1969). Survey also added detail, particularly in the countryside, which, as Bintliff et al. (2007) express, some validly view as the mirror image of the urban landscape and a reliable indicator of the health of local urban centres. The seminal article of Clive Foss on the fate of the post-Roman cities of Western Asia Minor (Foss 1977) became instantly fundamental to the debate of the scope and scale of urban decline. It remains so. Work has progressed, notably at Miletus and Amorium, the latter especially critical for the potential to illuminate conditions on the Anatolian plateau. The flurry of activity elsewhere in Turkey is likewise impressive – one needs only to peruse the table of contents of the annual Turkish archaeological bulletins to see how much work is being done there. With so many of the sites for which Foss derived his intriguing title 'Archaeology and the "Twenty Cities" of Asia Minor' largely unexcavated today, just as they were nearly forty years ago, the debate on urbanism in this corner of the world reminds one somewhat of the endless see-sawing of scholars on the Justinianic Plague; either you agree with Foss or you do not, but there is very little to go on to convince believers on either side to join the other camp (see Chapter 3).

As recently as the 1990s, Byzantine archaeology was viewed as a field (if it was even considered such) with quaint interests belonging to a different age. In a striking window into this state of the subject and how outside professionals conceived it, *The Oxford Companion to Archaeology* (Fagan 1996) entry of 'Byzantine archaeology' included the subheadings 'Decorative Arts', 'Fortifications', 'Ancient Synagogues' (!), and 'Byzantine Monasteries'. This is not a criticism of the specific volume but rather a point intended to highlight the relative backwardness of the field(s) concerned by those who study Byzantine material culture. In many of its interests and tenets, Byzantine archaeology has changed little since 1950. Byzantine archaeology does not exist at all as an academic field or discipline if the criteria as such depend upon an internationally recognized centre of funding, support, and scholarly interaction, or the publication of a marquee journal.

In the 1960s and 1970s, a new generation of academic historians, generally trained in Marxist historiographical and anthropological approaches, renewed efforts to establish a framework from which to investigate material culture and the economy. Theirs was a western hegemonic rather than nationalist approach. Archaeological practitioners of these decades were the students of the mature years of historians, such as Hobsbawm in Britain and the masters of the Annales School of the medieval world like Duby in France, whose shadow falls over the sweep of the discipline today. As wide reaching as such scholars were, it is fascinating to note that none other than Duby said of Byzantium, 'Il n'y a pas' (Cameron 2014) – that is, it does not exist as part of the history of medieval Europe. In Byzantine studies, the new generation included Évelyne Patlagean, whose initial scholarship centred on inequality as current in the historiography of the day, which stressed social history and history from below as opposed to the staid political narratives and 'great man' history of the preceding generations. In her first monograph, *Pauvreté économique et pauvreté sociale à Byzance 4ᵉ–7ᵉ siècles*, Patlagean (1977) was among the pioneers who used economic inquiry as a foundation from which to understand wider social structures. Her work continues to be heavily cited and her methods and subjects of inquiry have been widely followed. In material cultural studies, Cécile Morrisson began her vast contributions to Byzantine studies through numismatic studies; branching out from the objects themselves to archaeological context and then to wider questions of economy. Her work is of immeasurable value and has done a great deal to establish serious economic study of Byzantium. In the German-speaking world, the Austrian Academy of Sciences has also added steadily to the sub-disciplines required to embark on the study of the imperial economy, namely numismatics and sigillography, the two advanced by Werner Seibt (2002), Cheynet and Sode (2003), Nesbitt et al. (1991–2009), and others who have added to the seal studies of Zacos et al. (1972–1985). Also, there is the *Tabula Imperii Byzantinii*, a magisterial work of historical geography whose first volume, dealing with the early modern era on the island of Euboea, appeared in 1973 (Koder 1973). Since then, the series has helped greatly to advance our knowledge of the physical space of Byzantium. The critical spadework done by the above-mentioned specialists and many others has permitted much greater insight than was previously possible.

The symbolic, structural or post-processual archaeology of the 1980s, as advanced by the Cambridge School in Britain, aimed to critique the New Archaeology (Hodder 1982a, 1982b), which emphasized a dialectical approach to assessing the role of social construction, the individual, and the environment in shaping past societies. Historical and symbolic contexts were therefore of considerable interest to many British archaeologists of the era and remain so today. In historical materialism circles in the Anglo-Saxon world, the 1980s also marked another first. This was the attempt at an economic treatment spanning the entire existence of the empire by Michael Hendy (1985). This work has yet to be updated or superseded. Hendy's north star was numismatics and a dataset dominated by coins, texts, and seals. Archaeological excavation and survey plays only a minor supporting role in this study, which impresses today with its scope and the range of learning clearly on display. When Hendy's *Studies in the Byzantine Monetary Economy* appeared, there was scant interest in medieval archaeology in Western Europe, and much less in the states whose territory formerly belonged to Byzantium. Since the appearance of Hendy's work, and sparked in particular by the work of Hodges and Whitehouse (1983), specialists have made wide-ranging contributions within their disciplines and to the economic and social study of the empire as a whole.

Archaeological work in the lands of the former Byzantine Empire has progressed as well. This is especially the case in Turkey, which encompasses the area of the empire's former Anatolian heartland. Excavations at Amorium (see Chapter 3) have entered their third decade, though now under Turkish rather than British direction. Other major cities continue to be studied as well – Ephesus, Miletus, and Corinth to name only the most venerable of them. Alongside these are many shorter-term field projects in the Balkan states, Greece, and Turkey. The expansion of higher education and the growing number of Turkish scholars has resulted in an expansion of fieldwork. The recent spectacular discovery of the Theodosian Harbour (see Chapter 5) underscores the potential of Turkey to yield surprises that could greatly aid our conception of the empire. Many western scholars cannot access much of their production due to a lack of familiarity with the Turkish language, and other work remains difficult to access owing to limited publication. Nonetheless, in the coming decades Byzantine studies will be increasingly driven by scholars from the rising states and economies of Eastern Europe, countries who view Byzantium as integral to their history and identity.

Archaeologists of Byzantium do not generally balk at the 'Dark Age' label (Ivison 2007), even while embracing continuity and a certain degree of economic vitality (Lightfoot 2012). Likewise in a recent discussion of urban sites of Byzantine Asia Minor, Niewöhner et al. (2013: 101) also use the term. 'Iconoclast' as a category of periodization is not common among archaeologists. Rather than 'Dark Ages', many prefer 'early medieval' and this somewhat neutral terminology is probably the more common form of periodization in archaeology, although even scholars who prefer this to 'Dark Ages' or 'dark ages' find themselves using the latter without apparent reservation (Zavagno 2009). In large part, this is not due to a lack of debate among scholars but due to an especially pronounced paucity of evidence compared with the sixth century, for which a number of narrative histories survive and there are many more extant remains of material culture.

Transformation and decline

Few subjects energize the intellectually curious as the fall of the Roman Empire; properly the collapse of Roman political power in the western half of the Mediterranean epitomized by the single most shocking event of imperial history – the sack of Rome by the Goths under Alaric in 410. The shock and awe of the barbarian capture of the heart of the world, spectators to which forgot that no emperor had ruled from the Eternal City for a century and a half (in 286 Diocletian had moved the government to Milan and it never returned). These concepts regarding the classical city will be discussed further in Chapter 3.

Scholars have debated intensely the nature and pace of change in life before and during the period under discussion, as well as how we should label the constellation of phenomena that symbolize these differences. In simple terms, the spirit of the discussion is animated by the fall of the Roman Empire, '... the greatest, perhaps, and most awful scene, in the history of mankind' in the estimation of Gibbon (Gibbon and Bury 1906: 6: 645), whose *History of the Decline and Fall of the Roman Empire* was first printed in 1776–1789. As far from Gibbon as scholars today purport to be, I have noted above how we remain wedded to our times and prone to a different though equally potent set of biases. The application of post-modern approaches has helped establish a new framework of discussion but hardly solved all problems; we need to remain cognisant of our own theoretical shadings and limitations. Given the title of this book, I would do well to heed my own advice, dependent as its title and conceptualization is on traditional concepts and ways of seeing.

In the mid twentieth century, cultural relativism entered scholarly and popular discourse as academics freed themselves of parochial particularistic models and attempted to assess societies in history and archaeology on their own terms, albeit through a humanist and enlightenment filtered lens. It is natural, of course, to question the possibility of objectivity in process and the discovery of archaeological truths in a restrictive, natural sense. Instead, different truths ultimately reflect different perspectives and starting points. The difficulties in which scholars were enmeshed by cultural (and moral) relativistic views was recognized long ago (Barnett 1948). If we accept that any archaeological or historical understanding is ultimately constructed – our interpretations are simple cultural refractions or reflections of self – we reach an intellectual cul-de-sac. At best this can inform us and make us keenly aware of the limits of archaeology and places the discipline within broader discussions of theories of knowledge. Simply put, my approach is conditioned by an awareness of all of these debates together with, I hope, some grasp of my personal limitations and a hope to contribute to an examination that will be refined, debated, and revised by others.

Scholars of late antiquity, foremost among them Peter Brown, deserve enormous credit for rescuing from the dustbin of historiography the last centuries of Roman rule, still sometimes referred to as 'Le Bas-Empire' in the Francophone world. After many years of neglect, the study of 'late antiquity' has in recent years become dominant within ancient history. When not long ago my present university wanted to hire a Roman historian, few applicants had studied 'traditional' Rome – that is, the Rome of 'Le Haut-Empire' or the centuries of the political apex of the Roman state from the time of Augustus through the Severans (193–235). Le Haut-Empire ends with the third century crises that afflicted Rome. Cultural relativists may object to any analyses employing such stark periodization as wholly unsuitable, pinned as they are to the back of notions of 'decline'. Such approaches often bind us to conceiving the whole of society in the light of more traditional historical inquiry, such as military affairs or political narratives. We may then be blinkered to observing entire strands of life, which, in fact, might be quite vibrant. An illustrative case may be seen from the end of Byzantium itself, when the Paleologan era brewed an effervescent literary and artistic stew in the Balkans even as the political situation of the empire was terminal.

As the Roman Empire was an empire of cities, continuity of occupation in the urban environment from late antiquity through the early medieval era as well as the nature of that habitation have, understandably, been a lightning rod for discussion (this will be discussed in more detail in Chapter 3). Champions of the transformation model or 'non-fall' model (Brown 1978) tend to approach the problem from an assumption of the durability of place and cultural elements like cultic practice, sacred space, and natural advantage. Whittow (2001) notes that the abandonment of the decline paradigm as an overarching discursive framework is important because its utility belonged to another era, an era of imperialism beyond which we have moved or at least are attempting to move. Regarding specific sites on which a larger picture of continuity in late antiquity and longer is built, Eger argues that Antioch remained an important city in the early medieval period (Eger 2012: 19–20); and Magness (2003a) reads the evidence from the Levantine coast in a positive light as well, arguing that the absence of evidence in no way supports views of settlement impoverishment or cessation. Others (Vanhaverbeke et al. 2007: 641–42) urge us to consider the city over *longue-durée* and in the context of wider settlement activities. Viewed in this manner, the Hellenistic–Early Byzantine form of urbanization was an 'unnatural' form of human activity in Anatolia at least, with villages and dispersed settlements in the countryside being 'natural'. 'Yes, there was decline in late antiquity, but it was limited to the cities' (Vanhaverbeke et al. 2007: 642). This is a thought-provoking way of viewing the overall health of communities of the era (see Chapter 4); like any approach, it carries its own problems. It also highlights a division in the 'transformationists' – those who note that there were particular aspects of life that changed for the worse relative to the past, but that overall society as a whole did not suffer slow disaster. As Liebeschuetz recognized, our understanding of city life in late antiquity is ineffably imprinted by the written record and, in this way, the 'transformationists' are throwing us back onto more purely archaeological and anthropological models and means of inquiry, which themselves take on the trappings of neutrality and eliminate many of the (presumably false) impressions scholars have gleaned from the written sources. Finally, those arguing against 'decline' wish to be free of a term that has become, as Cameron argues, 'far too emotive to be useful' (Cameron 2001: 239).

Critics of the choice of 'transformation' over 'decline' are many and their arguments likewise forceful. Liebeschuetz has maintained support of the traditional 'decline and fall' model of the Roman Empire via studies that have focused on administrative, institutional, and other structural changes in Roman life, especially in the Roman city (Liebeschuetz 2001). Regarding the end of western Roman political power and its long-term ramifications for European history, Ward-Perkins (2005) embraced a materialist approach to which the use of archaeological data is especially suited. Ward-Perkins (2001), however, has elsewhere pondered that the old view of 'decline and fall' might be better considered from the vantage of 'fall and decline' – that is, that political shock destroyed the underpinnings of state control on which the superstructure of so much of Roman life depended. Although at variance in many ways, this is not unlike what Whittow argues: 'The Huns triggered one crisis; Muhammad's followers created the second. Rome did not decline, it fell' (Whittow 2001: 243). Those who argue for the traditional view of the 'decline' of the Roman Empire and its attendant negative consequences have an abundance of *negative* evidence – that is, the absence of imported pottery and other artefacts that support a picture of diminishing levels of public life. To cite but one example, decaying bathhouses are read as markers of lower hygiene and reduced everyday comforts, as well as signifying a decline in access to technologies that arguably made normal activities like eating, drinking, and bathing not only possible but more diverse, stimulating, and pleasurable.

This discussion has focused chronologically on the period just prior to that under consideration here, namely the fourth through sixth centuries AD. Nonetheless, the form and content of the debate is of the greatest relevance for the Byzantine East, where it is generally agreed that prosperity continued into the seventh century. The 'decline' or 'transformation' might be delayed by a century or two, but the same questions demand answers: Did the Byzantine state fail rather suddenly due to military or other pressures or some combination thereof? Did prosperity (whatever that means) fade with the weakening of the state, or before it and thus contribute to the fall? In other words, was there a Byzantine 'decline and fall' that ushered in the Dark Ages, a 'fall and decline' in the midst of these comparatively poorly chronicled centuries, or something entirely different – a slow transformation or group of changes in society which we have heretofore ignored or been confused about?

2

Material Evidence and Meaning

The material data of the early medieval period are especially challenging. The whole corpus of evidence, from texts to building inscriptions to ceramics and so on has been, compared with other eras, little examined. One scholar, commenting on the state of ceramic studies for early medieval Byzantine sites in the Aegean characterized the state of things as follows: 'In fact, to put it bluntly only a few studies dealing with Early Byzantine pottery of the seventh to ninth centuries from the Aegean area ... are anything more than groping in the dark' (Vroom 2003: 49); unfortunately, this still stands as a fair assessment across multiple forms of evidence. In this chapter, we will look at some of the major categories of archaeological material with a particular focus on pottery and coins, which are among our most abundant and best examined markers of life in the past. As will become apparent, the debate around each of these is uneven and the data themselves are problematic and, like data in most realms of inquiry, prone to be interpreted differently from one scholar to another.

Ceramics: overview

Many archaeologists are familiar with fine wares but possess only limited knowledge of coarse wares. Fine wares are distinguished from coarse wares by their finish, usually a slip or glaze that renders a glossy sheen and smooth texture to the finished product, and by their use as cups, dishes, and so on. The quality of manufacture and ubiquity of fine wares as well as their aesthetic appeal has led to their being relatively well studied. If we move beyond fine wares, the next best studied forms are amphorae used to transport and store dry and liquid goods. Other plain (coarse) wares include storage vessels and other utilitarian vessels. These types are usually less well known than fine wares, in part due to the methodological challenges that abound in making sense of Dark Age ceramic materials. *Pithoi* (also called *dolia*) are large bulk ceramic storage vessels usually buried in the ground. *Pithoi* and plain architectural tiles were central to village life throughout antiquity and into the early modern era but with rare exceptions (Arık 2007) these are unstudied. Consequently, over most regions of the former Byzantine Empire, the full complement of coarse wares used in everyday domestic tasks, including cooking pots, washing basins, pitchers, flasks, and a host of other food service vessels of the medieval table, are not widely known. The still more humble products, such as piping, mortaria, tiles, bricks, and other utilitarian types have received little to no attention. This is not to decry scholarship of the Byzantine world as fundamentally different from others; there are few coarse ware studies of any historical period from the Mediterranean and Anatolia. We simply lack the number of specialists with interests in these ordinary objects whose production and use were usually geographically quite localized. There are many arguments favouring a closer look at this entire category of 'pottery of the banal', including that coarse wares are ubiquitous on every archaeological site and represent the daily lives of the vast majority of the empire's citizens. The latter are especially difficult to access via texts and other means commonly resorted to. In most instances, the local nature of these ceramics permits the scope of coarse ware production and circulation to be understood within quite closed parameters. But for those who wish to understand more about daily life, especially among the poorer citizens of the empire, study of these utilitarian objects holds as-yet unrealized promise.

The great transition: the red ware tradition and its end

Ceramic objects have been part of shared Mediterranean exchange since at least the Bronze Age (Jones and Boardman 1986). At the start of the seventh century, much of the coastal Mediterranean shared a common ceramic culture of fine ware tablewares. These massproduced, fairly refined *terra sigillata* fine wares from Africa were made in red fabric and covered with a glossy slip (African Red Slip Ware, also referred to as ARS). ARS forms, such as the late type 107 bowl illustrated in Fig. 2, were generally used for formal dining or special occasions by those who could not afford sumptuous silver servings. In the eastern Mediterranean, these red wares, including Phocaean Red Slip Ware from southern Asia Minor (also called 'Late Roman C Ware') and possibly Cyprus ('Late Roman D Ware'), as well as Egyptian Red Slip Ware (ERS) circulated in many parts of the Mediterranean and even penetrated inland considerable distances from the coast, a clear sign of their availability, cheapness, and cachet among a range of people of different social and economic levels.

Scholars labelled African Red Slip Ware as such based on its region of origin and colour. ARS kilns were located in modern eastern Algeria and Tunisia where potters produced ceramics in well levigated fabric with small inclusions, unglazed but finished with a glossy red-orange slip. In earlier Gallic sigillata examples, the sheen and

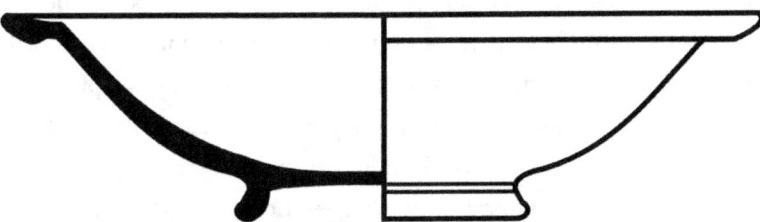

Fig. 2 ARS form 107 (Creative Commons).

colour of the pottery, which clearly played a large part in the popularity of these ancient terra sigillata wares, is due to the presence of silicon and aluminium oxide in the colourless glassy matrix that provided much of the lustre of the durable slip, and the presence of hematite crystals produced the red colour (Mirguet 2009); ARS and other terra sigillata wares were probably similarly composed. The sourcing and treatment of the clay as well as the application of the slips and methods of firing of late antique terra sigillatas indicate a great deal of shared knowledge circulated among numerous potteries. Likewise, the standardization of forms implies a significant amount of interaction and market awareness. This is true even at the end of the heyday of the red slip wares, evidenced by significant overlap of regional types from southern Italy and Greece (Arthur 2008: 163).

Although North African workshops also churned out lamps and other objects, the vast majority of their output was tablewares. North African potters drew upon earlier Gallic and Italian terra sigillata traditions in developing a host of attractive shapes. The appealing colour and generally sound finishing techniques clearly resonated among those of at least modest means, as the wares were exported in vast quantities. By the mid second century, North African producers shipped fine wares throughout the western Mediterranean. The introduction of ARS into the eastern Mediterranean soon followed and they came to dominate the market throughout the 'Middle Sea' and beyond, although in the northern fringes of the empire they never matched the popularity achieved in the Mediterranean because of the limits of the state-backed supply routes on which cargoes travelled.

The ubiquity of ARS, the longevity of the production sites in North Africa, and great variety of types that changed relatively rapidly has permitted the establishment of a clear and close chronology (Hayes 1972, 1980). Work on ARS has steadily advanced thanks to international interest and it is no exaggeration to say that ARS is the most intensively studied pottery type in the world. Strikingly recognizable even to the untrained eye, ARS and its eastern relatives have become critical diagnostic tools of chronology and trade contacts wherever they appear.

ARS workshops tended to be large-scale affairs; sherd scatters at some production sites sometimes cover several hectares. Manufacture also continued beyond the period of Roman political control of North Africa; this fact encourages us not to associate immediate economic collapse with administrative turmoil or replacement. The site of the city of Uthina (modern Oudna) in central Tunisia lay at the heart of ARS production due to its location within the region of Zeugitana dominated by Carthage. A kiln found at Oudna produced ARS until the end of Byzantine rule in North Africa in the mid seventh century and perhaps even later, although the presumed last phase of production would have been for local or regional consumption (Leone 2003).

In Byzantium, finds of ARS after 650 AD are uncommon. By the fifth century, ARS lost the bulk of the market in the eastern Mediterranean to regional competitors and local imitators. In southern Asia Minor around Pergamon, ateliers crafted Phocaean Red Slip ware ('PRS', also called Late Roman C Ware), which replaced ARS as the dominant fine tableware in the eastern Mediterranean by the fifth century. PRS was also traded widely in the west, with more than forty find spots in Italy alone; smaller quantities have been recovered on sites as far west as the Atlantic coast of Iberia and the British Isles (Reynolds 2010a). PRS production seems to have been more centralized than the rather diffuse networks of potters manufacturing ARS pottery but PRS kiln sites are insufficiently known to be certain of the organization and scale of production in Asia Minor (Özyiğit 1989, 1992; Vaag 2008).

Alongside PRS, Cypriot Red Slip Ware (CRS; or Late Roman D Ware, LRDW) is the last mass-produced regional fine ware to carry on the terra sigillata tradition on any significant scale in the eastern

Mediterranean. No kilns producing CRS/LRDW are known on Cyprus, but for decades morphological characteristics and petrographic analysis have indicated to scholars (Hayes 1972: 371–86; Lewit 2011: 315) that the island was a major production hub. Recent magnometric survey has revealed round updraft kilns in southern Asia Minor at Kadirgürü Mevkiisi; nearby production centres were located at the rural site of Gebiz, 35 km north of Antalya (ancient and Byzantine Attalia). These kilns were used to fire forms of LRDW and other wares, including pitchers and pilgrim flasks, the latter thought to have been made at Sagalassos in Pisidia. The number of ateliers, the range and variable quality of their production, as well as the sheer quantity produced – which was vast – indicate that this part of southern Pisidia was an important primary producer of LRDW ware. The prominence of Late Roman D form 9B (Hayes 1972: 381) indicates that many of these production sites continued into the seventh century (Jackson et al. 2012: 109). Until kilns are found elsewhere, Pisidia must be considered the primary production node of LRDW. At nearby Sagalassos just to the north of the kiln sites just mentioned, local ateliers made a regionally important fine ware throughout late antiquity (Poblome 1999, 2011), underscoring ever-changing regional production.

Other terra sigillata varieties from the end of antiquity are known, for example Askra ware from central Greece produced in the sixth to seventh centuries (Vroom 2005a: 40–41). Later forms of Egyptian Red Slip Ware ('B' and 'C') are comparatively poorly understood. They were apparently manufactured in the Nile Valley (Hayes 1972: 397–401) but a lack of detailed work has prevented a full morphological and chronological understanding of these forms. Given its circulation in Egypt and in many centres around the Levant, further study of ERS will help to expand our understanding of the early medieval transition there. Local red ware copies abounded in Italy and elsewhere. As ARS, PRS, and LRDW faded from the scene, their absence may indicate the decoupling of trade nodes that bound rural producers to slackening urban demand. But some provincial production centres continued to thrive in places like Italy, Greece, and Asia Minor, where late imitations of terra sigillata persisted into the seventh century. Thus demand was increasingly met by local or regional types as exchange networks became frayed, as in the case of Athens, Corinth, Delphi, and Demetrias, which continued through the sixth century (Petridis 2007a); their borrowing of forms from one another supports some local vitality and connectedness that flourished despite evidence of imported wares. Thus, we need to be aware of the fact that the symbols of external trade are not the only markers of cosmopolitan experience or wider cultural contacts or, more specifically, that 'self-sufficiency was not synonymous with isolation' (Petridis 2007b: 22).

Paul Arthur has identified key characteristics and changes in fine ware pottery at the end of late antiquity. Although the pace of variation differed by region, there was a general decline in the size of pottery workshops in the core of old Roman territories, particularly in North Africa where ARS was produced. In some areas, such as the former northern provinces of the empire, there was a rapid retreat of ceramic industries in part due to a precipitous decline of towns and thus the market to sustain professional potters evaporated. The range and complexity of tableware pottery forms decreased rather steadily. Red slip pottery produced in Asia Minor typically is generally of lower quality with thicker and more clumsily executed and coarser finishes, though still of an overall high grade of finish when compared with alternatives. Nonetheless, there was a general decline in ceramic manufacture from the fifth century onwards as indicated by the fineness and thinness of vessels (Arthur 2008: 169–71) and by wasters; sixth- and seventh-century waste was especially prominent on production sites (e.g. in Pisidia at the LRDW sites; Jackson et al. 2012) and probably indicates that skills were lacking among many workers or that there were technical issues with firing or both.

Other changes are also difficult to gauge in their meaning and significance. Footed pot forms generally disappeared (or the feet that do survive become much less pronounced), which may indicate a change in table manners, diet or both. A couple of decades after the Lombards invaded Italy in 568, only significant urban centres continued to import a mix of Mediterranean ceramics or produce forms sharing in the late antique *koine* of fine ware pottery. Cyprus, Egypt, Asia Minor, and some producers in North Africa continued to produce red slip wares into the seventh century but probably not deep into the century. An exception was Egypt where ERS continued to be produced, apparently in Upper Egypt (Hayes 1972: 387–401) into the Early Islamic period and the potteries there thus survived the seventh century and the transition to Persian, then Arab rule.

Terra sigillata forms became increasingly regionalized towards the end of the sixth century and then vanished altogether by the end of the seventh century (ERS continued later but lay outside the empire). Other fine ware types were new, such as painted examples made in Central Greece and Crete. These types were consumed as far afield as Constantinople, Egypt, and North Africa. The Greek forms, mainly tableware plates and dishes, were decorated with abstract floral and bird designs, while Cretan production included small jugs and other small closed vessels (Vroom 2005a: 43). Cretan production continued into the eighth century but likely did not continue much into the ninth; the ceramic tradition there split from its Hellenistic past during the years 828–961 (Vroom 2003: 49). Although painted vessels like these were new in their execution and artistic production, they were not unprecedented. Late antique painted pottery is known from Egypt and North Africa (Arthur 2008: 170–71) and especially from Palestine and Arabia, including the series of Jerash bowls belonging to the sixth to the first half of the seventh century; while Watson allowed that production may have trickled on after the mid seventh century, she notes that supposed eighth-century examples are poorly known.

Some forms of LRDW continued to be made into the eighth century, as Vroom favours for Limyra (Vroom 2007). Armstrong (2009) likewise contends LRDW continued into the eighth century and notes that other east Mediterranean wares also continued to be produced, including LR1 type amphoras and Dhiorios cooking pots. These types are apparently outliers rather than heralds of a significant wave of manufacture but important nonetheless to our understanding of the transition to medieval ceramics and economic forms. Similarly, in Palestine, the lacuna of eighth-century material is being filled by re-dating previously excavated material (Magness 2003a), but much remains to be done before we have a clear and convincing picture of the role and nature of red wares in the post-late antique Mediterranean.

This rather lengthy discussion of the red ware pottery tradition allows one to see how radical was the shift in fine ware production and circulation at the start of the medieval period. Pottery, one of the basic expressions of material culture, was transformed. In the majority of places, the centuries-old shared Mediterranean red fine ware tradition disappeared in the seventh century or the eighth at the latest. The seventh century is likewise the leading edge of the rise of ceramic techniques that typify the techniques of the Middle Ages. In the early medieval period, various painted or glazed white wares developed to replace terra sigillata. These forms employed less of the technical sophistication or standardization of late antique tablewares; neither did they circulate as widely or as long as their predecessors. Together they represent a ground-shift in tableware production to white fabric glazed forms that would prevail until the end of the medieval era. It should be stressed that the materials and techniques of medieval white wares and their relatives do not represent a clean break with the late antique pottery tradition, nor do they necessarily imply any revolutionary change but rather an evolutionary shift.

The fabric and finish of many ceramics did alter considerably. In Constantinople, Hayes noted the appearance of an intriguing minor form, Late Roman light-coloured ware, with analogues known from around the Black Sea region; based on the copying of forms of LRCW and fabric, he believed it belonged to Asia Minor. The incised decoration, inscribed with the sgraffito technique, include crosses and chase scenes, though too few examples are known to establish clear forms or dates, but white-bodied fabric jugs have been dated to the mid fifth to early seventh centuries (Hayes 1972: 408; Hayes 1980: lxviii; Hayes 1992: 7–8) and there are other tablewares from the beginning of the sixth century. White fabric pottery bearing traces of colour-coating appeared in quantity in deposits dated to the late sixth and seventh centuries at Saraçhane (Istanbul). In the capital, these plain white wares were shortly followed by the standard tablewares of the early medieval period: glazed white wares. The types and subtypes have been assigned different names through the years, making discussion sometimes complicated (for a list of types, see Vroom 2003: 369–74).

Glazed pottery

Among the more striking characteristics of early medieval ceramics is the use of lead glaze in Glazed White Ware (GWW or Constantinople Glazed White Wares – CGW to differentiate them from similar medieval types elsewhere). CGW I began to be made in the environs of Constantinople in the seventh century (Megaw 1975: 34) and continued into the late eighth. These vessels were covered with a slip then glazed with a lead glaze that ranged in colour from green to brown. The fineness of the clay and the finish of many CGW I wares was not less refined than the late antique red ware forms they replaced, and CGW I forms were not strictly tablewares. Additionally, the darkish brown/green glaze was apparently applied as a sealant rather than for decoration. Closed and semi-closed forms, such as cooking pots with lids, comprise the majority of early forms. Open forms, namely footed bowls and dishes, make up the majority of later CGW (Vroom 2005a: 63).

At Anemurium in southeastern Asia Minor, Caroline Williams (1977) analysed the finds from the excavation of a Byzantine well; coins of Heraclius found within the deposit indicate the well was sealed sometime between 630 and *c.* 700. Among the notable finds were fragments of a cooking pot with fine ridging on its upper sides. In its form it is similar to unglazed Cypriot examples from Dhiorios (Catling 1972: 11, fig. 7.P96) and the Kornos Cave (Catling and Dikigoropoulos 1970: 45, fig. 3.14). Early analogues are also known from the seventh century Yassi Ada wreck, which went to the bottom in about 626 (Bass and Van Doorninck, 1982). These wares were apparently imported from Constantinople and its environs from as early as the first quarter of the seventh century (Harrison et al. 1968: 203–5).

The precise origin of lead glazed ware is something of a mystery. Hayes (1992: 13) is sceptical of a western origin, although he allows that this technique may have arrived in Byzantium via Ravenna. Arthur (2008: 177) argues that glazing technology, which was used to decorate fine tablewares in certain parts of the Hellenistic and Roman worlds, entered the vernacular of Constantinopolitan potteries from the Danube or via Ravenna. Since there has traditionally been a close relationship between metalworkers and potters, especially in intersecting techniques such as the production of metal-based glazes, Arthur's theory is probably correct. One might look to sites like Sirmium, where glazed wares were common from the fourth century (Parović-Pešikan 1971: 35) or Ságvár (Tricciana) in Pannonia (Burger 1966). These regions are likely to shed light on the question of whether there was a connection between mining sites and ceramic manufacture. The glazes themselves certainly required considerable quantities of metals like manganese and lead or metal oxides like copper oxide.

There is also a possible link between glass making and glazing, which could be fruitfully explored in the study of wares of Byzantine and Islamic manufacture (Freestone et al. 2002).

During early antiquity, outstanding glazed wares were common products of Asia Minor, Mesopotamia, and Egypt (Greene 2007), but we lack a clear chain of evidence linking these types to those of the early medieval world. Glazed ceramics were prominent within late antique northern Italy, especially during the fifth century (Grandi 2007: 7). While northern production ceased in the seventh century, glazed wares made after this date crop up in eastern Sicily, an area closely connected to the capital. Whatever the origin of the technique, there were certain advantages to its use. Most slipped wares were porous whereas glazed wares were impermeable. Furthermore, lower firing techniques and reduced wastage due to cracking after firing were also practical advantages of glazed wares (Tite et al. 1998). In the Mediterranean and Aegean, the lower fuel burden of such production would have offered an advantage over other ceramics by decreasing the cost of labour and materials. It should be noted, however, that material reasons alone cannot have been determinative. As Dark has observed (2010: 118), coarse ware pottery continued to be manufactured and unglazed amphorae were made for transport and storage of liquids.

It is almost certain that no single reason underlay the adoption of white fabric pottery by early medieval Byzantines and many of their neighbours. One reason may well have been the look of the treated exterior itself; Liz James (1996) is certainly correct in her view that Byzantines found not only certain colours attractive, but also appreciated the brightness of objects, probably in part for their spiritual associations. Greene (2007: 666) cites competition from metal ware and glass as possibly thwarting the wider adoption of glazed wares in the early Roman era, and such competition undoubtedly continued into the Dark Ages and into the Middle

Byzantine era. Unless there were significant costs associated with glazed work or some reason for a greater negotiated cultural value than was usual for pottery, it is questionable whether metal and pottery ever really competed in the same space. It is also hard to consider even the finest and comparatively rare decorated fine wares as luxury objects. In certain contexts such as when they were imported, these vessels must have been prized as exotics or for the fineness of their decoration, but they would probably not have competed with metallic objects as status symbols among the elite. In clarifying these questions, more work on the Byzantines and Mediterranean peoples 'at table' such as that of Vroom (2003: 307–34; Magness 2010) would be helpful. Several Glazed White Ware forms, including cups, were clearly modelled on metal examples (Hayes 1992: 25). In this case, it is better to see ceramics as occupying a lower realm in the hierarchy of things, a cheaper facsimile of luxury for those who could not (or should not, perhaps in the case of monks and nuns) buy the 'real' thing.

White Wares of various kinds, both finely and more coarsely made in white or pinkish fabric, either plain or glazed, were the quintessential form of medieval pottery. Glazed types (Glazed White Ware I–IV of Hayes 1992) (Fig. 3) were manufactured throughout most of the history of the medieval empire, from the Dark Ages until the thirteenth century when Latin and Palaeologan rule coincided with changes in ceramic culture. White ware types, both plain and glazed, were probably made close to the capital, though kilns of Dark Age date have yet to be found.

Work at Corinth (Morgan 1942) and at the Great Palace excavations in Istanbul (Stevenson 1947) established the groundwork for our understanding of these Dark Age ceramics. Constantinopolitan Glazed White Ware 1 (CGW) represents the earliest type of medieval pottery – that is, a group of ceramic fine wares that owe little to the tradition of Roman red wares so prominent up until the sixth and

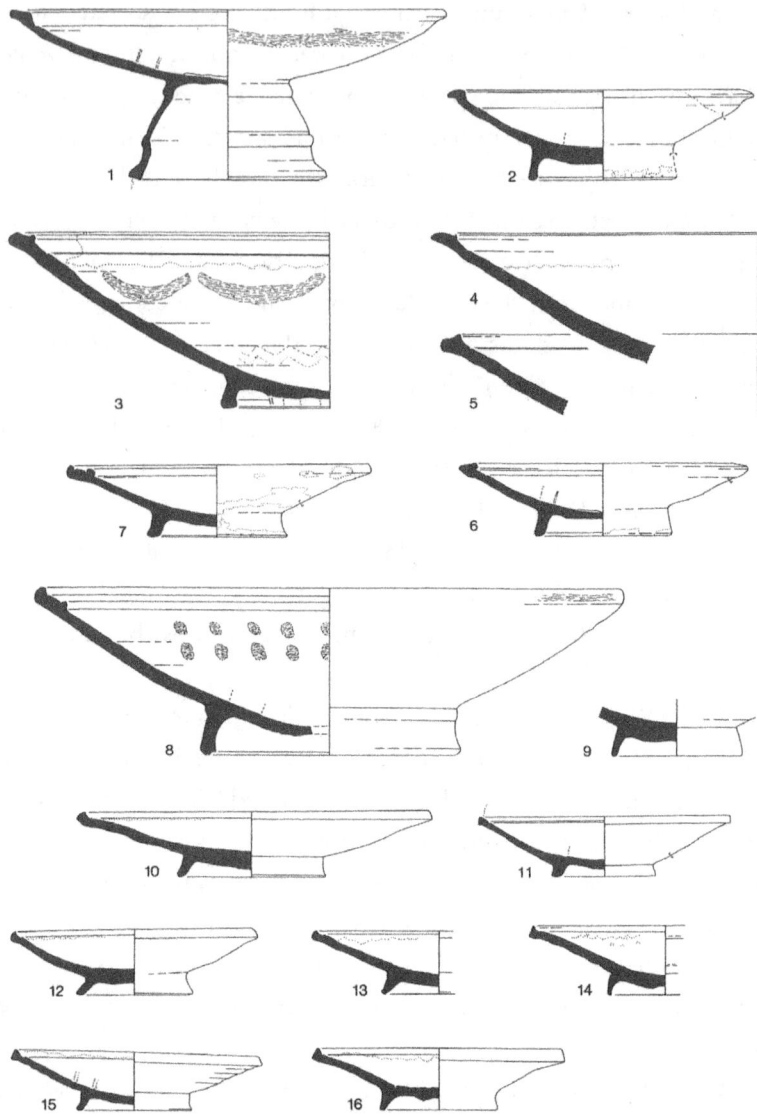

Fig. 3 Constantinopolitan Glazed Ware Pottery II (from Hayes, 1992, fig. 7, courtesy of Princeton University Press).

seventh centuries (Hayes 1992). Early type CGW I shares several characteristics with the vernacular of early medieval pottery elsewhere in Europe, namely its greenish to brown lead glaze also known from 'Forum Ware' in Italy (Vaag 2008) and similar Carolingian types, and may have influenced or been influenced by these. Seventh-century examples are undecorated but from the eighth century onwards, CGW I and CGW II incised decorations are common.

CGW II vessels were formed in fine white fabric and, like their predecessors, glazed in olive green or yellow glazes. The earliest of these dishes, bowls, chafing dishes, and jugs probably belong to the eighth century (Vroom 2005a: 75–77). By the ninth century a common variant, called 'Impressed White Ware', bearing stamped or moulded decoration, was also likely made in the environs of the capital. These wares grew more popular over time, it seems. Most of the impressed material from Saraçhane, where they comprise 12–15 per cent of all CGW II sherds (Hayes 1992: 19), belonged to the tenth century, indicating that decorated CGW II types were a major feature of domestic life in the capital, Greece, and the Aegean. In part due to the considerable amount of illegible material he encountered at Saraçhane, Hayes thought the stamps represented control markings but Armstrong, studying much better preserved museum examples, found these bore clear impressions and were decorative if not representative of the greatest artistry (Armstrong 2001). These designs of birds and hunting scenes or mythological creatures copied paradigms found in metalwork, especially the so-called 'Coptic' cast bronze ware (Hayes 1992: 17). Forms were generally conservative, reflecting perhaps both the needs and desires of both producers and consumers.

Other decorated variants of CGW forms II–V included Petal Ware and Plastic Ware (or Plain Glazed White Ware with plastic figural decoration) and Inscribed Ware (with lines etched into the biscuit-fired pots with a tool) (Vroom 2005a: 77). Impressed White Wares

(IWW) were either stamped or moulded with decorative motifs that included birds, the tree of life, and hunting scenes (Armstrong 2001: 67). An early dating for the production of IWW is favoured by Armstrong, who notes the appearance of impressed wares (CGW II) from eighth-century contexts at Saraçhane in Istanbul.

Polychrome ware, a term coined by David Talbot Rice (1928) to refer to a group of fairly rare, glazed ceramics with brightly painted decoration in multiple colours, found in minor quantities in medieval contexts in excavation. These appeared at the end of the Dark Ages at the earliest. Hayes dated polychrome wares found at Saraçhane to the eleventh and twelfth centuries, though only 1 per cent of the ceramics unearthed there (Hayes 1992: 35). Sanders (2003: 391) likewise believes polychrome pottery belonged to the eleventh century at the latest (Sanders 2003: 391). Tiles of similar fabric and decorative aspect from Constantinopolitan churches belong to the ninth century and later (Mundell Mango 2001). Dark (2010) believes that this evidence supports an earlier dating than that advanced by Hayes and Sanders. Particularly at issue is the dating of finds from the monasteries at Patleina and Preslav, which are traditionally thought by numerous scholars (Grabar 1928; Mijatev 1937; Kostova 2009) to belong to the very end of the Dark Ages, c. 900.

Since comparatively little work has been done on the early medieval tablewares, even one as important as Glazed White Ware, many questions remain unanswered. While Dark (2010: 122) has noted the dating of kiln furnishings from excavations of the Great Palace to contexts c. 1200, when large portions of the former seat of government were abandoned or dilapidated, earlier kilns producing GWW have not been found. The fabric comparison attempting to link Ottoman white clays to those of Byzantine period GWW has not, to my knowledge, been completed. Progress has been made in other areas: Günsenin (1995, 1998, 2001) and Armstrong (Armstrong and Günsenin 1995) have explored Middle- and Late-Byzantine kilns located around Ganos on the northwest shore of the Sea of Marmara. The earliest of the wares found there belong to the eleventh century, though it is hoped further prospection yields even earlier sites. While it seems nearly certain that the locus of production lay near the capital, kilns linked with Dark Age CGW remain unknown. Thus many aspects of production elude us, including the scale, its organization, the techniques employed, and the sources of raw material. Petrographic analysis via a combination of techniques offers our best opportunity to explore the sources of CGW and similar medieval pottery, though to date this analysis has been brought to bear predominantly on later examples of Byzantine pottery (Maguire 1995).

At Amorium, the significant discovery of a kiln in the Upper City that produced pottery in the eighth to ninth centuries has been largely overlooked. The kiln structure itself as well as wasters and misfired pots provide good evidence that the pottery's output included both unglazed and glazed wares in local red wares and painted as well as incised forms (Böhlendorf-Arslan 2004: 1:28). The Amorium kiln provides rare evidence of continued regional specialized production, as well as proof of close links with the capital and the exertion of its artistic influence: the decorative motifs and morphology of these vessels bear similarities to contemporary types of wares from Constantinople.

At medieval Butrint on the Adriatic in present-day Albania, Glazed White Ware imported from Constantinople or presumably its immediate hinterland is joined by red-bodied glazed wares of local manufacture as well as nearby southern Italy around Otranto (Vroom 2008; Arthur et al. 1992). One of the important excavated areas of the city was the so-called Triconch Palace, named for its impressive late antique triconch dining hall (Bowden and Hodges 2011). The Triconch Palace remained unfinished and ceased being an elite residence in the first half of the fifth century and was abandoned by the mid seventh century. From excavations at the Western Defences,

Vroom (2004) noted the presence of Glazed White Ware I (CGW I). In addition, locally made glazed wares in a red fabric indicate local imitation of imported forms from nearby Otranto and Constantinopolitan Glazed White Wares. Additionally, glazed 'chafing dishes' and portable cook wares were found. Chafing dishes have a vented bottom to which a heat source can be applied to a concave cooking surface above. Usually about 20 cm in diameter and topped by a separate conical lid, the cooking dish was probably used to fry foods or warm sauces using coals or some other heat source. It may also have been used as a small oven. At Gortyn on Crete, fragments of these lids probably belong to the mid eighth century (Vroom 2003: 56), while at Corinth local examples began to be made only in the ninth century (Sanders 2003: 390). Local glazed red wares from Corinth also appear beginning in the ninth century.

At Butrint we also observe the disappearance of open forms of pottery, such as dishes and casseroles, and their replacement with closed-form vessels like cooking pots; closed forms account for 96 per cent of the early medieval assemblage from the Triconch Palace area (Vroom 2008). Additionally, there was 'ruralizaton' of pottery making, including increased reliance on local forms and handmade wares, declining numbers of imports, and the appearance of sagging or round-based cooking jars. These cooking jars, as has been noted above, were often placed over a heat source, either directly or using a tripod. Sagging or round-based cooking pots became more common in the Mediterranean outside of North Africa towards the end of late antiquity; Arthur notes that this may well reflect a broad transition from cooking on stoves in private kitchens or in ovens to cooking in communal spaces over open fires or braziers and may reflect the products prepared in them as well as environmental conditions (Arthur 2005: 179; Arthur 2007). Moreover, small, round, peaked ceramic ovens (Latin *clibanus*; Greek *klibanos*) for baking or roasting became an important part of the culinary tools of the inhabitants at the end of late antiquity and the Dark Ages. Finally, we can note a gradual move towards self-reliance in pottery production, with the output of local and regional potters replacing the imports that dominated assemblages of late antiquity. Such local pots include plain wheel thrown wares and handmade types, the latter indicative of household rather than workshop production.

Many of the changes in early medieval pottery production and consumption observable at Butrint indicate that this minor provincial city fits into a general pattern observed in Byzantium. These include the end of terra sigillata imports in the seventh century or shortly thereafter; the appearance of glazed wares, both locally and regional imports from Italy and further afield in minor quantities from Constantinople or its environs; and striking changes in dining habits indicated by morphological shifts in cooking wares, including the appearance of chafing dishes and new closed forms whose shape probably indicates new quotidian food preparation habits. Also noteworthy is the virtual disappearance of mould-made lamps around AD 650 (Gill 2003: 68; Lightfoot 2007: 285). These lighting devices made in professional ceramic workshops were ubiquitous features of Roman life through the end of late antiquity. Their absence from early medieval Amorium and subsequent replacement at least in part with locally produced, cruder 'saucer lamps' and candles indicate a pronounced shift. As Lightfoot (2012: 224–26) has theorized, alterations in lamp use probably reflect the sorts of fuel used in lamps, as olive oil, a major trade item of Roman late antiquity, gave way to more readily available local products such as walnut or flax oil, or animal fats.

Coarse wares, which represented the majority of ceramics in use, are so-called due to the lack of fineness of clay and their general utilitarian rather than aesthetic appeal. Coarse pottery need not imply poor fabrication techniques or *only* local production, though it is true that coarse ware pottery did not circulate far from its place of manufacture. Some coarse wares continued to be traded over long distances during the early medieval period. At Limyra, for example, the share of coarse wares recorded by Vroom (2005b: 252) from the eastern part of the city amounted to 40 per cent of the total ceramic finds. Of these, 82 per cent were produced locally; however, about 7 per cent were imported, some from as far away as Syria-Palestine. Coarse ware types are generally far less studied than glazed examples, which are easy to recognize and have a fair body of literature with which to help in their identification and analysis. One area of coarse ware pottery studies has generated some debate, however – namely, how we are to understand the presence of handmade pottery.

At the close of late antiquity, handmade wares, always a part of the ceramic tradition, become more prevalent on sites throughout the Mediterranean. On Cyprus, such wares have been recovered in surveys and excavations at Amathus, Kalavasos-Kopetra, Maroni-Petrera, and elsewhere (Rautman 1998), and their appearance dated to the sixth century. At Sagalassos, coarse, thick-walled cooking pots were prominent in the post-Roman period (seventh to eighth centuries) (Vionis et al. 2009: 195). These pots were either handmade or thrown on a slow wheel; they were not kiln fired but rather fired in the open or in a bonfire. Parallel examples, mostly wheel-turned but with handmade types as well, are known from Cyprus; those at Kalavasos-Kopetra (Rautman 1998, 2003) were made beginning in the sixth century and continued to the last quarter of the seventh. This group of coarse wares includes several variant forms of basic cooking pots and some bowls. Wheel-turned analogues that include bowls with convex rims are known from the seventh century at Yeroskipou and Nea Paphos (Gabrieli et al. 2007). Forms from as late as the eighth century are known at Kourion (Megaw 1986).

So-called 'Slavic Ware' (also called 'Avaro-Slavic Ware') includes small vessels that were handmade or thrown on a slow wheel. These unglazed pots are generally about 20 cm high and appear in Dark Age

Greece at Corinth, Tiryns, Sparta, and Argos (Aupert 1980, 1989; Polou-Papadimitriou 2001), in the Peloponnese and in east central Greece at Demetrias and Hyettos in Boeotia, as well as further north at Thessaloniki (Vroom 2003: 107; Vroom 2005a: 49). This ware is made of quite coarse but diverse fabrics, tending to orange in colour, with lime or quartz inclusions (Vroom 2004: 318; Vroom 2005a: 49), coated with a grey-brown slip. Later examples are decorated with wavy bands of incised decoration. They are flat-bottomed pots with flared rims, sometimes with attached handles, but often lacking handles entirely. Other examples have a pair of handles attached at the flared mouth.

These little pots have been a magnet of scholarly debate ever since Aupert (1980) linked their appearance at sites in Greece with the sixth- and seventh-century Slavic intrusions into Greece mentioned in literary sources, including an invasion of 549 described by the sixth-century historian Procopius (*Wars* VII.38.21–23). Consequently, the text-led historical archaeology approach that has dominated most Mediterranean archaeology underpinned the nationalist-inspired association of (badly) handmade wares with aliens whose work was perceived to be at variance with the ceramic culture of the Mediterranean. Matters are complicated by the generally poor chronological understanding of 'Slavic Ware' and its mingling with local Byzantine pottery in assemblages. Subsequent careless interpretation by some (Vryonis 1992) has exacerbated the problem. Also problematic is a lack of any analogues to 'Slavic Ware' north of the Danube (Curta 2011: 418–20). There can be little doubt that the attribution of such material to Slavs or other outsiders of Byzantine culture should be discarded until there is a thorough re-evaluation of their excavated contexts.

Debate has also focused on the question of the meaning of increased reliance on handmade pottery, a practice far removed from the pan-Mediterranean trade and consumption of terra sigillata, amphorae, and a host of other products. On Cyprus (see Rautman 1998), local handmade pottery common in early medieval times (early seventh century and later, though chronological controls are often slack) is known from numerous sites, including Amathus, Salamis, and Ayios Kononas. A strap-handled cooking pot bears morphological similarity to a thin walled type from Constantinople. The Cypriot cooking pot is heavier, with thicker walls and made in local dark, coarse fabric. Local examples are known from Kourion, Kalavasos-Kopetra, and Maroni-Petrera and similar, contemporary handmade vessels are known from around the island. Rautman makes several important observations about these handmade types. For example, around AD 650 they existed alongside an abundance of wheel-turned pots from Cyprus and Palestine. These pots, made by local non-specialists near their villages for their own domestic needs, were influenced by eastern Mediterranean, commercially produced, wheel-turned varieties. In some instances, handmade wares neither disappeared from household use nor were they crowded from the market by specialist wheel-turned pots – Pantellaria ware, from an island off Sicily is cited as an example of handmade pottery produced and exported for more than a half millennium and found in fifth- to seventh-century layers at Carthage. Rather than viewing handmade coarse wares as 'debased' successors of specialized Roman production, we are urged to view these products as an integral part of local material culture in which these wares had specific roles that require no special explanation. The social and political upheavals at the end of antiquity and their economic knock-on effects (similar, Rautman notes, to the difficult era of transition at the end of the Late Bronze Age) are best understood within a framework freed from the narratives and judgements filtered through modern Eurocentrism: 'As a product of conditions faced and choices made by inhabitants of the rural household, handmade pottery offers eloquent witness to both the transitions experienced by contemporary society and the adaptive continuities that sustained it' (Rautman 1998: 98).

This view contrasts with that of Ward-Perkins, who holds a rather dimmer view of the prominence of handmade wares, noting that after the withdrawal of Roman political authority in Britain, the emergence of handmade pottery that had trended upward since the third century became complete. The collapse in demand for specialist, wheel-turned pots and professional potters was so severe that wheel-turned pottery was not made in Britain for another three centuries (Ward-Perkins 2005: 118). Cyprus lay close to flourishing centres of Islam and the Byzantine mainland and thus shared more fully than did Britain in the Mediterranean ceramic tradition. Nonetheless, along with the changes to fine wares, the Dark Age shift in pottery is repeated in Byzantium over multiple forms of material culture. While differences in culinary habits and ethnicity or identity undoubtedly explain many alterations, the broadest and most sweeping changes evidenced in ceramics are related to a less connected and less economically prosperous Mediterranean. In this trend, Byzantium and its Aegean and Anatolian core were no exception.

Coins

Coins are archaeological markers of a multiplicity of economic, social, and cultural elements. Numismatists who study coins as objects engage with individual coins from numerous, increasingly sophisticated perspectives, including via iconographic, propagandistic, and mechanical perspectives. Economically coins facilitate the movement and storage of perceived value – the perception of their worth is of course culturally constructed. Coins have no intrinsic value in the societies that choose to utilize them and it should be remembered that before the Classical Greek expansion and eventual dominance of Hellenism throughout the Mediterranean and Middle East, coins were not a fundamental part of exchange. By any standard, contemporary or otherwise, the world of late antiquity in the eastern Mediterranean was highly monetized. The fifth- to seventh-century Byzantine state struck millions of coins representing an outpouring of rivers of gold and copper (really bronze or other copper alloys, which is why the two terms 'copper' and 'bronze' are sometimes used interchangeably in the literature). The gold reform of Diocletian and Constantine, in which the *solidus* (Greek *nomisma*) was struck at 72 to the Roman pound, was made possible by imperial seizure of specie as plunder from internal military enemies, temple reserves, and the hoards of political rivals (Hendy 1985: 284). Base metal coins, mainly copper, provided the means of daily transactions and several reforms across the fifth to sixth centuries aimed to create more useful denominations and alter the ratio of gold to copper. Such reforms were likely made for fiscal reasons (official pay and taxation) and not out of concern about trade or other economic issues. The rhythm of coin production and movements were managed by the state, though as in any traditional society, controls over the movements, melting-down, sale, and forgery of coinage were imperfect to say the least.

Broadly speaking, archaeologists analyse coins based on the context of their discovery. There are two basic categories: isolated (or 'stray') finds that are devoid of a clear archaeological context, even though they may be found during archaeological fieldwork, and excavated coins. Coins recovered during field survey or coins excavated from layers that lack clear stratigraphic sequences are examples of stray finds. Isolated finds may also be encountered outside of any known archaeological context entirely, for example in the form of single coins turned in from a known location by metal detectorists. Coins without any provenance are essentially worthless to archaeologists, though they may be of value to numismatists and are thus of value for economic analysis (Gândilă 2009). Hoards of coins, concealed by owners in the past and never recovered, do not fit neatly into either category. The majority of hoards come to light only by their being dug outside of a controlled excavation and these offer limited data. Other hoards are discovered during excavation and thus can tell us a great deal about the conditions of their assemblage and concealment.

Coins with scant archaeological attributes, for instance examples found in the top level of an excavation where they may be residual, are useful. Coins within good archaeological deposits are relied upon as critical indicators of date; although the sophistication of relative ceramic chronologies has allowed for increasingly nuanced dating, coins remain a vital component of describing and interpreting archaeological sites. In older excavations in which medieval layers were published after a fashion, notably Corinth and to a lesser extent Athens, coins were often the only chronological indicators available. Such dependence is not without controversy: Magness (1993, 2003b) has argued coin finds have led to false dates and that coins are often inferior to tightly controlled, stratigraphically verified ceramic markers.

In addition to their assistance in establishing site chronology, scholars generally accept coin evidence as representative of economic activity, especially market exchange not directly tied to the state. The conventional view, best expressed by Hendy (1985: 619), 'that the seventh century must have witnessed an economic and financial crisis of fundamental proportions and long-standing nature', can be sustained by the coin finds from Corinth. The absence of coin finds, coinciding with the political tumult that engulfed the empire, has been used to reinforce the picture of decline. The case is not so clearly cut and dried however. Hoard finds provide a good example where new methodologies are being applied to revise the traditional view. Data from hoards have often been used to support interpretations of traumatic events, especially barbarian invasion (Blanchet 1936;

Metcalf 1962: 14–20), such as in places like Greece and the Aegean where hoards of the late sixth century are linked in the literature with invasions of the Slavs (MacDowall 1965: 264; Nystazopoulou-Pelekidou 1986), Persians (Caramessini-Oeconomides and Drossoyianni 1989) or Arabs (Metcalf 1962). Morrisson and colleagues (2006) maintain the view that hoards are useful indicators of invasion and civic disturbance. Recently, however, this view has been challenged and some scholars have increasingly viewed hoards as complex indicators of selective processes by their owners. In some cases, it is clear that these collections are something akin to a savings account or bankroll for a tradesman or merchant; as Curta (2011: 84) argues, 'it is unlikely that such hoards were collections hastily put together at the time of their burial. The year-by-year sequence of coins strongly suggests that the accumulation in each of them was a slow, gradual process, which may have taken many years.' What was the fate of coin production and distribution? What can the archaeology of coins tell us about the state of the early medieval Byzantine economy? The coins themselves attest a total overhaul of the minting network in the seventh century and near-simultaneous changes in coin types and in the rate of monetization of the empire.

Changes in minting locations and coin types may offer some information, as does the relative frequency of the coins themselves. During the reign of Heraclius, military emergency led to a reconfiguration of the network of coining establishments. Constantia on Cyprus and Alexandretta ad Issum (today Iskenderum), Jerusalem, and Isauria served as makeshift mints to coin for the pay of troops and bureaucracy during the Persian War (Morrisson 2002: 913). Eastern mints at Cyzicus and Nicomedia ceased output in 629, as did Thessaloniki, although the latter functioned again briefly under Theophilos (829–842). Constantinople supplied the bulk of coins throughout the subsequent centuries, at least to the Balkans and Anatolia, whereas the western themes were served by sundry mints in

Sicily and Italy, which ebbed and flowed depending on the political fortunes of the empire (Morrisson 1994). In 616, the coining of the silver *hexagram* accompanied the halving of government salaries, and in 621 Heraclius was forced to melt down church plate to produce the hexagram; its coining was abandoned during the reign of Constantine IV (Yannopoulos 1978), eventually to be replaced by the *miliaresion*, modelled on the Arabic dirham beginning with the emperor Leo III in 720 (Gordus and Metcalf 1970).

The extraordinary efforts to which imperial officials resorted is evident in the introduction of new coin types, the (re-)introduction of silver coins, and in the melting down of church plate, statues, and roofs. Alongside these measures we find numerous overstrikes, counter-strikes, and the re-uptake and re-coining of older coins. All of these measures demonstrate both monetary crisis but also a strong will to maintain a monetized fiscal system, however curtailed. Minting of gold continued unabated (*solidus, semissis, tremissis*), as did that of copper. The state maintained a high-quality gold coinage that suffered only minor loss of weight and purity: beginning in the 680s, when the full impact of the Arab Conquests was felt and which resulted in an attendant reconfiguration of Byzantine state structures, there were only minor weight decreases and debasement. The solidus of AD 491–668 weighed 4.41 g and was of 98 per cent purity; beginning in the 680s, the weight was cut to 4.36 g and the purity decreased to 96 per cent (Morrisson 2002: 928–29). The weight of the copper *follis*, the principal copper denomination, declined steadily from 12 g during the reign of Phokas (602–610) to a paltry 3.6 g around 660: each debasement may reflect a general lack of minting control (Grierson 1968: 22) but these declines are more likely a direct response to fiscal and political crisis (Morrisson 1994). These examples show serious fiscal challenges as well as basic disruptions of bullion stocks, no doubt mostly due to the cessation of tax revenues from the former eastern provinces, as well as loss of access to mines in the former eastern regions of the empire. We must be cautious in our views of metal shortages, however, as the influx of new metal into the system is generally thought to be quite slight, between 0.34 per cent (Guerreau 1986: 258–59) and 1 per cent annually (Poirier 1985: 84, fig. 35).

We must also be cautious in relying on archaeologically recovered coins, as there are a number of major stumbling blocks to our understanding of the relationship of found coins, the size of the currency stock in circulation, and consequently the fiscal and economic health of the empire in the seventh to tenth centuries. No thorough study of Byzantine coin dies has been conducted and thus there is great uncertainty regarding the total output of coins. The rate of contemporary loss of coins and thus the loss of bullion stock is also highly uncertain. Finally, the question of the proportion of original medieval coins discovered on excavation today introduces another challenge: for late medieval Cyprus, for example, Metcalf and Pitsillides (1992: 4–5) reckon that only one or two out of every thousand silver *gros* coins struck survive. Similar rates of survival are to be expected for much of the early medieval Mediterranean.

To a great extent, the archaeology of the coin supply mirrors the production problems outlined above. While it must be recalled that coin supply in provincial and remote areas was always lower than that of urban centres, there is a pronounced universal downward trend in the finds of coins after the reign of Heraclius. In part this is due to a bias: Heraclius perhaps doubled the supply of coins annually during the years 610–632 (Morrisson 2002: 937). The massive flow of Heraclian issues created a clear bubble and these issues may have remained in exchange (especially coppers) long after the 630s; a hoard from Palestine indicates that copper issues may have circulated for as long as a century (Bates and Kovacs 1996: 173). Copper and silver would have been especially challenging for imperial authorities to remove from the monetary arena, as they were not normally swept up as tax. This fact, rather than a global shortage of bullion within the empire, may explain the emergency measures like those of Constans II in melting down church roofs in Rome (Mango 1963: 58).

Our lack of knowledge and the hindrances of scattered and uneven archaeological data aside, on present evidence the eastern provinces of the early medieval empire seems to have suffered a relative dearth of coinage. By the mid seventh century, in cities like Athens, Corinth, Aphrodisias, Ephesus, Pergamon, Priene, Sardis (Morrisson 2002: tables 6.1–9), and others, coins vanish in the archaeological record. While those who study the issue accede to this general trend (Metcalf 2001), its precise implications remain opaque. These results have been taken by some earlier historians (Charanis 1955) as connoting an economic chasm into which the entire empire plunged, while others were more sanguine and believed that Byzantium continued to have a 'developed' monetary economy (Ostrogorsky 1959: 64). The situation in the western Mediterranean offers an interesting contrast; supply there is largely uninterrupted, a fact not lost on scholars who view the fundamental issue as the status of a gold-based economy, which continued unabated and is acknowledged by pessimists represented by the likes of Vryonis (1963). If present archaeological data of coin finds broadly reflect regional patterns, as has been argued for other regions – namely Anglo-Saxon England (Naylor 2007) – then Anatolia and the Balkans suffered a currency inversion from the mid seventh through the early ninth century, and some areas experienced a much longer tightening of supply. The effects of the dearth of coins would have rippled throughout the fiscal structure and the wider economy, making life in the eighth century look rather different than that of the sixth.

When coins are found on Dark Age archaeological sites, their significance remains an open question. Some, such as McCormick, see coin finds within an economic picture that he believes portrays a renewal of investment and trade in the Gulf of Corinth around 830 at the latest (McCormick 2001: 536). In such an interpretative framework, coins recovered from specific archaeological contexts indicate some sort of commercial (i.e. non-state-directed) economic activity. Curta (2011: 138–40) interprets the coin data quite differently, linking the surge indicated by the issues of Theophilos (829–842) and others to military action against Slavic rebels. These conflicting interpretations are unlikely to be resolved without considerable advancement in both numismatics and excavation data, but it should be noted that in other ancient environments coin circulation patterns fail to match other evidence for trade. Thus, the relationships of coins to the movement of goods and people and to the wider economy are all in doubt and require much more work before we can draw firmer conclusions.

Glass

Early medieval glass continued the tradition of Roman glass production. During late antiquity, glass was apparently too expensive for the very poor but accessible to those of middling incomes (Antonaras 2010). Commenting on Sardis, von Saldern (1962: 5) exclaimed 'the extensive use of window glass is astonishing; in Sardis it must have been relatively common and cheap at this time'. Whether the cheapness and ubiquity of glass remained the norm in the seventh to tenth centuries is not known for certainty but while some Byzantine scholars have considered glassware as luxury items, others conclude that the range and commonality of finds on medieval sites indicates that there was a range of cheap items (Lightfoot 2005). The effect of the loss of Levantine glass-producing centres after the 630s needs thorough investigation; certainly the output of these places was vast. At Jerash, by no means a huge city, the excavators report glass deposits up to 0.25 m deep north of the Church of St. Theodore (Meyer 1988: 184). While glass production declined significantly at Sardis, the medieval settlement remained a local producer (von Saldern 1962).

As with other finished goods, access to these objects depended on where one lived; a recent survey of the archaeology of Epirus lists no certain finds of glassware on early medieval sites (Veikou 2012: 238). Certain types of glass are attested in early medieval Byzantium and were apparently common items. Among these were cups, goblets, lamps, windows, and bracelets. Other products in daily use were game pieces, unguentaria, and medicine flasks. At Amorium, most glass belonged to the Middle Byzantine era (post tenth century) but a small body of material is dated to the seventh to tenth centuries, indicating that local sources could be accessed.

Metalwork

Like glass objects, Dark Age finds in various metals have not received due attention. Relatively few pieces from the period occupy the display cases of museums and the sample to discuss is rather small. Consequently, it is easy to forget the vast array of medieval objects made of metal: crosses, candelabra, lamps, basins, bowls, cruets, censers, braziers, pitchers, buckets, jewellery, fixtures, and hand tools are examples of metal items for daily use of the early medieval period. Our understanding of their significance, trade, and details of their manufacture are hindered by the lack of provenance and clear dating of many of the best preserved (presumably) medieval pieces (Bénazeth 1991). Everyday objects such as nails and other simple metallic objects have warranted scant scholarly consideration. As Mucahide Lightfoot (2003) notes, the numerous buckles found at Amorium and in the nearby Afyon Museum show how neglected the study of such objects is. A sizeable proportion of the Amorium buckles belong to the seventh or eighth centuries. Elite objects in silver are rare for the Dark Ages but somewhat better studied. One well-known silver example is the so-called 'Ewer of Zenobius', dated to the seventh century. With its inscription quoting Psalm 29 and 'Lord help your servant Zenobius. Amen' (Metropolitan Museum of Art, Accession 17.190.1704; Bálint 2000: 185), the ewer was probably part of an elite 'Avar' treasure. Control stamps on the base of the vessel indicate the Ewer of Zenobius was made in Constantinople; unfortunately, these control stamps cease after 661 (Mundell Mango and Boyd 1993: 215). In the fourth to seventh centuries, silver, especially from the mines of Cilicia and Isauria, was worked into a vast number of ecclesiastical and secular objects that circulated in large numbers and over much of Eurasia (Mundell Mango 2009b). The surviving objects indicate that the output of eastern workshops was truly massive, as do textual records indicating spoils of war measured in tons of silver heisted from cities like Edessa by the Persians (Whittow 1990); their use no doubt facilitated because the state did not rely on silver until the seventh century. The question of the quantity of the output of silver work in the seventh to tenth centuries is impossible to assess at present due to the rarity of identified finds. Among these are a set of four church vessels belonging to the eighth or ninth centuries (now in Geneva), the silver cup of the Grand Zhupan Sivin of Bulgaria dated *c.* 865 excavated at Preslav, and a similar example from Gotland in Sweden (Mundell Mango 2009b: 227–30).

A number of loosely dated copper alloy, especially bronze cast and hammered so-called 'Coptic' bowls, illustrated by an analogue recovered from Amorium (Fig. 4) survive in Dark Age burial contexts throughout temperate Europe, especially along the Rhine and in Anglo-Saxon burials as well as in Italy. Various forms of cast bronze, flat-bottomed bowls, finished by lathe-turning and hammering are represented among these. Most bowls have triangular or omega-shaped handles attached near the rim; handles were applied either with solder or with lugs attached into either side of the body of the bowl (Harris at al. 2006). Classified according to morphology and assigned by Werner to Egyptian manufacture (Werner 1957, 1961),

Fig. 4 'Coptic' style copper bowl from ninth-century Amorium (courtesy of The Amorium Excavations Project).

scholars today remain at odds about their precise origin. Early medieval copper vessels are relatively rare finds in the eastern Mediterranean, which has led to speculation that they were not made in eastern workshops and considerable disagreement surrounds the use of the term 'Coptic' for material (Périn 2005) spread over a considerable extent of space and time. An example of a copper bowl excavated from Pella in Jordan in destruction layers associated with the earthquake of AD 749 (McNicoll and Smith 1982: 140, pl. 59) indicates that such items were common but valuable everyday items in Byzantium likely to be used over long periods of time and melted down once they could no longer be mended. A similar copper alloy basin was found at Amorium in destruction layers related to the sack of 838 (Ivison 2007: 51 and fig. 23). The problem rests more with our understanding of specific types and their cultural origin – for example, Carretta (1982) argued that hammered bronze vases interred with Lombard notables in the seventh century belonged to a Lombard or general Germanic tradition rather than the Byzantine world, though others excavated in the west, notably cast pieces, were presumably of eastern origin. Bronze bowls and a pitcher from excavations in Rome at Crypta Balbi and the discovery of 'Coptic' bowls in a shipwreck off Camarina, southern Sicily, indicate to some a south-Italian production centre in the sixth to seventh centuries (Zagari 2005: 110). Increasingly, it seems that scholars believe assigning the origin of these copper alloy vessels should be approached in a more sophisticated manner. Based on technique of manufacture and in light of other known Mediterranean metalworking traditions, some of these vessels were possibly made in the Germanic successor kingdoms (Périn 2005).

Such metal wares hold tantalizing clues about such fundamental issues as migration, settlement, self-identification of the producers and consumers of these goods and those who displayed and interred them, as well as their wider contacts. The persistence in the highlands of Albania in the seventh century of a popular dress accessory, the bow fibula, enlarged and slightly modified from its sixth-century predecessor, is telling. In this instance, the large implement may be an outward marker of a relict population of Roman soldiers or administrators or locals who self-identified with these (Curta 2013a). The deposition of 'Coptic' bowls in western graves, for example, may indicate more sustained trade or diplomatic contacts than usually considered likely. The closing of the Mediterranean trade, a theme of scholarly debate since Pirenne, may be further underlined by exploration of these elite metal wares. In order to achieve this, however, we need much more analysis and clearer chronological controls.

Other categories of material evidence: stone, bone, and other materials

Besides its use as building material, the evidence of worked stone from the empire indicates that its inhabitants continued several classical traditions, including large practical items such as troughs and basins, decorative marble flooring and cladding, especially in ecclesiastical spaces. The late antique technique of cutting polychrome marble tiling to shape a figural or geometric pattern seems to have survived into the early medieval period. Fragments of *opus sectile* known from Hagia Sophia, Bizye (Bauer and Klein 2006), may be as early as the ninth century but their precise chronology remains obscure. *Opus sectile* is likely the type of pavement recalled in texts relating the decoration of the palace of Basil I (842–867) and the Nea Ekklesia (Mango 1972: 181, 194). In Italy, *opus sectile* incorporating Proconnesian marble from Prokonnesos in the Sea of Marmara, was laid in the nave of the Abbey Church of San Vincenzo Maggiore in the ninth century (Hodges 1997; Hodges et al. 1997), indicating that the art and something of the marble trade was still alive in the former territories of the empire. The mosaic arts, which show such bloom in the eleventh-century churches of Hosios Loukas and Nea Mone on Chios (Evans and Wixom 1997: 12), could hardly have sprung from nothing; the specialization of such knowledge implies at least some level of workshop production across the seventh to tenth centuries in continuing ancient production of tesserae and their application. Stone was also used in ways that are probably unexpected by people of the twenty-first century used to synthetic and metal materials in utilitarian and even luxury roles: common or semi-precious stones were used in jewellery and in personal and architectural decoration. Steatite (soapstone) was used to imitate ivory in icons and plaques as early as the tenth century and probably earlier (Beckwith 1970: 107). Stones were used as metallic moulds for metal and ceramic production, for ship anchors, and for a range of other practical applications, such as grinding grain.

There are numerous other categories of material evidence long overlooked in our discussion of early medieval Byzantium. As with the other types of evidence we have noted above, none of these are terribly easy to approach. Due to limits of space, I can offer nothing more than a cursory view here and describe some of the potential approaches below, though see Decker (forthcoming) for a more detailed series of investigations. Animal bone and ivory were used for an array of objects including buckles, inlays for furniture and implement handles, gaming pieces, and tools such as spindle whorls, combs, and archers' thumb rings. Judged by their ubiquity in archaeological sites, worked bone tools and decorations were a normal part of the material culture of Byzantine Dark Age society. In their humble forms, they were used by all social strata in utilitarian objects or as decorative pieces imitating more sumptuous items made from ivory or more expensive materials, such as ivory icons and plaques represented by the tenth-century examples from Dumbarton Oaks and other precious ivory pieces (Evans and Wixom 1997: 154). On display with these items are a range of expressions of status exemplified by the selection of their material, their uses, and the effort expended in making them. Were elite objects like ivory panels made alongside simple bone combs? It seems likely, but until workshops producing ivory come to light, we are unable to capture much of the information these finds promise.

Textile fragments offer another set of material data from which to view glimpses of aspects of the early medieval period. Material from the seventh to ninth centuries is rarely preserved. At Amorium we are fortunate enough to have carbonized fragments associated with the destruction of the city in the Muslim attack of 838. Likely materials from the Amorium assemblage including wool, silk, or hair were in mainly Z-spun fabrics (Z twist yarn was spun on the wheel clockwise) traditional to Anatolia, and weaves belonging to the early Byzantine tradition of cloth manufacture imply production within the empire at minimum and probably within Anatolia (Linscheid 2003: 190). Conditions unfavourable for the preservation of cloth and consequently their rare discovery in most of the former empire should not blind us to the potential promise of these primary sources to cast light on numerous questions, many already recognized in other archaeological and anthropological disciplines (Fulghum 2001–2002; Weiner and Schneider 1989). Closer analysis of pieces like the famous (probably ninth century) Charioteer silk of the Aachen Munster Treasury conducted by Muthesius (1993: 43; Muthesius 1997: 173; cat. M29–30) allows considerable insight into the imperial cloth-making industry and the technology of production, as well as control and circulation of elite items. To date, however, data on more common cloth remains elusive.

3

Cities

It is safe to say that no other area of Byzantine archaeology has generated as much debate as the fate of the classical city, and for good reason. The Roman Empire was an empire of cities. How does one define the Roman city? It was a locus of permanent or seasonal residence for the elites of surrounding areas, an arena of entertainment, of competition among the families who dominated the major political and social networks and whose statues and inscriptions were knotted in the public spaces to proclaim their goodness and value to their peers and rivals. The city was the home of the gods where local cults were celebrated in the temple precincts. Even modest temples, gilded and graced with finery, their sacrifices smoking and smouldering in the air, imbued a pungent sacred odour to the streets when crowds of the great and the good and their social inferiors gathered in civic solidarity. And the Roman city was a place of government in which most centres had the basic structures of law; the hall of judgment in a basilica or a forum where cases were heard, lawyers, judges, and notaries in attendance. By the second century, most Roman cities carried on the sacred Hellenic tradition of athletic contests and spectacle, especially horse racing in which factions – the Greens, Blues, Whites, and Reds – stabled their animals and maintained a web of supporters and clients. Even provincial cities like Jerash in Arabia, El Jem in Tunisia, and Carnuntum in Austria possessed amphitheatres hosting displays of blood sport. The city was a market, a node of specialization of both workers – from tinkerers and clothing makers to hucksters of wheat, wine, and vegetables – and merchants from afar carrying more exotic wares. Even the most humdrum little Roman cities, like the agro-towns littered throughout ancient Africa Proconsularis, now modern Tunisia, were fine alternatives to the chaotic, free-range, and open vastness and mountain strongholds of the past. Cities knitted together unruly clans and federations. Often to be seen was the Roman fist: the parade of the curials and their tax-collecting troops, the tramp of seconded soldiers policing the countryside, the hated surveyor and assessors who measured and recorded the land to the last foot and registered hearths and heads for taxation. But along with the limits on civic freedoms came running water, aqueducts with their soaring water bridges and piped water to fountains, eye-catching nymphaea, and public baths and latrines.

Roman elites urbanized Western Europe, inculcating populations from North Africa to Germany of the habit of living in cities. To say that cities were the sinews of the empire is not an understatement – they were the nerves and senses of the state as well. The Romans settled their colonists in cities, established their administrative apparatus within them, and endowed them with public buildings, many of considerable opulence and beauty. The agonistic exhibition of elite culture – witnessed today in the organization of public space, the arrangement of temples, and arrangement of inscriptions – bears testimony to the richness and vibrancy of many of these settlements, even in provincial areas like North Africa, where Latin and Roman culture made rapid headway among the chief men of the autochthonous inhabitants, or Asia Minor where a city like Melitene (today Malatya in eastern Turkey) grew from a post servicing the needs of a legionary garrison. Most cities were provided with aqueducts, public baths, and often had sewers that benefitted public health and made life much more pleasant for their residents. Temples and cult sites where the public celebrated feast days with food provided by the temple treasury or elites, helped to allay pressures on the urban poor and provided an arena for charitable distributions by polytheist patrons. Many cities had resident doctors paid at the public expense and all had schools at least for primary education while others, like Alexandria and Beirut, hosted skilled practitioners and teachers of medicine, philosophy or law. Public libraries were common, as were gymnasia where mind and body could be exercised. Theatres and odeons provided venues for plays, musical performance, and hosted the travelling companies of actors common throughout the empire. The amphitheatre hosted beast shows and gladiatorial combats. Especially in the third and fourth centuries, these sometimes featured Christians and other deviants exposed to cruel justice. Cities also boasted brothels and public markets and, as late antiquity progressed, increasingly hosted industrial activities of all kind in the suburbs and sometimes even within the confines of fortified precincts.

By the end of late antiquity, especially in the sixth century AD, the city was where the bishop resided, sovereignty having been transferred from the emperor to God. If the bishop defined a city, then a whole clutch of new cities appeared, mostly in areas that had hitherto been backward and rural, like Cappadocia where Gregory of Nyssa famously carped about his see of Nyssa, a cow town in Cappadocia. Many of these places, like Mampsis in the Negev, Caričin Grad (Justiniana Prima) in Serbia, and Zenobia in Syria bore only scant resemblance to even middling provincial cities; they were small, often not much larger than a village, and their most prominent building tended to be a church. The civic focus of these late antique cities was the Christian ecclesiastical complex, while many were fortified with massive masonry walls. By the fifth century in many regions the old bouleteria were in weeds and as Christian mores spread and the authorities centralized financial and political power, the hippodromes, theatres, and other trappings of agonistic polytheism and civic pride and display vanished with them. Of the plethora of specialized public spaces of the ancient city, those most likely to survive in the late antique city included the halls of administration, such as the old civic basilicas or praetoria, and the baths. As the latter usually required running water, aqueducts were often sustained in support of the baths and public fountains. One suspects that other uses were made of these waters, including for domestic and industrial purposes. At Caesarea, portions of the aqueduct were maintained into the seventh century (Porath 2002) while the aqueduct on Gortyn in Crete apparently functioned in some way into the eleventh century (Pagano 1992).

From this overview one can easily see how germane the city was to Roman governance, identity, and sense of belonging. The regular planning, similarity of public spaces and amenities, access to goods, and representation of the Roman state provided by these centres helped to unify the empire, at least at the level of the elites who governed it. The desire for the well-off especially to mingle with one another and partake in civic values in such places as Timgad (ancient Thamugadi) in Algeria and Mogontiacum (today Mainz in Germany), if only on a seasonal basis, was for centuries key to the continuation of Roman governance. Thus, the mutation of civic life and the disintegration of Roman authority have been closely linked in the literature. As one scholar has noted regarding the question of urban decline,

> At the centre of this debate lies the city. It is central because Roman civilization in its broadest sense is frequently regarded as an urban civilization; central because it is argued that the culture whose passing Procopius is assumed to be mourning was one only fully possible in a classical urban context; and central because cities, as relative concentrations of population, wealth and social interaction, can perhaps be treated as diagnostic of trends less visible elsewhere (Whittow 2001).

For the late antique East, the debate is complicated and at the risk of oversimplification here, we will summarize some of the major contributors and their thoughts in what has been a brisk trade of late. The views of Liebeschuetz are perhaps most emblematic of the declinists, a group who considers that the Roman Empire declined and fell and who may or may not think that alongside the political decay there were transformative structural changes in society that accompanied it. Liebeschuetz argued that the later Roman Empire (AD 300–700) experienced a profound unravelling, the threads of which might be seen in the end of the erection of public inscriptions, or at least a considerable curtailing of these. The death of the 'epigraphic habit' as these carvings are termed, presaged 'the decline of the city as a political community and of the institutions and social and political attitudes which had found expression in the putting up of public monuments' (Liebeschuetz 2001: 12). At the heart of decay were administrative changes that eroded the responsibilities and powers of local elites, on whose civic engagement in urban space the empire had relied for centuries. As the imperial officials sought to centralize authority, the role of the decurions, the local officials and city councillors who wove the mesh of administrative fabric within the provincial cities became fraught with risk; much was demanded of these officials but there were greater rewards to be found outside of the civic structure in the imperial service or Christian church (Liebeschuetz 2001: 104). The effect was to create a government of 'notables', including bishops, rather than decurions (Liebeshuetz 2001: 122–24). These notables were ultimately less useful to the state than their predecessors were and made the cities less useful to the state as well. Symptoms of these changes included fundamental alterations in Graeco-Roman cultural expression (the end of the shows, cessation of civic monumental building, alterations in artistic representation of Greek cultural forms, and so on) that progressed at different rates and affected each region somewhat differently, but the end result was the regionalization of the former territory of the empire. Telling, according to this view, is that the recovery of early Byzantine Anatolia was administered not from cities but from the *themes*, which were essentially military structures.

Other scholars have articulated similar views of the state of affairs prior to the arrival of Islam, notably Hugh Kennedy, who sketched the decline of urban settlements in Syria. Kennedy argued that the cities of the eastern Mediterranean witnessed a general curtailment of monumental building in late antiquity and the dereliction of major spaces of former prominence within the civic life of the empire, notably theatres, none of which were built in Syria later than the third century and few functioned in the sixth century (Kennedy 1985: 7). Drastic changes in urban planning and the failure to maintain the open, regular plans of the urban grid are visible in the archaeological record of the Byzantine period and thus were underway already prior to the arrival of the Arabs (Kennedy 1985: 12). The arrival of the mosque and its usurpation of the role of the church as the focus of life for the Muslim community cemented these changes, which were both structural and organic. Much of Kennedy's thesis, although not all of its particulars, has met widespread approval, especially among scholars of Islamic history and archaeology. Magness (2003a) proposed critical re-dating of sites throughout the Levant in her rejection of the notion of economic or social decline in the East. Likewise, Walmsley maintained that there was broad continuity across the southern Levant in social and economic forms that had been unfolding for centuries and rejects the notion of a decline prior to and after the Muslim arrival (Walmsley 2007). With the recent reassessment of much of the material evidence of Syria-Palestine by Avni (2011, 2014), the 'continuitists' have made an even stronger case. Scholars now widely hold the view that the lands under Islamic political control enjoyed continued prosperity and vibrant social and cultural life.

In Byzantium, the picture is complex. The fall of the Levantine provinces to Islam in the seventh century was the latest of a series of shocks over the century that began in the 530s. These included a series of earthquakes, the great pandemic of AD 542 – the 'Justinianic Plague' – invasions by Slavs and Avars in the Balkans, alongside the devastating war against Sasanian Persia (602–628), all of which strained the resources of the empire. But did this century also witness the progressive degrading of civic and economic life in the cities of the empire? In the 1960s and 1970s, scholars such as A.H.M. Jones (1964) hypothesized a general terminal decline of the whole of the Roman world over the third to the sixth centuries AD, helping to institutionalize the dominant view of the death of the empire in circulation from the time of Edward Gibbon's *Decline and Fall of the Roman Empire* (1776). In a seminal article 'Archaeology and the "Twenty Cities" of Asia Minor', Clive Foss (1977) posited that the Persian and Arab invasions of Anatolia led to terminal decline in the cities of western Asia Minor. In this article Foss proposed a different chronology, with eastern urbanism resembling the classical model surviving into the seventh century. Foss addressed the great ancient centres of Ephesus, Smyrna, Miletus, Sardis, and Pergamum, among others. In his investigation he utilized a combined material approach that included data from architecture, ceramics, and coins. This novel method prompted archaeologists to make use of more of the data available to them in seeking answers to the major questions they posed.

Most major Byzantine cities have been continuously occupied since their founding. Nicaea (Iznik), Nicomedia (Izmet), Smyrna (Izmir), and Ancyra (Ankara) are presently densely occupied and have been the subject of negligible archaeological work. In Constantinople, apart from the rare medieval buildings, the only traces of the old city fabric appear in the form of disarticulated architectural fragments and other stray finds, supplemented by occasional emergency excavations that often remain unpublished. From written sources it is known that the capital remained inhabited during the early medieval period, of course, and it remained the pre-eminent city throughout the history of the empire. However, the precise nature of Dark Age life remains elusive and in order to gain some comparative perspective it is necessary to turn to other provincial centres.

In the Balkans, which would play an increasing role in the history of Byzantium beginning in the ninth century, decades of excavation and survey have produced hundreds of publications in multiple languages, making it difficult to extract a coherent picture of early medieval settlement. Recent approaches have stressed the importance of regional studies, which allow a finer-grained approach to settlement than assessing the Balkans as a whole (Dunn 1997, 1999). It seems therefore sensible to examine briefly cases of Balkan urbanism from which to derive a clearer image of the fate of the city in the peninsula and the overall pattern of Dark Age settlement.

Balkan urbanism: the cases of Nicopolis, Butrint, and Corinth

Nicopolis ad-Istrum

At the far end of the empire and on one side of a broad spectrum of cities is Nicopolis-ad-Istrum, subject of excavation by a joint Anglo-Bulgarian team from 1985 to 2002. Nicopolis lies on the west bank of the Iatrus River near the confluence of the latter and the Rositsa River in Moesia (modern Bulgaria). Around AD 110, a colony of Roman veterans from western Asia Minor established themselves and the city grew quickly. Despite the nature of its citizens (discharged veterans and their families), not terribly common throughout the east, the modest size, plan, and agrarian outlook of Nicopolis is certainly reflective of most cities (Fig. 5). It had a regular plan and a range of public buildings, including an agora, a basilica, bouleuterion, temples, baths, and an aqueduct. At its peak the walled *urbs* covered an area of about 21 hectares (Poulter 2007a: 72). Nicopolis was therefore a small Roman city in area and population; its excavator estimates only a few hundred people lived there (Poulter 2007a: 68).

Approximately thirty large houses accounted for 35 per cent of the space inside the city walls; these dwellings, with stone foundations, mud brick walls, and tiled roofs, were nonetheless far from grand

Fig. 5 Plan of Nicopolis (Andrew Poulter).

urban villas. With their lack of central heating, annexes with beaten earth floors, and evidence for the harvest and storage of wheat, rye, millet, and pulses among other crops, these urban villas resemble large farmhouses. However, the city was well connected with the material culture of the Roman world. Imported fine ware pottery arrived from Italy and North Africa. Oysters were imported from the Black Sea, and glass came from abroad as well. Local industry was modest: minor metal- and bone-working are evidenced primarily in the southern, poorer suburb. Local red slip ware, imitations of well-known African Red Slip types, were produced but this pottery output apparently faded at some point before AD 400. Activity from around the agora continued – new building is attested there around the time of Constantine I; the odeon was in use in the fourth century, and coins indicate maintenance and business activity until the mid fifth century (Vladkova 2007: 208–9). In the early fifth century, the building of a *proteichisma* (outerwork) in mud brick and widening of the defensive ditch was followed around AD 447 by the destruction of the same structure by fire; thick deposits of ash and collapsed debris in the agora and bath complexes likely indicate a conflagration engulfed and destroyed the classical city. At the same time that Roman Nicopolis experienced this fire and subsequent abandonment, its hinterland underwent far-reaching changes as well. The villas of the Roman era town were abandoned around the mid fifth century, probably in response to Hunnic incursions that followed the widespread disruptions caused by the passage of the Goths through the region. With the collapse of the regional villa economy, such settlement that remained moved to smaller hilltop hamlets of uncertain duration, but probably not lasting beyond the sixth century (Poulter 2002: 26–9).

Sometime in the later fifth or early sixth century, after several years or several decades of abandonment, the re-founding of Nicopolis commenced. The Byzantine city occupied the former southern extramural suburb; settlers clearly selected this site for its defensibility.

A strong circuit wall about 2.5 m thick comprised mortared rubble core faced with small, cut limestone blocks and bonded with thick mortar. These limestone courses alternated with bands of brick, five courses thick (Poulter 2007a: 75). There were three identifiable gates and fifteen towers, some of which were excavated and one of which – Tower 8 – was a huge affair, a 9.3 m wide pentagonal bastion; indicatiing that it and its presumed twin (Tower 9) flanked the main gate to the settlement on the east.

The centerpiece of the settlement, the Large Basilica (one of two churches excavated, the other from Area K in the southeast quarter), was a timber-built church with a polygonal apse. Internally the church was arranged with a central ambo, screened aisles and chancel, along with rooms flanking the apse. Elsewhere in the settlement, three long blocks of buildings running west to east along the centre of the site have been interpreted as barracks or storerooms. But resistivity survey data suggest presumed workshops and churches stood in isolation, without any dense housing quarters or monumental public buildings.

Economically the picture of Byzantine Nicopolis is one of small-scale craft and artisanal production with metal working for domestic use; the scant waste and metallic objects do not allow a clear picture but do not suggest any kind of sizeable surplus production. Farming and fishing remained the primary pursuits but the foodways of the settlement altered substantially from that of the prior city. The Byzantine era inhabitants relied more on rye, millet, barley, and pulses than had their predecessors. Significantly, millet was a crop adapted to a shorter growing season and was grown in the summer months, often after the harvest of a winter cereal and could be used as a grain or fodder crop. The adaptation of millet and rye to cooler conditions may also indicate a climatic shift or other subsistence strategy based on cultural preference or security concerns. In any case, the cereals from the later phases of Nicopolis were not preferred by Romanized populations in the Mediterranean and would therefore not be likely to have found an export market there. The ceramic picture is also revealing with a diminished range of imports and reliance on Aegean products indicative of a rather narrow axis of supply, interpreted by some as the involvement of the state in transporting goods to Nicopolis (Karagiourgou 2001). By the end of the sixth century, Nicopolis was no longer occupied and the lack of destruction evidence and careful removal of metal and architectural components suggests planned abandonment rather than a catastrophic end to the site.

Byzantine Nicopolis fits fairly well into the picture of the lower register of Byzantine urban settlements exemplified by Caričin Grad in Serbia (Bavant 2007), Zenobia (Halabiya) on the Euphrates (Lauffray 1983–1991), and others. In their present states, these cities resemble little more than fortified ecclesiastical compounds and military cantonments.

Butrint

Butrint (ancient Latin *Buthrotum*, Greek *Bouthroton*) lies astride a promontory along the north bank of the Vivari Channel to the Ionian Sea and thence the Adriatic. Butrint was part of ancient Epirus and is now within the borders of Albania. The city is almost 8 km (5 miles) from the island of Corfu, from which the polis alleged it was founded in the seventh century BC. As it lay on a peninsula, Butrint had to be compact. The wall-circuit was just under 1.5 km; expansion therefore had to be extramural and the environment favoured development to the south onto low-level ground on the opposite shore of a channel, where excavations were also conducted in the Vrina Plain. By the second century, Butrint prospered, at least in part due to the presence of a healing cult of Asclepius. In addition to the temple, the classical and Roman city boasted the civic architecture typical of its peers, including a central theatre. The Romans granted the city colonial status, an important honour and a relative marker of status among foreign cities. Although Butrint does not feature prominently in the literary record of the imperial era of Roman history, we can be reasonably certain that it continued to prosper through late antiquity.

A major seismic event struck in the fourth century but the city recovered, as exhibited by long-distance trade links with both the western Mediterranean (predominant until the late fifth century) and the eastern Mediterranean, before declining after AD 550 (Hodges 2013: 18). The fifth and sixth centuries witnessed, then, the last burst of monumental building activity for about two centuries. At this time the new lower city walls were built, the northern portion following a good deal of the classical city outline (Fig. 6). The new circuit excluded the suburbs of the Vrina Plain, which the excavators conclude had been an integral part of Roman Butrint (Molla et al. 2013: 261). A variety of masonry techniques and uneven use of material and mortar throughout indicate that various teams of masons worked on various portions of the wall. The square towers, typical of late antique Byzantine fortifications, and numerous gateways made an impressive boundary and testify to the continued vivacity of the site. At least four churches – the Acropolis Basilica, the Gymnasium Church, Great Basilica, and Diaporit Basilica – served the intramural area, and two additional churches were found in the Vrina Plain, a basilica and a chapel (Greenslade et al. 2013: 59). Construction of the Acropolis Basilica was a considerable undertaking involving the clearance of earlier Roman building remnants. The Acropolis Basilica has been thoroughly excavated; it measures 33 × 22 m and is orientated east–west and is thought to have been constructed largely from the private funds of the individual whose crypt was located in a room accessing the narthex from the southwest (Greenslade et al. 2013: 57). Such private church building was commonplace in late antiquity. There was also a tower house of several storeys built over newly terraced space

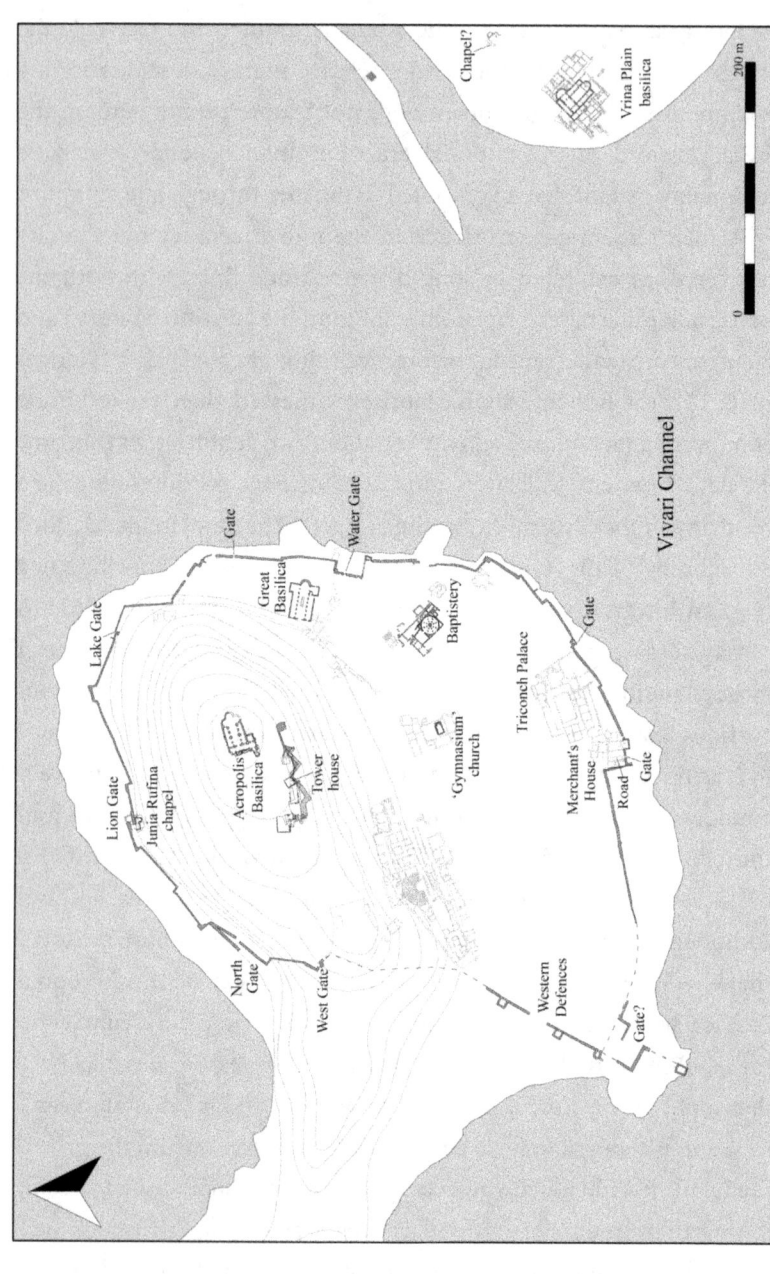

Fig. 6 Butrint: City and Vrina Plain in Late Antiquity (courtesy of the Butrint Foundation).

indicating domestic dwellings of some stature on the hill overlooking the lower city.

Inside the sixth-century walls, a shift in values is expressed in stone: the old gymnasium contained a church. The acropolis possessed a basilica and a chapel on the north side rather than the old cults of Greece and imperial Rome. The so-called 'Great Basilica' lay at the foot of the acropolis hill on the eastern edge of the city. As Hodges (2013: 12–18) has noted, the late antique planners took great pains to include the lower city within the wall-circuit despite issues of waterlogging of some of the buildings on ground nearer sea level. The connection with the sea implies the continued reliance on the Adriatic and Mediterranean as sources of food and trade goods. By the first quarter of the sixth century, the grand domus of the Triconch Palace, never completed after its initial massive expansion of AD 420–480, hosted communities of fisherman and craftsmen (Bowden 2011a) within its impressive crumbling walls and was accompanied by inhumations and robbing of masonry until it was abandoned by the seventh century.

The fourth-century earthquake presumed to have struck Butrint inflicted grave damage on the aqueduct of the city, evidenced in the nature of the collapse of several of the masonry piers that carried the line across the Vrina Plain and into the urban area (Wilson 2013). With the failure of the water system that fed the monumental nympheum and other fountains in the city, a major facet of life characterizing the Roman and late antique periods came to an end. In the extra-mural area of the Vrina Plain, at least one grand villa was perhaps abandoned in response to its reliance on water from the aqueduct (Greenslade 2013: 138), although it was fairly soon reoccupied. This villa site evidenced conversion into an ecclesiastical complex in the late fifth century and served as such into the mid sixth century; fire damage from this horizon may indicate violent destruction of the site.

In the city centre, the 'Triconch Palace' was largely remodelled but, for reasons that remain unclear, left incomplete in the fourth century. Likewise, the adjacent domestic complex, labelled 'the Merchant's House' whose oldest contexts belong to the fifth century, was modified over the succeeding century (Fig. 7). Among the changes was the building of an additional storey on the south boundary of the complex. In this vertical addition of space, the Merchant's House and neighbouring Triconch Palace shared in an increasingly common architectural expression of late antiquity (Bowden 2011d: 315–16). At the end of the seventh century, there is no evidence the Merchant's House was occupied; no coins belonging to Heraclius or his immediate successors were found, but there were small quantities of eighth- to tenth-century ceramics. As Hodges (2011: 322) warns, 'A few sherds of 7th-to-9th century pottery from the Triconch Palace (and Merchant's House) excavations do not equate to urban continuity.' He further notes, 'By the early to mid 7th century Butrint probably amounted to little more than a modest village within the ruins of the Graeco-Roman city.'

Only sparse evidence of Dark Age Butrint has come to light. On the acropolis hill, the eastern regions settlement trickled to naught by the end of the sixth century. So too over much of the lower city, which, although not wholly abandoned, was sparsely occupied. The walls of the so-called 'Western Defences', excavated Towers 1 and 2, provided evidence of domestic occupation perhaps indicative of a civilian group making use of the former fortifications. Among the finds are three-spouted pots and locally made braziers that were, as noted above (Chapter 2), characteristic markers of changing dining habits in the early medieval era. In the late eighth century, a fire consumed both structures simultaneously and destroyed them. Evidence for Dark Age occupation elsewhere in Butrint is minimal – scant finds of pottery indicate low-intensity occupation from the seventh through the ninth centuries and only a few sherds

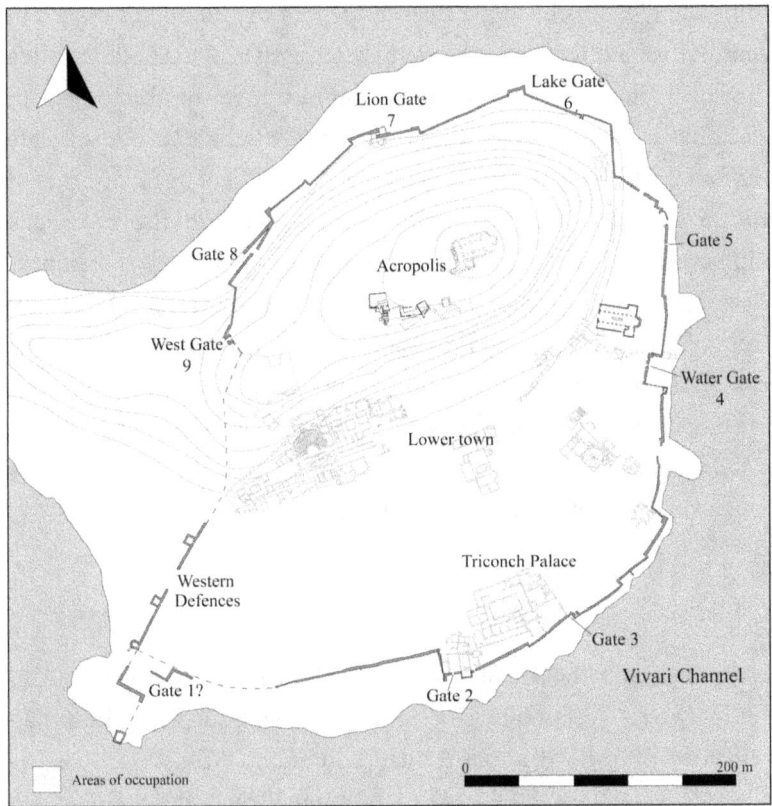

Fig. 7 Early Medieval Butrint (courtesy of the Butrint Foundation).

belonging to the tenth and eleventh centuries were found in the towers (Kamani 2013: 252).

Medieval written sources mention Byzantine Butrint only rarely. St. Elias the Younger was detained as a spy at Butrint and his near contemporary Arsenios of Corfu (876–953) noted the marine wealth of the town. The archaeological signature of activity grows stronger in the tenth century when the volumes of coins and ceramics indicate year-round occupation and considerable economic activity (Hodges 2011: 324). The place where St. Elias was held has been hypothesized to be the *oikos* in the Vrina Plain, which, in the middle of the ninth century, replaced the sixth-century ecclesiastical complex with a possible official residence and administrative headquarters. In addition to the church, which was partly rehabilitated, an elite residence (*oikos*) was built. Several lead document seals discovered within the *oikos* indicate high-level contacts with the provincial military governors (*strategos*) of the western themes of the empire. These may imply that imperial administrators governed the region from the *oikos* rather than the citadel (Greenslade 2013: 150–55). The colonization of medieval Butrint by the Byzantine authorities seems to coincide with the reign of Leo VI (886–912), whose rule witnessed a cultivation of the ideals of the Roman past and the project of *renovatio* of the old boundaries of the empire (Tougher 1997).

Corinth

Far to the south, the fate of Corinth was similar to its northern Balkan counterparts. A famous city in classical antiquity, Corinth had remained prominent under Roman dominion (Williams 1993). The enviable position of the city is best exemplified by its maintaining two ports, one on the Gulf of Corinth to the west at Lechaion, 3 km from the city centre, and a second on the Gulf of Megara to the east at Kenchreai, 10 km from the centre (Fig. 8). In the fourth century, Corinth was the capital of the province of Achaia but by the sixth and seventh centuries the city was in recession. It is possible that by the end of the seventh century the locus of settlement had shifted to Acrocorinth, the fortified citadel of ancient Corinth that lay about 4 km by road from the city forum, but this is pure speculation. In any case, evidence for seventh- and eighth-century building and economic activity is scant in the lower city agora (forum) where most excavation work has been conducted. As early as the ninth century, a period of extensive building began that culminated in a twelfth-century city

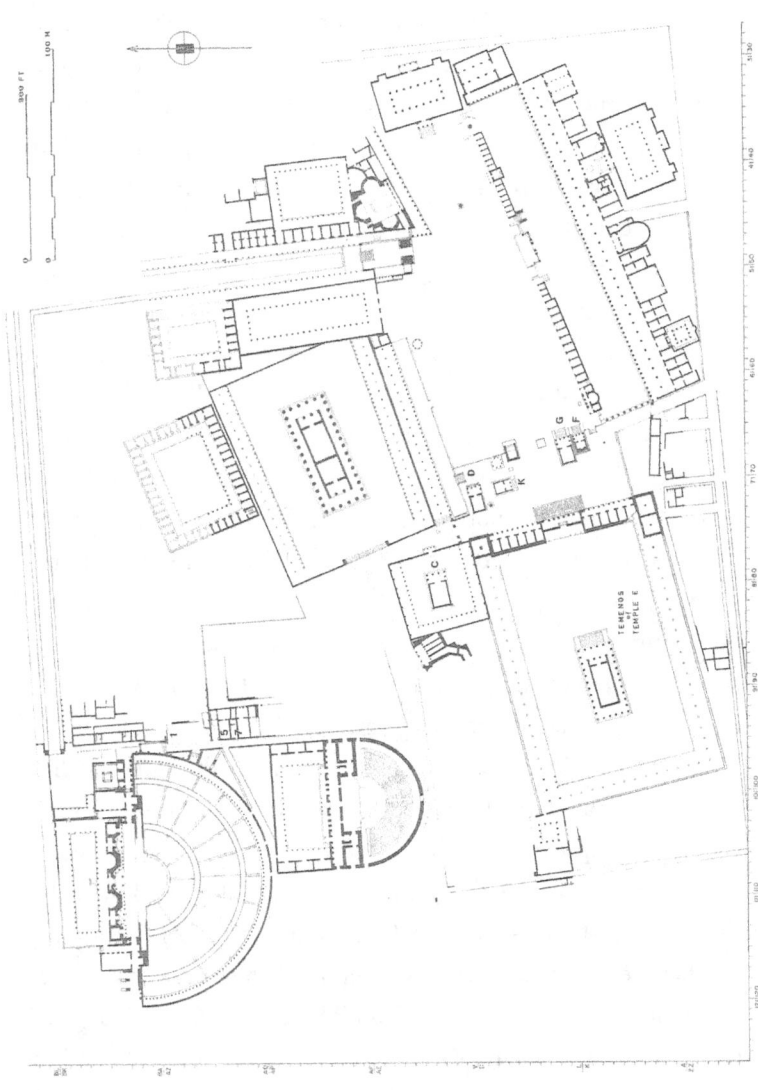

Fig. 8 Roman central Corinth (plan of Roman Corinth, courtesy of The American School of Classical Studies at Athens).

absent of any obvious signs of central planning with irregular thoroughfares and few public spaces apart from churches and small squares.

Late antique Corinth (Fig. 9) was remodelled sometime in the late fourth/early fifth century. New city walls were built in late antiquity; Tim Gregory dates the refortification to the late fourth century based on an inscription dedication (Meritt 1931: 141, no. 245) to 'Theodosius, renovator of Corinth' by the quarriers, carters, and marble workers but this may equally refer to Theodosius II (408–450). These fourth- to fifth-century walls enclosed a smaller area than previously occupied by the classical city. Gregory (1979) restored a sweeping perimeter that enclosed the forum and most of the settlement. This impressive but speculative restoration has recently been challenged: Sanders (2003) thinks the late antique circuit was much smaller and enclosed a fraction of the area of that presumed by Gregory. Most striking is that the circuit newly hypothesized by Sanders leaves out all known late antique churches and the old heart of the city, the Roman commercial forum/agora.

The nature of sixth-century occupation is unclear: the so-called southeast building by the Basilica of Julian revealed signs of domestic occupation in the sixth century (Scranton 1957: 42). A house was squeezed into the east side of the Peirene fountain, the latter of which was apparently maintained in some fashion as a public watering place. A house by the Apollo Peribolos to the north is also reported but not published from early excavations in the area of the latrine. Still further north on the east side of the Lechaion road, the Great Baths were given a new service area in the sixth century around the same time a new pool and a bench were installed along the west wall. Not much later, access to the Lechaion road was blocked by a lime kiln and the latrine by the colonnade was no longer maintained past the early seventh century (Biers 1985: 12–13, appendix 3). Recent excavations of the Panayia Field to the southeast also yielded fairly rich materials

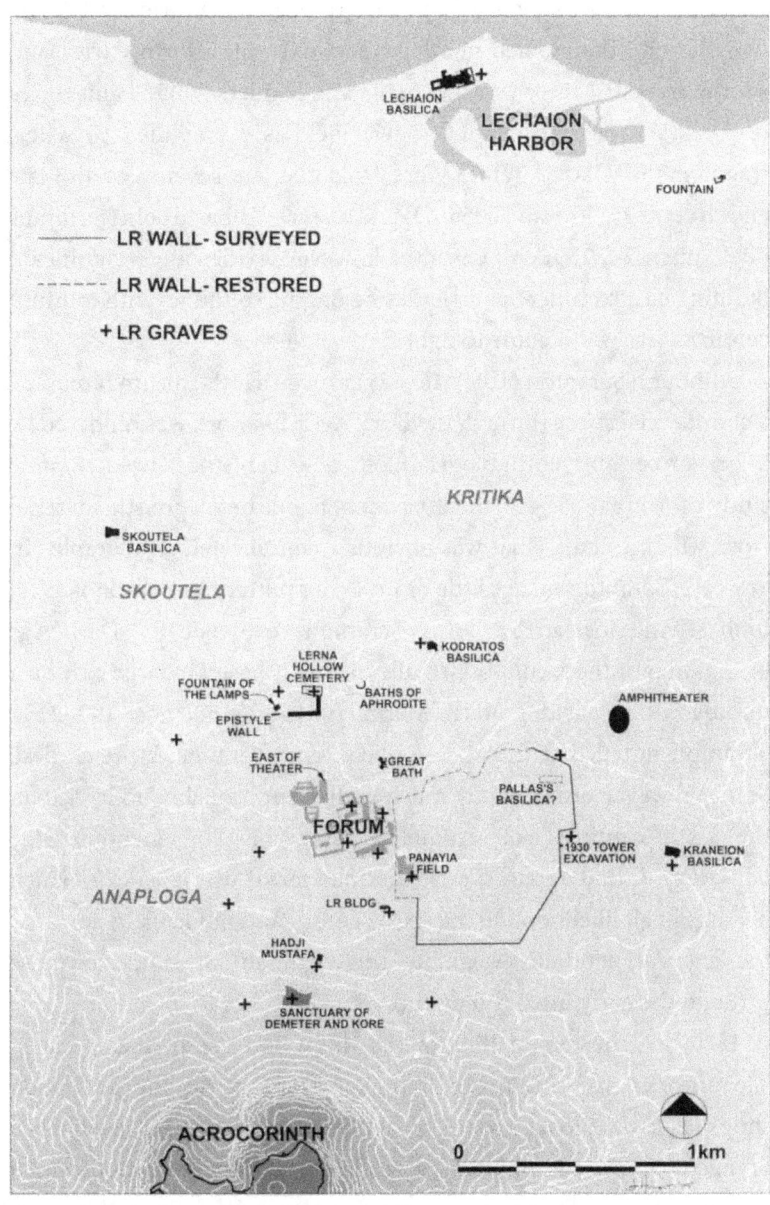

Fig. 9 Corinth in Late Antiquity (after Warner Slane and Sanders 2005, fig. 1, courtesy of The American School of Classical Studies, Corinth Excavations).

and part of an urban villa of the fifth to seventh centuries, indicating that the city maintained good connections with North Africa and southwest Asia Minor (Warner Slane and Sanders 2005). Faint traces of Dark Age activity from Panayia Field is exemplified by a few fragments of Glazed White Ware from the late seventh or the late eighth century (Vroom 2005a: 63) and an early 'Abbasid coin (terminus post quem of 750). At Corinth, however, evidence of significant building and commercial activities belonging to the seventh to ninth centuries has yet to come to light.

Although Scranton (1957: 46–48) argued that the forum remained a commercial space through the Dark Ages, his work was hindered by a lack of ceramic chronological control: except the flawed ceramic study of Morgan (1942), the excavators had little diagnostic material from which to date what was obviously complicated stratigraphy. In any case, Scranton makes little or no use of pottery as a chronological tool, relying instead on coins. Scranton's evidence for Dark Age occupation of the forum is virtually nil and is based in large part on a number of undated graffiti (Meritt 1931: 125–30, nos. 198–215). Scranton noted that these were likely tenth century at the earliest. Some, however, are certainly much earlier but probably no later than the sixth century. For example, inscription 208 mentions the *boukellarioi* (body guards; a late antique term) of the *eparch*, which belongs in all likelihood to the sixth century and not later. In any case, these graffiti lend no weight to the argument of continuous use through the early medieval period.

Likewise, the remodelling of the shops and use of the so-called 'Governor's Palace' and 'prison' in the central portion of the old Roman shops is also without chronological certainty. So, too, is the evidence of medieval fresco found in the so-called 'palace', the remains of which Scranton assigns to the tenth century at the earliest. From the entire agora, the only good relative chronological indicators available to the excavators were coins; those mentioned are nearly wholly from the tenth century and most are much later than this. It is difficult to sustain the optimistic view of Sanders (2003) and especially Brown (2010), the latter of whom takes Scranton's poorly controlled excavations in the area of the forum to indicate that this area remained 'at the core of bathing, fountain, and industrial installations' (Brown 2010: 236).

In Greece, late antique burial practices, especially the role of extramural cemetery basilicas, changed considerably in the Dark Ages. Intramural inhumations became common, as did burial within derelict churches. The function of cemetery churches beyond the sixth century is a fraught issue and needs to be explored on a case-by-case basis rather than assuming their wholesale continuity or dereliction. Barrel-vaulted burial chambers became rare (Veikou 2012: 71), apparently reserved only for the wealthiest strata of society who wished to make special statements of their identity within the community. In their place were cist graves (simple stone- or rubble-formed coffins set into the ground surface), no longer marked by tombstones. There was also a general diminution in the number of grave goods; this is especially true of pottery and lamps. Buckles and other personal adornments are also rarely found, though these continued to be deposited (Poulou-Papadimitriou et al. 2012). At Corinth, while the precise chronological end of the major classical cemetery north of the city is uncertain, at least seven clusters of burials dating from the sixth to eighth centuries were scattered throughout the agora, including a well-known burial of a warrior, possibly a Slav warrior, as some have argued that the Slavs sacked the city in AD 584 (Aupert 1989) despite there being no written reference to Corinth specifically. It should be noted that the city circuit as recently redrawn by Sanders would have excluded the whole of the forum and its burials. Among these burials is the famous 'wandering soldier' inhumation, a tile-lined grave found in the colonnade of the South Stoa (Davidson 1974; Curta 2011: 103), a male burial initially interpreted as a Slavic, Avar or Bulgar warrior (Setton 1950: 520). Neither the 'wandering soldier' nor the near contemporary graves thought to be warriors due to their interment with spearheads and other weapons, were interred within or near a known church (Curta 2011: 106).

While these burials are no longer interpreted as evidence of Slavic sack of Corinth, they cannot really sustain the notion of a thriving community in the heart of classical Corinth either. Rather, their presence may indicate, as do abundant coins of Constans II (641–668), seventh-century military activity and therefore continuing state interest in Corinth. Wherever we find the military, we find the administrative apparatus and support staff to sustain settlement. The military presence is probably the best indicator at Corinth to date for the persistence of economy and state in the early Dark Ages, but whether this kind of evidence indicates permanent urban or suburban life is an open question.

Corinth did remain a bishopric through the challenging years of the seventh and eighth centuries. Although several churches appear to have been used in the medieval era, none belong to the city centre, apart from the putative church hypothesized by Scranton (1957: 9–11) inside the converted Julian basilica delineated by an apse constructed of spolia after the earthquake of AD 375, as well as inhumations in chambers added to the western wall to create a regularly planned crypt with at least three burials. This identification of the conversion of the Julian basilica is absent or downplayed in later literature (Scotton 1997: 19–20), but with so much of the medieval data poorly or not recorded at all, we will probably never grasp the nature of this conversion. Other known churches were far removed from the old commercial heart of the city. The Kraneion basilica church, 1.3 km from the forum, was built in the sixth century in the midst of a cemetery, but that it experienced continuous use until the thirteenth century (Brown 2010) is doubtful, although a burial in the northern aisle of the basilica was apparently of the eighth century (Vikatou 2002). Without a fuller analysis of pottery from the excavations of the old city centre, we must rely on the coin finds: one coin of Justinian (527–565) is followed by a hiatus in the numismatic material until the eleventh century when an anonymous follis represents renewed activity (Pallas 1976: 179). There were probably periods of abandonment and dereliction of most of the churches in Corinth but at this stage neither continuous use nor periods of abandonment can be assumed and more work is needed. The St. Kodratos Church (to the north of the old forum by the Lerna Spring, 0.65 km from the forum) was built sometime during late antiquity and is again asserted to have continued in use into the thirteenth century (Pallas 1977). Within the basilica, a marble lintel bearing the name Kodratos belonging to an early phase of the church (which presumably served as a pilgrimage shrine) allows us to link the sanctuary and the nearby sacred spring to the cult of St. Kodratos, martyred in Corinth in AD 258 (Landon 1994: 258). The church remains may support the presence of St. Kodratos as a late antique cult figure and thus one whose veneration continued to flourish in Dark Age Corinth. Moreover, the vita of Kodratos is found in a tenth-century manuscript and the spring and its saint were noted by Joseph the Hymnographer (d. c. 883) in the ninth century at the latest, by which time the Christian cult had taken over the spring to the west previously belonging to an ancient healing cult, badly damaged and largely filled in during the fourth century (Landon 1994). The large basilica at Lechaion by the western harbour was started in the late fifth century (coins of Zeno in the foundations) and completed in the sixth. Judging by its size and splendour, Lechaion was probably the archepiscopal church until it was abandoned in the seventh century (Pallas 1977).

Based on the find of a tile grave in the central apse that contained a coin of Leo VI (886–912) (Scranton 1957: 42), it seems clear that the so-called Bema church, built into the converted Bema in the former Central Shops area, was in use in the late ninth or early tenth century. During this era, the church probably functioned as a cemetery sanctuary. The derelict Roman West Shops area was partly re-used in the tenth century, perhaps again as commercial spaces, although the chronology of this region, as with so much of the site, is unclear. A pottery kiln installed in the ruined entrance of Temple D functioned in the tenth century or more likely the eleventh century, prior to the building of the Monastery of St. John, which destroyed it. The western end of the medieval marketplace is presumed to lie over the north of the previous Roman bema on the south of the agora (Morgan 1939: 262). Coins (type unspecified) of Constantine VII and Romanus II (945–959) were found embedded in medieval construction in this area, loosely affiliated with 'shops' (a dubious interpretation of the structures using *spolia* from the old bema complex). Also in the western end of the old agora, excavation revealed the southern extension of the monastery with its Church of St. John Theologos and a nearby wine press and possible tavern – the *floruit* of these latter structures was in the eleventh century (Scranton 1957: 76). Around 1100, Corinth was once more at a peak of prosperity even if the exact nature of urban development cannot be ascertained; certainly Morgan's plan of 1942 is optimistically clear (Fig. 10).

Although the transition from the late antique to the early medieval countryside will be treated in more detail in Chapter 3, a brief glance at the hinterland of Corinth is instructive. The rural areas outside Corinth seem to have experienced a downturn at the end of the sixth century, although we need to await the full results of the Eastern Korinthia Archaeological Survey to advance our understanding of this. While the Swedish excavation of the Pyrgouthi Tower in the southern Argolid revealed scarce evidence for agricultural production in the late antique (fifth to sixth centuries

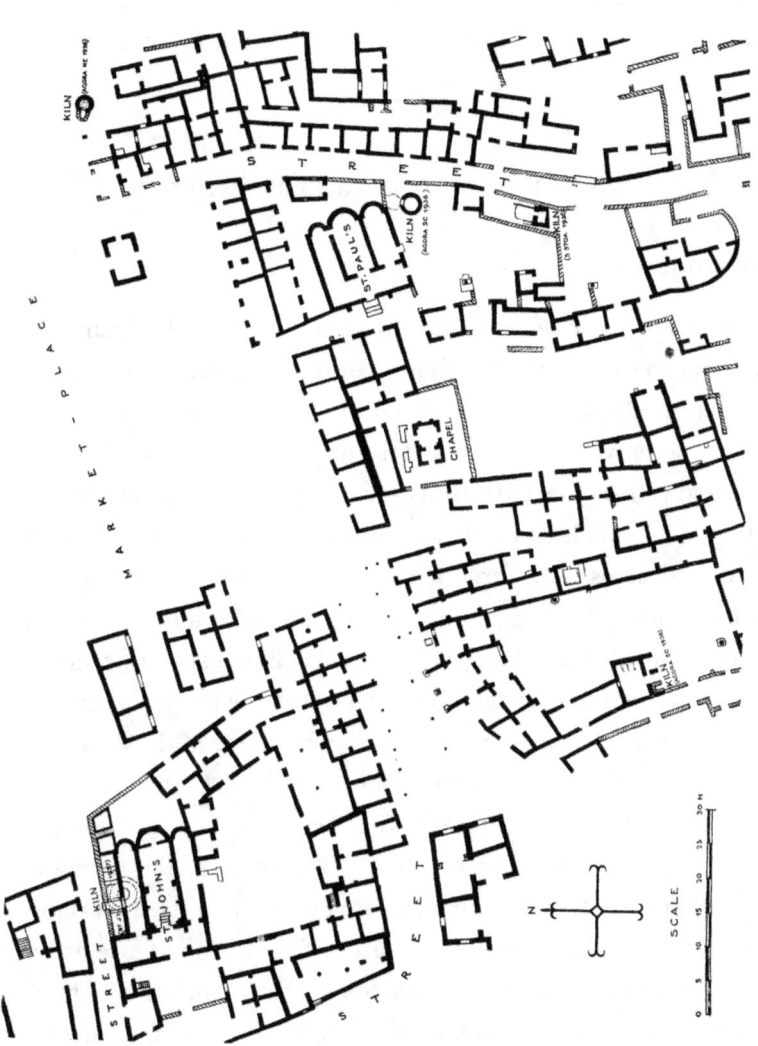

Fig. 10 Central Corinth c. 1100 (after Morgan 1942, fig. 1, courtesy of The American School of Classical Studies, Corinth Excavations).

AD) countryside of southern Greece, there are no indications sites like Pyrgouthi were plentiful in the Corinthia during the sixth and seventh centuries. Limited survey data indicate a recession around the seventh century, with the majority of villa sites abandoned and a landscape reflecting the near-death experience of the ancient city.

Anatolian urbanism: Amorium and Hierapolis

Amorium

An interesting case of profound urban continuity is Amorium (or Amorion, now by the village of Hisarkoy east of Emirdağ). Amorium is somewhat atypical in that it possessed the advantage of being, like Corinth, a provincial capital but somewhat disadvantaged when compared with coastal cities by its situation on the Anatolian plateau on the frontier of Galatia and Phrygia. Amorium lay on an important trunk road across southern Asia Minor; its role in the imperial communications network was partly responsible for it becoming the thematic capital of the Anatolikon, probably in the seventh century. The city endured Arab attack in 644 and 646 and in the ninth century was the home of Michael II (802–829), who founded the 'Amorian' dynasty. Excavations have been ongoing since 1988. Amorium was probably a Hellenistic amalgamation of Phrygians and Greek-speakers; by the second or first century BC at the latest, Amorium was a *polis* (Jones 1971: 60). During late antiquity, it possessed a bishop (suffragan to Pessinus) and was a place of some importance as its substantial remains attest. Kedrenos states that Amorium was built (*ektísthe*) by Zeno (474–491), while Arab authors attribute its construction to Anastasius (Ivison 2007: 35). The lower city alone covers 75 hectares. At the end of the fifth or beginning of the sixth century AD, Amorium was extensively remodelled. Builders constructed a new city wall, a spacious basilica, and a sumptuous set of baths. All of these, in one way or another, were maintained for some three centuries until their destruction by fire in the first half of the ninth century. Amorium seems also to have maintained its late antique grid.

The first of these, the city walls, created a defensive circuit some 3 km long (Fig. 11). Only a portion (Trench AB) has been excavated. It was built in large limestone ashlars at the foot of the barrier, with alternating limestone and brick banded work above, as at Constantinople and elsewhere. The wall was strengthened using many polygonal and circular towers. According to the tenth-century Persian author Ibn Khordadhbeh (de Goeje 1889: 79), the city possessed 44 towers; 20 have thus far been discovered via survey. The excavated example, a triangular structure protecting a gateway, is similar to towers at Corinth and Thessaloniki, both of which apparently belong to late antiquity. The walls of Amorium were maintained into the ninth century; a paved area was added to the sixth- to ninth-century buttressing behind the gate (excavated at AB) to create an apparent double-gateway.

The lower city church was of basilica type and occupied an area of 600 square metres. The church was richly decorated as indicated by the use of significant quantities of imported marble and the finds of large numbers of mosaic tesserae, probably from the original vaulting as it belonged to pre-collapse levels just above the Phase 1 floor level (Harrison and Christie 1993: 149). This floor, judging by the number of cut marble tiles found, must have originally been of *opus sectile* type. Although not a large church by late antique standards, the building is nonetheless rather typical in scale and appearance to many provincial churches of its age. More important, the *ekklesia* was apparently maintained into the ninth century; buttresses comprised of *spolia*, for example, strengthened the nave at some point between the sixth and ninth centuries; similar to the alterations made to

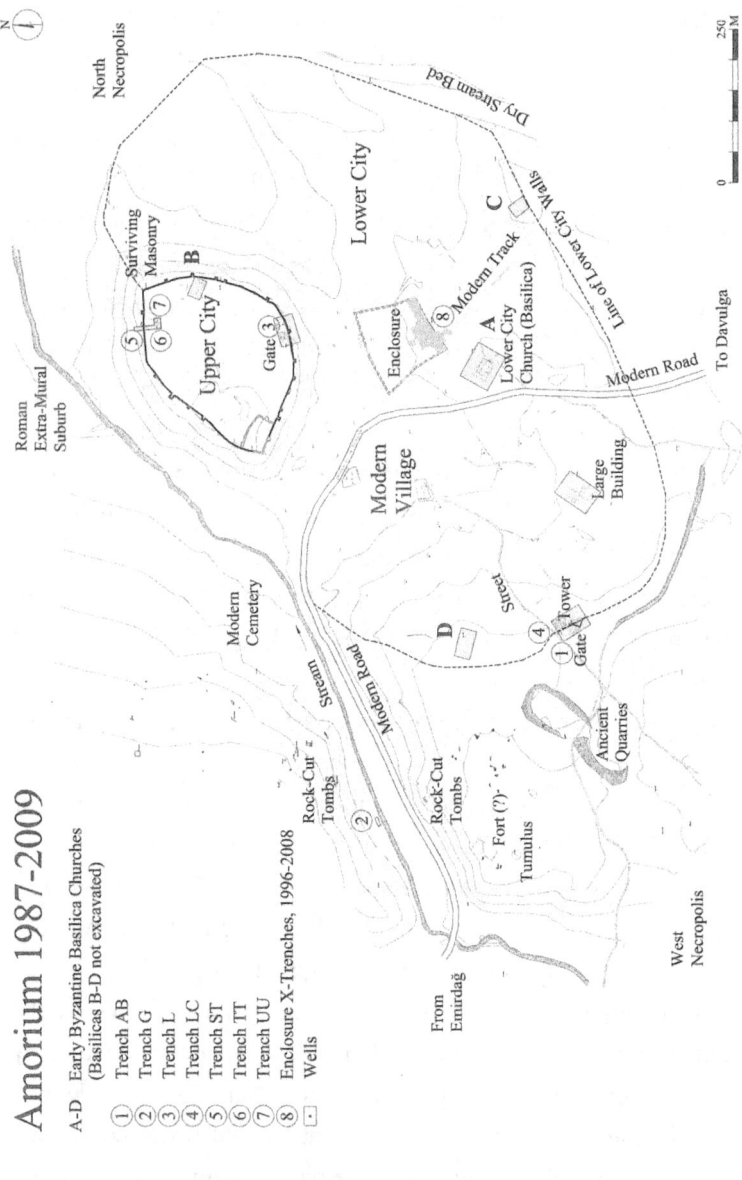

Fig. 11 Plan of Amorium (after Lightfoot and Ivison 2012, fig. 1/1, courtesy of The Amorium Excavations Project).

surviving churches in Constantinople, Thessaloniki, and Cuman'in Camii in Attaleia (Ivison 2007).

The bathhouse (Fig. 12), one of the more prominent sights as one approached the city, was impressive. It boasted a domed *apodyterium* (the space for changing and socializing) with a column topped by basket capitals and was surrounded by a court and auxiliary buildings. The impressive apodyterium was systematically stripped of many of its architectural elements and walled off from the rest of the bath. A small hoard of bronze coins, among them a type 2 AE follis belonging to the reign of Leo IV (778–780) found at the bottom of a robbed water basin, indicates this downsizing occurred sometime in the eighth century (Ivison 2007: 45). Nonetheless, the rest of the bath remained open. Evidence of repair of the hypocaust within the bathing area suggests routine maintenance: *spolia* and recycled ceramic water pipes were used to replace some of the *pilae* in the hypocaust beneath the tepidarium and the caldarium, a flue was

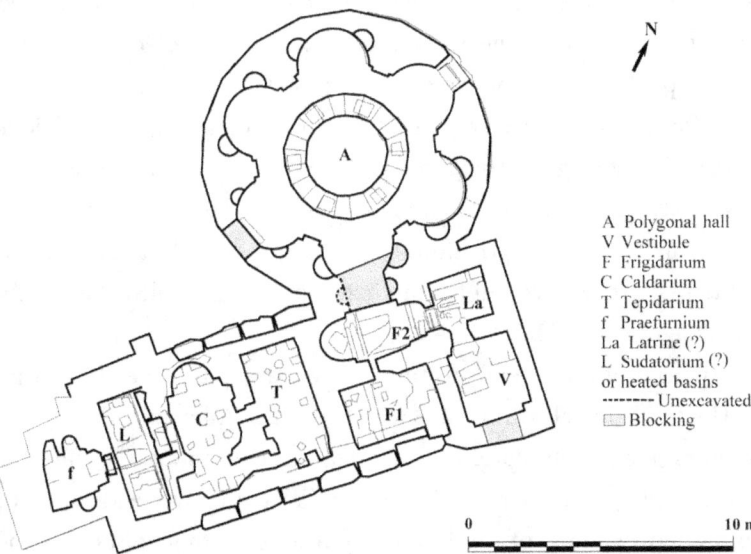

Fig. 12 Plan of Amorium baths (courtesy of The Amorium Excavations Project).

repaired (again utilizing spolia), while the exterior northwest corner was provided with buttressing.

The city has yielded some surprises, among them the lack of an aqueduct, no trace of which has been found. Amorium would thus be the rare city that relied on the abundant groundwater to supply the bathhouse (or bathhouses, as it is probable in a city of its size there was more than one) and its domestic and industrial needs. Amorium may have been chosen as an administrative and fortified centre in part because of this abundance of fresh water, which could not be cut off during a siege. Especially intriguing is the discovery of a small kiln in the upper city that produced glazed wares imitating Constantinopolitan glazed white wares: no tableware production sites are known for the latter, which leaves Amorium as a rare provincial example of continuing professional pottery production, albeit modest (Böhlendorf-Arslan 2004: 222). Of further note, Amorium remained monetized throughout the early medieval period. Small change coins were found in abundance; most of the numismatic material recovered – 232 of 309 coins – belong to the ninth to eleventh centuries (labelled 'Middle Byzantine' by the excavators; Lightfoot 2002). Nearly all coins are copper issues and thus small change used in everyday transactions and for the most part represent normal losses (e.g. not obvious hoards). Other signs of medieval economic activity were noted in the lower city: glass making was probably performed in or near the walled enclosure area, while agricultural processing, especially a great deal of wine making, was certainly conducted inside the walled lower city (C.S. Lightfoot 2003, 2007).

The end of the early Byzantine city was dramatic. In 838, an army led by the caliph al-Mu'tasim (838–842) sacked Amorium; the written sources portray this episode as devastating, with thousands killed or taken captive. Whether the collapse and charring over wide areas of excavated portions of the lower city belong to this episode as the excavators suggest is open to debate. These finds are striking: thick ash layers indicative of fire, destruction, and collapse were found along the lower city walls. Charred timbers inside the triangular tower yielded C14 dates of c. 800 AD. Unusual finds, such as intact metallic objects like the copper alloy bowl (noted in Chapter 2) may also support the occurrence of a sudden catastrophe in which valuables were left behind. Immediately behind the lower city wall, other chronological indicators include globular cooking vessels typical of the eighth and ninth centuries and coins of Nikephoros I (802–811) and Theophilus (dated 829–830). Thick layers of ash indicating a conflagration are also found in the bathhouse and its immediate quarter; coins again belong to Theophilus or the Amorian dynasts (Ivison 2007; Lightfoot and Ivison 2012).

Resettlement of Amorium, or the return of citizens who had fled, apparently began soon after the sack. Ibn Khordadhbeh (de Goeje 1889: 74), who wrote in 846 and relied in part on reports of al-Jarmi, a Muslim who had been held captive by the Byzantines from 837 to 845, noted the sack of the city along with Ankyra by al-Mu'tasim, but he gave no indication that either city was ruined in his day. Instead, he numbered Amorium among the seats of the 'patricians' of the empire, each of whom commanded ten thousand troops. If Ibn Khordadhbeh's evidence is valid, then Amorium was never wholly abandoned in the wake of the Muslim siege of 838. In fact, archaeological evidence indicates that the city was active again soon after, with considerable infilling and new construction datable to the late ninth or early tenth century when the enclosure of the lower city was apparently built. Inside the enclosure are traces of both tenth- and eleventh-century activity, including glass production. Earlier economic activity near this spot had included wine presses of the seventh to ninth centuries. No full survey of the hinterland of Amorium has been conducted and without one the city cannot be fully understood. Hopefully, the Turkish archaeologists who have taken over the Anglo-Turkish excavations will complete this crucial piece of the puzzle.

Hierapolis

The remains of the ancient city of Hierapolis (Fig. 13) lie 350 m above sea level on a travertine terrace formed by the precipitation of mineral from the adjacent hot springs of modern Pammukale, opposite the Turkish city of Denizli. Hierapolis was a classical polis from at least the second century BC, when Antiochus (222–187) established the urban plan that underpins the ancient city partly uncovered today. But use of the site stretches deep into antiquity when the Phrygians utilized the thermal springs and established the reputation of the settlement as a cult centre and healing shrine. While the hot springs assured a steady trade in people seeking healing for their ailments, the city also commanded a portion of the fertile Lykos river valley and the surrounding uplands, whose fecundity supported thriving agriculture and stocking that underpinned city life. In late antiquity, Hierapolis was a thriving centre, 'a focus for wool production, teeming with merchants who plied their trade from Italy to the Orient along routes that ran west down the Meander valley to the Aegean, or east onto the Anatolian plateau and beyond' (Arthur 2012: 277).

The classical city was first explored in the nineteenth century by a German team whose work was continued by Italian archaeologists into the 1920s and 1930s (D'Andria 2006). Work resumed in the 1950s, with work since then focusing predominantly on the monumental centre of the city, whose layout belongs to the Flavian rebuilding of the city following the earthquake of AD 60 (D'Andria 2001: 99). This city was organized around the main north–south axis, a broad avenue, the plateia that was some 13 m wide. From the plateia radiated secondary streets 3 m wide. The Flavian rebuilding included the large agora, which occupied 476,000 square metres (170 × 280 m) from a total urban area of 800,000 square metres (0.8 of a square kilometre), which reflects the extent and grandeur of the city and the

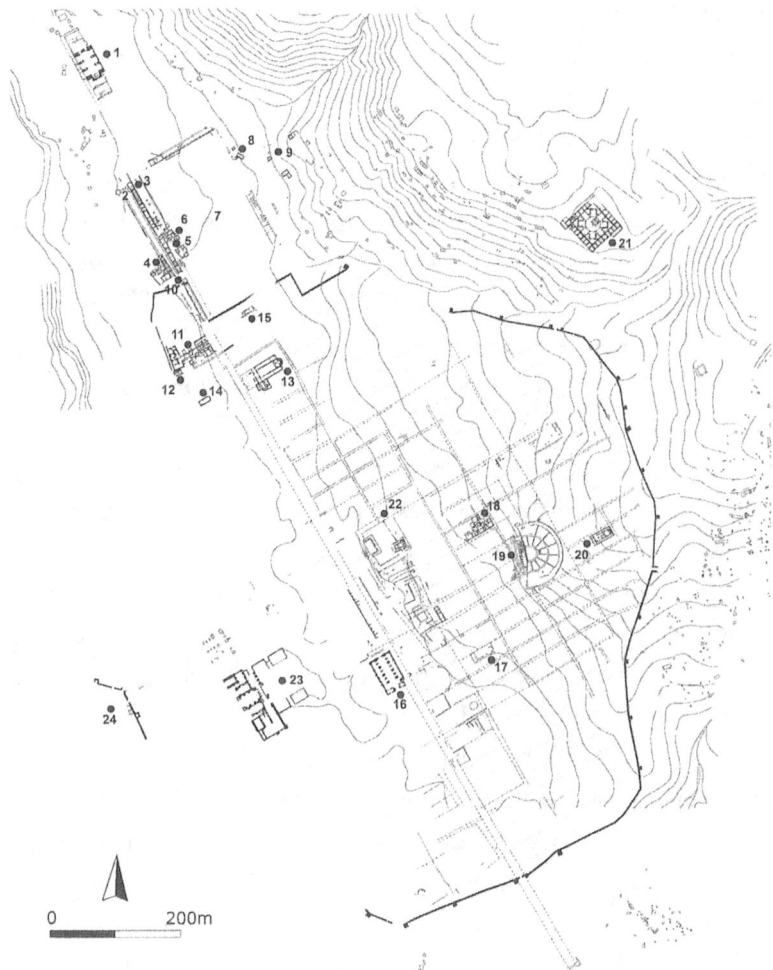

Fig. 13 Plan of Hierapolis (Archivio MAIER and Paul Arthur).

lavishness of imperial support, which also included equipping the city with a new theatre (D'Andria 2001: 104).

An earthquake again struck in the mid fourth century that caused widespread damage, and considerable rebuilding followed. In contrast, no monumental rebuilding of the urban core followed a seismic event in the seventh century (De Bernardi Ferrero and Verzone 2002). Around the late fourth century, as at Corinth and elsewhere in Asia Minor, the citizens of Hierapolis erected a powerful circuit wall. Tellingly, the wall left out the older Flavian agora, which by now had become an artisanal quarter for the production of finished goods for local consumption and export. Numerous lime kilns slaked much of the rubble from the collapsed agora into lime (Mastronuzzi and Melissano 2007).

Early in the Christian era, the city developed an association with the cult of the Apostle Philip. Contemporary (or nearly so) with the erection of the city wall, the Hierapolitans built large urban and suburban Christian sanctuaries; the former is the fifth-century Cathedral, a large (48 m long) basilica. Atop the nearby necropolis to the northeast of the city, the community built the monumental Martyrium of St. Philip. The martyrium was a domed square with an octagonal interior (D'Andria 2001: 113; Arthur 2012: 278), perhaps planned and executed by an architect from Constantinople (Verzone 1965). This spectacular building, more than 50 m on a side, dominated the city below and was the clear focal point of cult life as well as a major pilgrimage centre, no doubt intended to rival the shrine of St. John at Ephesus (Arthur 2012: 278). In the fifth or sixth century, a church was also constructed above the Severan theatre. Other public building in the fifth and sixth centuries included at least one major bathhouse built over the debris from the earlier fourth-century earthquake that had levelled the Flavian agora. This bathhouse, with its vaulted roof and longitudinal axis, prefigured the medieval *hamam* of the Islamic world (D'Andria 2001: 113).

Some dwellings in the classical *insula* blocks west of the Severan theatre have been investigated, specifically the high-status 'House of the Ionic Capitals', erected in the second century, restored after the fourth century earthquake (Zaccaria Ruggiu 2007), and transformed through a substantial refurbishment in the fifth and sixth centuries.

During the latter rebuilding, the peristyle was closed off and converted into the public area of the house, indicated by its separate entranceway and stone seat. Rich decoration in fresco and *opus sectile* indicates that the domus continued to be a high-status residence. The so-called 'House of the Doric Courtyard', another elite residence, was also restored following the fourth-century earthquake. Like its near-neighbour above, in the fifth or sixth centuries the House of the Doric Courtyard was sumptuously decorated with a lovely fresco simulating a marble peristyle (Zaccaria Ruggiu 2007).

The Phrygian neighbour of Hierapolis, Laodicea-ad-Lycum, and other *poleis* in Asia Minor, such as Ephesus, Sardis, and Aphrodisias, suffered at the hands of the Persians around 616; at Laodicea the burned quarters were never rebuilt. No coins after the reign of Phokas (602–610) have been found at Laodicea and other material seems to be wholly late antique as well, indicating widespread abandonment by the early decades of the seventh century. Large-scale Turkish clearance of Laodicea-ad-Lycum cannot offer certain clues of how damaging the Persian attacks were or if there was any later occupation. Trouble came to Hierapolis in heaps as well. Besides the Persians, there was a major earthquake that destroyed the Martyrium of Philip and much of the monumental centre of the late antique city (Cormack 1991: 120). The dramatic fashion of the collapse of major civic structures at Hierapolis indicates that sometime in the mid seventh century, yet another devastating tremor shook the settlement, again levelling a civic centre that to all appearances had been thriving just prior to the event. The lack of subsequent urban renewal stands in vivid relief against the prior destruction/revival episodes (Arthur 2012: 279). In all probability Hierapolis was part of a fraying urban network whose major economic sinews were slackening; during the distresses of the seventh century, these cords proved too inelastic to handle the buffeting they received. Dark Age Hierapolis was much different than its late antique predecessor. The cathedral had two religious enclosures fashioned out of its side aisles but was never fully repaired; instead, it became a burial church, with inhumations in the southern aisle and narthex, as we saw in the Bema Church of the re-purposed agora at Corinth. The late antique church above the Severan theatre was also brought back into reduced use – its side aisles too were blocked off and partitioned into small rooms. After the mid-seventh-century seismic event, housing was installed into the northern branch of the *plateia* thoroughfare. The spot was probably chosen because it was level and relatively free of the heaps of rubble from fallen monumental public structures; it was beyond the capacity of the citizens to clear this material. The small rectangular structures they built into the *plateia* included storage bins and domestic quarters; a number of houses of probable early medieval date, abandoned during the tenth century (Arthur 2012: 283). The emplacement of a sizeable walled area, called the *kastron* by the excavators, and domestic re-use of portions of the late-antique bathhouse, indicate continuing activity in the northern sector of Hierapolis. Local pottery production continued in the eighth century and later. By the end of the tenth century, some new disaster led to the abandonment of many of these early medieval domestic structures.

By looking at the seventh- to tenth-century lives of cities in the Byzantine world, we can draw lines more clearly between the late antique *polis* and the medieval city. To describe most early medieval urban centres in the empire, the English word 'town' would perhaps be a more useful term than 'city' or 'polis', as these settlements typically lacked the size, population, and civic and economic sophistication associated with either of the latter terms (Haldon 1999). But this would have been true of the great majority of cities in the sixth century as well. Interpreters of the changes like those that transpired at Nicopolis, Butrint, Corinth, and Hierapolis – though not, apparently, Amorium – have examined such features as the reduction of the circuit walls of cities, the rejection of classical models of monumental architecture, intramural burials, the Christianization of sacred space, and the militarization of the city. These features are each or together used to assess the nature of the late antique city, nearly always in light of its classical predecessor (Lavan 2009). However, the nature of these changes and their pace differed by region and should not necessarily be seen as a continuous phenomenon. Imperial fortification of Amorium and Corinth, while apparently nearly contemporary projects, nonetheless have little else in common and the subsequent fate of the two cities differed markedly from one another.

As noted above, some scholars, such as Haldon (1999), posit that fundamental structural changes influenced the change in cities as they lived at the end of late antiquity. In this view, cities were essentially superfluous to imperial goals after the seventh century, by which time they had lost their functions as administrative nodes and the interface between the state and its constituent elites and in turn between those elites and their dependents. While we have noted above the 'declinist' and 'continuitist' views, these rather black and white characterizations are being continuously reassessed. A full autopsy has yet to emerge but broader regional studies, as in the work of Anna Leone (2013) for Africa and Ine Jacobs (2014) for Asia Minor, underscore the regional approach that will shape the debate for years to come.

Our methodologies continue to improve, but in the end, large-scale excavation is probably the only way to discover traces of urban life in the Dark Ages (Hodges 2013). Great leaps in our ability to identify medieval ceramics, in our understanding of past environments, and accumulated knowledge of Dark Age material culture have enabled us to make pronounced advances in understanding the complexities of early medieval Mediterranean urbanism. It is especially thanks to methods pioneered in northern Europe, that the ephemeral materials of construction and daily life are finally a growing part of the repertoire of excavation throughout former Byzantium. Despite these notes of progress, there remains a chord of dissonance and the strain of real challenges. Many cities – and even entire regions – remain a blank slate, with little or no archaeological publications from which to analyse their Dark Age character, and no prospect of any fieldwork on a substantial scale. Nor can we rely solely on remote sensing or field survey to reveal the complexities and address the multiplicity of questions we continue to ask of this period. Have we simply overlooked the occupation evidence of the seventh through ninth centuries at cities that we believed to have been abandoned at this time? After all, it once appeared that Sagalassos was abandoned at the end of late antiquity. If we examined them with greater care, might we find those sites we believe were unoccupied after the sixth or early seventh centuries to have been occupied after all? Pessinus, for example, immediately springs to mind as a possible test case: it seems to have been largely deserted in the sixth or seventh century. Maybe the ongoing work there will prove otherwise but it seems unlikely. As Hodges (2013: 19) put it so starkly, at Butrint the excavators found 'the Byzantine Dark Age by digging for fourteen years, seven of which saw excavation on a very substantial scale rather than cheaper, non-intrusive methods such as field survey or geophysics'.

But what can be learnt from these cases about the nature of urbanism and its transformation from 500 to 1000? To state the obvious, not all cases were equal. Both Amorium and Corinth were governmental centres and they were clearly given due attention by the state; the refortification and rebuilding within the walled areas of fifth-century Amorium and Corinth are good examples of this, but this cannot be the whole story. Nicopolis, an average place and not part of an important administrative or military command network, witnessed investment, but it was not sustained after the Danube *limes* were deemed untenable.

Instead, we witness contraction of the urban areas as defined by the city walls and little clear evidence of suburban domestic activity at a high level in the seventh to ninth centuries. At its lowest ebb, the

Byzantine city is a set of walls protecting a few hectares and a church. At Butrint, environmental stress and insecurities led to the desertion of much of the site not much later than the final abandonment of Nicopolis. However, the debate needs to move away from simplistic notions of continuity versus decline to a proper understanding of each city and region, first on their own terms and then as part of a whole. Amorium, like Gortyn on Crete, Thessaloniki in Greece, Constantinople, and probably Corinth offer clear examples of continuity of vibrant urban forms in the early medieval period. Others fared more poorly or failed altogether. But cities failed in antiquity as well as the present day – one has only to drive through the American Rust Belt to see this first-hand. The question remains what exactly we make of the fabric of these cities as recovered by archaeologists and what these remains tell us of forms of public, private, and sacred spaces, planning, and economic activity, as well as civic and social life.

As noted, certain elements of late antique urbanism certainly endured at larger and more important sites, sometimes, as at Amorium, with quite striking claims to continuity. The focus of excavation and consequently our notion of the Byzantine city of the seventh to ninth centuries is one focused on churches with some public bathing establishments as true public spaces. But the country has invaded the city already by the fifth century (indeed it must have done so earlier). At Nicopolis there was a decidedly rural aspect to the houses; at Amorium wineries, potteries, and glass works lived cheek by jowl with the church and bath and the ancient grid may or may not be observed – it often was not by the sixth century. These pragmatic details, a functional city life in which the sharp distinctions between city and country had dulled, where the citizens lived and worked behind the relative safety of massive curtains of stone, have many parallels both in space and time. The successor to Dark Age urban centres, the Byzantine urbanism of the eleventh and twelfth centuries, where towns like Corinth thrived, owed much to the late antique and

Dark Age transformations noted above and little to the classical *polis*. As in the contemporary West, the urban core of the Byzantine city under the sway of the dynasty of the Comneni (1081–1185) outside of a few major *metropoleis* like Constantinople and Thessaloniki, was a hive-like affair with houses, monasteries, workshops, agricultural installations, stables, and administrative buildings packed around market and ecclesiastical spaces.

4

The Dark Age Countryside

Settlement in Dark Age Byzantium: debating the meaning of the evidence

As stressed in Chapter 2, archaeologists have obsessed over the fate of the city. Exploration of the rural milieu has produced but a sliver of the archaeological record and the countryside is nearly always constructed as hinterland rather than a multivariate space with interesting and potentially revealing things to say about Byzantine life and society. Precious few rural excavations have been conducted. Worse for the student of Byzantine archaeology, it is a struggle to think of a rural site excavated with the aim of elucidating the Dark Age period. Assumptions based on interpretations of written texts, survey data, and comparative data substitute for a broad, securely dated base of evidence. The classical urban and architectural archaeological framework from which most Byzantinists work is inadequate for the task to hand, namely the exploration of largely ahistoric landscapes, which are better served by approaches and methods adopted from other regions and disciplines, namely northwest Europe and prehistory, respectively.

As noted in Chapter 3, there was generally a less sharp distinction between urban and rural spaces in the early medieval world than in the more concentrated settlement era of the fourth to sixth centuries. In fact, Veikou urges a departure from a conception of space for the early Middle Ages from that based on large, fixed central places to one recognizing a 'flexible organization of habitation' (Veikou 2009: 51).

What is at stake here, to be clear, cannot simply be the view of a baseline settlement; there are bound to be disagreements about what life in a landscape described by such models resembled. In any case, in no medieval city, no matter how large, was one insulated from country life. The sights, sounds, and smells of rustic life were apparent everywhere: market stalls sold local grain and other foodstuffs, and the streets would have reverberated with the braying and plod of donkeys and mules carrying passengers and cargo. And sheep, pigs, and other domesticated animals would have been herded into pens ready for butchery and sale in the city's markets. While a strict urban–rural dichotomy is too limiting, the imperfect picture of early medieval settlement that we possesses does support the notion of the countryside as a major focus of human activity dominated by pastoral, forest, and agricultural activity.

No people or no perception? Field survey and the construction of the Dark Age countryside: potentials and problems

In lieu of expensive excavation of sites, archaeologists have relied on field survey to fill in the great gaps of the Byzantine countryside. Before discussing what we currently believe we know about the countryside of the seventh through ninth centuries, a brief look at field survey is required. For the sake of simplicity, I will refer to 'survey' and its cognates to represent the subfield of archaeological investigation whose principal characteristics are the mapping of terrestrial surface artefacts (underwater survey is a different matter entirely) and non-intrusive means of inquiry. Over the past half century, survey has changed tremendously and in the process become an integral part of the fabric of discourses of Mediterranean archaeologies and histories. The strengths of survey have long been recognized: access to regions where excavation is impractical, the ability to traverse and record information from large surface areas, and document material markers from many centuries. The potential of survey to chart the ocean of the countryside – though usually in reference to how that ocean washes the islands of 'urban' life – has led to its entrenchment in and has given rise to a body of self-aware, self-critical practitioners whose methodologies are constantly challenged, undermined, and re-invented. The caricature of early survey as 'blokes in khakis staring at the ground' is not entirely baseless. Walking while scanning for visual indicators of flint industry, worked stone, ceramics, and architectural fragments was (and is) a key attribute. In large part to respond to criticism, scales have often diminished and extensive approaches have given way to intensive approaches.

Since most surveys are diachronic and record medieval material, how surveyors determine the nature and meaning of such scatters of past anthropogenic material has some bearing here. In most cases, 'site' is used to designate 'clusters of artefacts that, on the basis of their composition and contextual association, are assumed to represent the visible material remains of either short- or long-term, and often multi-phased, places of human settlement' (Bevan and Conolly 2004: 129). For some, a 'site' is determined in the field in the moment of encountering what the surveyor judges to be a concentration of material sufficient to warrant the 'site' designation (Mattingly 1999). Absent a uniform agreement about how to characterize different features, as with chronological periodization, chaos results. For instance, Pettegrew (2002) criticized the tendency to classify large rural artefact clusters as 'farmsteads', which should be interpreted and labelled with a greater awareness of the process of site formation and patterns of domestic use and re-use. Off-site formation of low-density 'background' pottery in particular has been highly debated for the classical Greek countryside, with some proposing that sherd scatters are reflective of manuring and thus markers of agricultural praxis

(Wilkinson 1982; Snodgrass 1994; Forbes 2013), while others view with scepticism whether manuring alone could have led to the deposition of such scatters. Forbes (2013) hints at the problem as it relates to Byzantine archaeology; for example, a dearth of such scatters from areas like Boiotia where settlement spanned multiple eras, including the medieval. The implications are far from minor, relating as they do to settlement density, intensity of land use, and livestock regimes. The relevance of the answer to these questions has a lot to do with how we conceive of the Dark Age landscape.

Others prefer to focus at the level of individual artefacts and their relationships to one another and to the rest of the environment in what has sometimes been (confusingly) termed 'siteless' survey, and thereby adopt terminology intended to avoid the perils of applying common but problematic labels to findspots, thus the use of terms like 'Abnormal Density Above Background Scatter' (Millett 1991: 23). In the Eastern Korinthia Survey, artefacts with a putative date and function were classified as 'chronotypes' within a system where artefact recording was more intensive than many similar projects, although collection of objects found during field walking was quite restricted. One significant achievement of this approach, as argued by the project leaders, was the ability to be 'source critical'; for example, the investigators demonstrated that an abundance of recognizable artefacts from the Late Roman period (described below) produced an exaggerated picture of settlement intensity in Corinthia (Caraher et al. 2007) during late antiquity.

Extensive surveys, like those of Adams (1965) in Lower Mesopotamia, covered vast territories before returning to assert control over the dataset using smaller, more focused reconnaissance and excavation. Similar work touching on the Balkans led to debates about collection of data, their interpretation, and even the value of information claimed by such means. One might include in this the still indispensable, magisterial *Tabula Imperii Byzantini* (TIB 1976–), which, although best categorized as a work of historical geography, remains a starting point for investigating the settlement history of Byzantium as well. In the Aetolia Survey, for example, the surveyors covered an area of 60,000 hectares and recorded 452 sites (Bommeljé and Doorn 1987), while the University of Minnesota Messenia Survey catalogued 455 sites in an area of 380,000 hectares (McDonald and Hope Simpson 1961, 1964, 1969). For those interested in broader issues, this kind of work remains valuable both for approaching past landscapes and also for understanding evolving methodologies. Surveys aiming to record all periods without claiming total coverage continue to be conducted but these, too, tend to have intensive sampling strategies built into their research frameworks. The general move towards intensive survey, involving capturing to the fullest possible extent a record of all material markers from all periods in the target area, has become the norm over the whole of former Byzantine lands. Although this is not the space in which to debate the effectiveness or lack thereof of survey material, it is important to briefly consider some of the competing thoughts on approaches to survey and the nature and value of survey material.

Over the past three decades, survey methodologies have evolved greatly. Archaeologists have access to more tools and analytical possibilities than ever before. Methods such as geophysical and geomorphological surveys, 3D scanning and modelling, photogrammetry, and remote sensing through a variety of approaches such as Historic Landscape Characterization (Fairclough 2006; Turner and Crow 2010), are today a part of many survey projects. Older approaches, such as ethnographic and historical methods remain vital. Although intruding less into the discussion of Byzantine archaeology, precisely because so few archaeologists focus on the period as their central research area, issues of the labelling and interpretation of sites have nonetheless played a role in Mediterranean archaeology. For example, debates about the definition of what comprises a 'site' and its analogue, 'off-site' artefacts, continue. Bintliff (2000: 41), for example, prefers the Continental approach via the Sielungskammer ('settlement chamber') framework in which loci of natural resources, such as fertile soil and water, tend to attract settlement. Over the *longue durée*, while precise centres and concentrations may shift within them, the settlement chambers witness fairly continuous activities.

Large-scale survey often leads to contested results, as demonstrated by the Archaeological Survey of Israel. In the 1990s, the Department of Antiquities published a series of archaeological gazetteers that aimed to cover the whole of the country and make the results accessible in Hebrew and English. The resultant publications are informative and invaluable and form the basis of a view of much of the settled landscape of ancient Israel. However, regarding the crucial seventh- to eighth-century span coinciding with the advent of Islamic rule, some of the published results have been challenged. For example, the material recovered from the area of Shivta (Baumgarten 2004) indicates a dramatic decrease in settlement in the Early Islamic period. Material from elsewhere in the Negev suggests that decline did not occur over most of the region. Settlements did abate in some places during the early Islamic era, but Avni argues that the sharp decline posited by survey from places like Shivta and especially in the Upper Golan and Galilee has been grossly overstated (Avni 2014: 208). The disparity further supports the already widely held belief that a comprehensive view of the evidence on a regional case-by-case basis is required. To gain greater clarity of settlement activity, we should be more attuned to the nature of site formation, ceramic chronology, and open to enhanced survey techniques. Unfortunately, the kind of fine-grained detail permitted by the evidence from Israel is lacking over most of the Balkans and Anatolia. Archaeologists in Israel have increasingly supplemented data from excavation, which has allowed for a much better understanding of local and regional ceramic patterns and, on older sites, permitted rectification of chronology (Avner and Magness 1998; Magness 2003a, 2003b).

In the northern Balkans, survey data from the countryside correlate with those from excavated urban sites, indicating that the Dark Ages came to the Danubian region in the fifth century. Survey of the Lower Danube between the Roman military installations at Novae and Iatrus indicate that the villa culture established there largely through the emplacement of discharged veterans during the second and third centuries was destroyed by Gothic and Hun military invasions by the fifth century (Conrad 2006; Thomas 2007a, 2007b). The local villa economy of the hinterland of the small city of Nicopolis-ad-Istrum had also collapsed by the mid fifth century (Poulter 2007a: 79–82). If the recent interpretation of Curta is correct, the countryside of the northern Balkans was largely devoid of settlement from the retreat of the Byzantine state in the sixth century until the eighth century (Curta 2013b). At the present time, there is much debate about the complete alteration of life along the inland portions of the Danubian region.

Due to a lack of excavation outside of classical cities in the southern Balkans, one must presently rely on survey evidence for the late antique and early medieval periods. As archaeologists started to practise intensive survey widely in the 1990s, the results of these regional surveys surprised. In the southern Argolid, the authors remarked 'nothing in the recorded history of the period prepares us for the dense settlement and intensive use of the countryside the evidence of the survey has demonstrated, but with hindsight the sharp change can be understood' (Jameson et al. 1994: 404). The Boeotia Survey likewise noted strong increases in the Late Roman (300–650 AD) period (Bintliff et al. 2007); similarly, the Northern Keos Survey (Cherry et al. 1991) recorded a sharp spike in site numbers, albeit from a small sample of sites from the Early Roman (1–300 AD) to the Late Roman (300–700 AD). Data such as these from survey work throughout Greece emerged in the 1980s and 1990s. Their results demonstrated noteworthy uniformity regarding an abundance of Late Roman material in the landscape, which in many ways was unexpected. Prior to the 1990s, the Late Roman period was thought to have been economically and socially moribund – the notion that the record really reflects 'no people' or depopulation – a state of affairs based primarily upon readings of the written sources. In the face of the material data, the narrative of Late Roman decline shifted to one of Late Roman settlement and economic expansion (Kosso 2003). Reactions were not long to follow. In rejecting a simple 'boom' of late Roman expansion, those working in the Corinthia attempted to smooth what are essentially problems of conceptualization and periodization (i.e. the distribution of artefacts across chronological thresholds which themselves are imposed and problematic, as discussed in Chapter 1). But to mitigate the apparent biases within the material signature of the Late Roman era, especially in reference to the Early Roman era, is not without peril. The impulse to somehow even out perceived disparities is accompanied by the view that we may simply not be able to properly identify material from the missing or 'under-represented' eras because of methodological blindness – or the 'no perception' side of the debate.

As noted above, after the sixth century well-known imported red ware ceramic types diminish and consequently survey data are less helpful. A few examples will suffice to demonstrate what at first glance appear to represent major declines in activity but which others see as revealing potential deep structural problems that bedevil the record. For example, the Argolid Exploration Project recorded 99 total Late Roman (AD 400–650) sites and 59 Middle Byzantine-Frankish period sites (650–1500 AD) (Jameson et al. 1994: 229, fig. 4.4). The Berbati-Limnes survey of the northern Argolid recovered only one fragment of seventh- to eighth-century Glazed White Ware pottery (Hahn 1996: 424, 432). The Southern Euboea Exploration Project recorded ample Late Roman (AD 400–600) sites, but just 2.5 per cent of these continued into the Early Byzantine era (AD 600–1000) (Kosso 2003: 39). The Boeotia Survey recorded a strong settlement signature in the Late Roman era (AD 250–600) and a sharp drop thereafter; the same is true of the Patras Survey (Late Roman era 300–650 AD) (Pettegrew 2006: fig. 4.1). Results like these have led some, such as Gregory (1994, 2004), to comment on the sudden shift from apparent dense settlement accompanied by prosperity to a sparsely inhabited, apparently materially depleted environment. Alcock (1993) argues that Roman imperial intervention created structures that fundamentally reconfigured the countryside. This influence did not survive for long the collapse of centralized political power – in Greece this would correlate with sometime in the seventh century – and the Roman nadir was followed by a reversion to more dispersed settlements characteristic of the pre-Roman environment. The tapering of material markers whose very dearth becomes a scaffold for the edifice of the Dark Age façade has led to considerable hand-wringing on the part of scholars wondering where all the people have gone.

Even those who practise survey and believe in its usefulness acknowledge fundamental problems with current practices. In Greece, there is a near-universal failure to identify early medieval material or to date finds beyond the nearly useless category of 'medieval', or worse, ignoring the thousand years of the medieval past altogether (Bintliff 1999, 2000; Vionis 2013), and in many parts of Cyprus the criticism of Rupp (1986) has yet to be redressed. Although there have been conscious efforts to address this issue in Greece and elsewhere, especially Cyprus where there is evidence of progress, results have been uneven at best and progress in detecting Dark Age evidence slight (Given et al. 2013: 335). To this point, surveys have not detected a significant habitation signature over much of Greece after the sixth century. Of the intensive surveys to report post-Roman materials, all ten indicate a precipitous drop in the number of sites marked by early medieval pottery (Kosso 2003; Pettegrew 2007). On the face of it, Dark Age Greece, like the northern Balkans, seems to have undergone a near-total reconfiguration of rural habitation or the disappearance of the majority of its settlements sometime during the seventh century. The evidence from coin hoards is no more encouraging. The number of hoards from Greece whose latest coins are datable from the century of 711–811 is just seven. This stands in stark relief against the 82 hoards whose latest coin belonged to 518–618 and the dozen with latest dates of 618-680 (Curta 2011: 113, table 3.1).

This picture is unsettling, implying as it does that Greece apparently suffered a depression in the seventh and eighth centuries. Pettegrew (2007) argues that the prime fault in the survey data lies in recognition and recovery of ceramics: on the one hand we fail to recognize relatively poorly studied forms from pre- or post-Roman times, while on the other inflating Late Roman settlement and prosperity values. Without a doubt the record is skewed, sometimes drastically so, by this breakdown in the chain of the recovery process. A little evidence is a dangerous thing, however, and while it is nonsensical to think of Greece as completely emptied in the seventh to ninth centuries, it is less waggish to suggest that there were fewer people living in the southern Balkans in the eighth century than there were in the sixth. Pettegrew (2007: 779) simply defers the end of the 'busy countryside' until the seventh or eighth century when the 'lights of the Corinthian crossroads dim and go out'. Likewise, Joanita Vroom, based on her experience in Aetolia, raised the possibility that people in upland areas have traditionally possessed a fundamentally different material culture *vis-à-vis* pottery than lower-lying regions. One might assume this to be true of any inaccessible landscape. Ceramics were simply cumbersome and replaceable by skins and other storage and transport objects (Vroom 1998) and thus the lack of pottery in the archaeological record demonstrates only a different domestic material basis rather than an absence of people.

Scepticism of the accuracy of the survey data as providing proof for both the Late Roman settlement 'boom' and the early medieval 'bust' that followed has led some to cast aspersions not only upon the methodologies of survey as noted above, but also the value of the data thereby obtained. The most critical recent assessor of survey and its application within Greece is certainly Guy Sanders (2004). Sanders notes conflicts resulting from reliance on imported pottery; the landscape of the Lakonia Survey appears to be abandoned by c. 400 (Lawson 1996: 123), whereas on Melos imports continued to c. 850 (Renfrew and Wagstaff 1982). For Sanders, unlike Pettegrew, it is not primarily about our recognition (or lack thereof) of pottery. The problems are much more involved. Most surveys are poorly conceived and executed; while purporting to be multi-period, they focus on one era of interest to the detriment of others. Surveys often use poorly trained staff (Sanders 2004) and are too likely to focus on concepts of urban 'hinterlands' and problems related to urban concerns. Moreover, do surface finds really represent subsurface strata (Alcock 1993: 50–53)? If finds lying on the ground do represent human activities within our indicated chronologies, in what way and to what extent do they do so? The deep ploughing over a considerable portion of the Boeotian Survey area has not been adequately addressed, although scholars are clearly aware of what such annual churning must do to 'sites' based on diagnostic sherds, which tend to be smashed by ploughing but not completely pulverized (Winther-Jacobsen 2010). In some instances, ploughing is likely to have doubled the number of sherds visible on the surface (Forbes 2013: 586) over more deeply ploughed fields and over-representation may be an even greater problem than dispersal and loss (Poulter 2007b: 592–94). These problems are not easily confronted. Moreover, since survey has often been conducted with reference to urban excavations, what about those periods or regions where settlement was more dispersed? Urban models certainly do not apply to the less densely settled spaces of the countryside. Finally, the easy assumption of pottery = sites = people is clearly flawed as its negative analogue (Sanders 2004). Unfortunately, with excavation becoming increasingly expensive, and European and North American government and university budgets more constrained, survey is likely to remain the dominant means by which settlement history is constructed in the foreseeable future. Beyond cost, another simple reason why this is likely to remain the case is that final reports from surveys are published at a much higher rate than those from excavations.

We know of course that rural Greece and the Aegean were not completely depopulated, but the dearth in the material record is acute in cities and even worse outside larger settlements. For the seventh century, at least, ceramic studies and excavation has made limited progress. Based on 'site' numbers from survey alone, the settlement picture of seventh- to ninth-century Greece is quite grim. Due to some of the methodological concerns just noted, Veikou (2013) urges a return to qualitative rather than quantitative discussion when interpreting the post-sixth-century countryside and in this she is certainly right. Veikou further notes evidence of activity throughout Greece in the form of church construction and burials. From her detailed study of Epirus, though, the results are again sobering: one church restored in the seventh century and four in the eighth. In light of the inherent problems built into the current survey data, we must look elsewhere in the archaeological record for signs of vitality that some scholars assume to have persisted after the sixth century.

Many sixth-century cemeteries in Greece go out of use *c.* 620 and extramural interment places were replaced by intramural locations. Smaller sites not associated with classical cities (and thus 'rural' for our purposes) with burial fields are known at Tigani on the Mani Peninsula. In Lakonia, the church established in the late sixth or early seventh century served as a burial place apparently prior to its renovation in the twelfth century (Drandakis 1976; Drandakis and

Gioles 1980; Drandakis et al. 1981). Among the finds of the dozen burials excavated on Antikythera, one produced a seventh-century buckle. At Drymos in Thessaloniki, a cist grave outside the apse of a fifth-century Byzantine church was used for a second burial sometime in the seventh-tenth century. To the west of Thessaloniki at Edessa in Greek Macedonia, other grave sites are known with solidly dated seventh-century objects. But the proxy evidence from burials and finds within them is slender and confirm only a general picture of region-by-region activity in Greece (Veikou 2012). Although it is good to have confirmation that the landscape was not completely depopulated (something that to my knowledge nobody has ever proposed), so far we have been unable to really distil the disparate data into a fine-grained picture of settlement. Excavation of rural domestic sites in Greece is rare and recognition of material from the seventh to ninth centuries equally infrequent (Kourelis 2003). In light of the relative paucity of material evidence for Dark Age domestic and agricultural life, historians relying on sparse textual evidence have dominated discussion of the countryside. The debate, in so far as scholars take interest in rural matters, is about oscillations in populations and their extent and timing. In the case of the presumed demographic drops that accompanied the abandonment of some cities entirely and substantial parts of others, the countryside is often viewed as having suffered a similar fate (Kaplan 1992).

Within the precinct of the temple of Zeus at Olympia in the Peloponnese, a sixth-century village flanking a church was replaced at some time in the seventh century by a new settlement. This village was peopled by outsiders who cremated their dead and whose material culture indicates a different identity from that of those who had farmed the area in the sixth and seventh centuries. Several scholars take these newcomers to Olympia to be Slavs (Völling 1995, 2001) who lived peacefully among the Greek Christian inhabitants (Malingoudis 1981; Sanders 1995; Avramea 1997: 86), but strong parallels from the Olympia material with contemporary objects from the western Balkans and from the Avar khaganate (Vida and Völling 2000) indicate an intrusive presence (Curta 2011: 125). Around the derelict Temple of Zeus, excavators found evidence of seventh-century domestic structures. At Aphiona, a portion of the approximately fifty burials, which included male, female, and subadult inhumations, belongs to the seventh and eighth centuries (Bulle 1934: 219–22; Curta 2011: 121).

The Swedish excavation at Pyrgouthi (Hjohlman et al. 2005) in the Peloponnese recovered a tower farmhouse whose latest period of occupation apparently ended sometime in the early seventh century. The site thus offers a rare occasion to say something about the agricultural regime as practised in the southern Peloponnese during the transformation of Byzantium. Faunal remains indicate that animal husbandry on the site focused largely on ovicaprids (sheep/goat represent 39.1 per cent of the finds), while swine (15.4 per cent) and cattle (13.6 per cent) played a secondary role (Mylona 2005). Equids (donkey, mule, and horse) were also present. As elsewhere in Greece and the Aegean, the profile of Pyrgouthi indicates a reliance on sheep and goats primarily for milk and wool with meat a secondary product, while cattle were used for traction and probably milk as well; secondary products from bovines would have included bone and hides. Finally, the relative abundance of pigs as an animal of secondary importance is unsurprising; hogs are less versatile than cattle and require more water than goats, for instance, but reproduce and grow relatively rapidly, offering a good source of protein and calories.

The crop regime at Pyrgouthi resembles that from elsewhere in the contemporary Byzantine world (Decker 2009). A reliance on olives, legumes (e.g. chick peas, lentils, bitter vetch, dwarf chickling), and grains such as emmer- and durum-type wheats, *Triticum turgidum* and *T. carthlicum* (Pollard wheat or possibly Persian wheat), six-rowed hulled barley (*Hordeum vulgare*) (Sarpaki 2005), and oats was common over much of the empire. Among the interesting possibilities at Pyrgouthi is the presence of Persian wheat, which is known only in its area of origin in Iran and the Caucasus and in one putative site in Neolithic Britain. Its positive identification at Pyrgouthi would therefore be highly unusual. Unfortunately, progress on Byzantine archaeobotany lags, and despite all the possibilities these remains hold and even when well done, interpretation of specific cultivars remains controversial (Hillman 2001).

Nonetheless, it seems the inhabitants of seventh-century Pyrgouthi practised similar forms of rotation and inter-cultivation among fruit trees known from modern Greece and from ancient sources. So too was the cultivation of grape vines and wine making; the presence of a press indicates a certain level of sophistication and expense, as wine can be trodden in a variety of large receptacles such as plastered basins, rock cuttings or tubs, or a fixture like the small niche-like treading area in the corner of the farm tower at Pyrgouthi. Interestingly, although the output of this press setup was modest, there is nonetheless evidence that this rather remote, unpretentious site was fully integrated into the late antique economy, including consuming (re-using?) LR2 amphorae (Hjohlman et al. 2005). Unfortunately, the viticultural tools and remains of wine presses and storage jars from Pyrgouthi and Olympia (Völling 1995, 2001, 2002) do not provide evidence for agriculture very far into the seventh century.

More data from excavation are available from Italy and the Adriatic as well as the islands. In the Salento of southern Apulia, there is considerable archaeological and environmental evidence for thriving agriculture. Excavations at Supersano (Arthur et al. 2008, 2012) revealed traces of wine making via the remains of crushed grape remains, olive, quince, and cornelian cherry. The settlement was abandoned sometime during the eighth century. On the opposite shore of the Adriatic, excavations of a late antique ecclesiastical complex on the Vrina Plain abandoned *c.* 800 and re-occupied as an elite residence *c.* 830 (Greenslade and Hodges 2013) preserved a similar mélanges of crops. Millet was present in the sixth century and also in later medieval contexts, while free-threshing wheat varieties and barley were present throughout the late antique and ninth and tenth centuries, as were grape and fig (Livarda, forthcoming). On Crete, a great deal of recent work aids discussion, though one still encounters the regrettable neglect of medieval periods as around Kavousi at the eastern end of the island (Haggis 1996: 373, n. 3).

Paolo Orsi (1942; Arthur, forthcoming), whose numerous publications on Byzantine topics were in many senses ahead of their time, provided archaeologists with a different framework whence investigation has proceeded. Indeed, on Sicily perhaps more strongly than anywhere else in the empire, there is evidence of a smooth transition through the sixth to eighth centuries as the countryside is generally viewed as having remained well populated (Molinari 1994). Fortunately, there is a great deal of recent material to be worked through and analysed in a synthetic manner by someone in the future. The nature of Dark Age archaeology on Sicily may in no small part be due to the fact that the great ancient *poleis* of the island remained occupied through the present day. This has led to more interest in outlying sites and a de-emphasis on rupture and decline. In any case, there seems to be little debate among Sicilian archaeologists that Byzantine Sicily of the seventh to ninth centuries was relatively healthy. Pelagatti and Di Stefano (1999) have published work on the architecture of the village of Kaukana on the south coast dated to the seventh and eighth centuries. The site served as an anchorage for coastal trade and the remains of fine stone houses suggest a certain prosperity. Not far inland, a fortified farmhouse complex (30 × 17 m) with a tower belongs to the seventh or eighth century. Throughout many parts of rural Sicily, it seems there was broad continuity in settlement activity from the sixth to eighth centuries. The band of villages that fairly evenly cover the southeastern landscape from just north of Syracuse to the southwest at Kaukana are nucleated agricultural and herding settlements whose builders demonstrated a preference for limestone upland environments, perhaps on account of security and dry environmental conditions (Messina and Di Stefano 1997). In the Platani Valley around Agrigento in the southwest, a similar situation prevails: Arab- and Norman-period sites replace Byzantine villages, farms, and small open settlements, which were dispersed across the landscape in the seventh to ninth centuries (Rizzo 2005).

As noted above, Cyprus has long been at the forefront of challenging the picture of Dark Age gloom. McClellan and colleagues (1995) argued for changes in land-use strategies in response to the collapse of regional markets, and there is certainly much to favour this view. Lower proportions of pottery finds datable after the sixth century may be due to the presence of an increasing number of handmade ceramics, which investigators are likely to consider prehistoric (Rautman 2003). Despite increasing recognition of probable continuities in local production, archaeologists have been unable to fill in the 'gap period' in the Byzantine countryside. Even recently, methodologically aware teams like those of the Troodos Archaeological and Environmental Survey Project in northwestern Cyprus have been unable to advance the 'no people' versus 'no perception' debate very much, though its investigators conclude that many late Roman ceramics must go deep into the seventh century (Given et al. 2013: 335). The same holds for rural sites discovered during survey of the Vasilikos Valley (Rautman 2005). Excavations of rural sites like Kalavasos-Kopetra, Sirmata, and Maroni-Petrera indicate a general decline in activity *c.* 650. Pottery at the latter included late forms of Phocaean Red Slip Ware (form 10), which was produced at least into the seventh century but perhaps later; there the coins also indicate abandonment in the seventh century. But in other areas the Cypriot countryside appears more dynamic. The South Basilica at Polis-Chryochous, for example, exhibits a different experience with extensive rebuilding (more architecturally expansive than refurbishment or remodelling) representing a portico extension to the south and a barrel-vaulted roof sometime in the mid seventh century, as revealed by the finely controlled ceramic assemblage (Caraher et al. 2013). In the northern part of the island on the Karpas Peninsula, Stewart (2008, 2010) has argued that the barrel-vaulting replaced timbered roofs in the local churches in the seventh or eighth century, indicating considerable rural resources and vitality. In many ways, these examinations build on earlier work.

On Crete, the scholarly consensus until recently was of a seventh-century deterioration in living conditions and urban life (Di Vita 1985; Tsounkarakes and Chrysos, 1988) owing to its general malaise as elsewhere in the empire as well as episodes peculiar to the island, such as the earthquake of 670 (Di Vita 1996). This picture is being somewhat modified via new approaches that stress stratigraphic and spatial awareness (Zanini 2009). In western Crete, surveyed remains of putative farms indicate several modest late antique dwellings with some material suggesting these households were connected to the wider economy at least into the early seventh century (Raab 2001), although there seems to have been less activity than in the century prior. Modest homes and a 'village-like' character of the townscape of Gortyn in the seventh century are interesting facets of architectural change amidst local vitality that ceramic evidence (including imports) indicates continued into the third quarter of the seventh century (Zanini and Costa 2011). Also intriguing are the material remains of agricultural and herding activities within the Pythion quarter of Gortyn (Zanini 2009; Zanini et al. 2009), where piles of bones indicate butchery of sheep/goats, a feature of 'ruralization' noted elsewhere (see Chapter 3). This underscores once more the inability of the categories 'urban' and 'rural' to adequately describe early medieval settlements. As Cosentino has noted, Gortyn promises to inform our understanding not only of Byzantine 'urbanism' but of different economic, social, and morphological features that are its corollaries (Baldini et al. 2013: 241–42); here again I would rather we choose a different expression than urbanism but there is no ready substitute to hand.

Turning to Asia Minor, the evidence of the seventh to ninth centuries is equally challenging to recover. As in Greece, there are numerous surveys – far too many to discuss or even enumerate here – of varying methodology and quality of analysis. Only highlights will be noted alongside the salient features of the overall debate about Dark Age life in Asia Minor. The narrative of urban decline dominates and this discourse is underpinned further by a relative absence of Dark Age material in the countryside as well. Nonetheless, a sampling of archaeological work reveals evidence for continued occupation in many regions. Dozens of survey projects, many undertaken by Turkish archaeologists, have covered a sizeable portion of the landscape. However, these surveys really are a mixed bag, focusing on anything from Neolithic artefact scatters to Greek inscriptions, often with little regard for any material or features outside of these rather narrow remits. Most surveys that report Dark Age material are, like those in Greece, the offshoots of classical site excavations. Despite their central role in Hellenistic urbanism and the great classical cities that subsequently flourished there, the western coastlands are comparatively under-explored for the Byzantine era, especially in the countryside. Detailed survey work is rare and extensive studies and reconnaissance work in the model of city and hinterland dynamics understandably frames discussion. Preliminary work from the Granicus River Valley near Troy probably well represents the region from Bithynia all the way to the south coast with late antiquity fairly well represented, but the seventh to ninth centuries and later either absent or poorly represented at best. In the Granicus Valley, the city of Ilion gradually shrank in population while the countryside of the eastern Troad seems to have become more densely populated, perhaps due to migration as a result of earthquakes and malarial conditions (Rose et al. 2007; Rose 2011). In Bithynia, the evidence from survey does nothing to sharpen the picture, although some environmental studies help. In the historical record, Bithynia was prominent and contained major administrative centres like Malagina and the medieval town of Apollonia, which lay on a promontory on the western edge of its eponymous lake, today Lake Uluabat. The wall of Apollonia possibly had a seventh- to eighth-century phase (Foss and Winfield 1986: 138) but these stylistic grounds are not supplemented by survey pottery. Interestingly, French work in Bithynia published no pottery from the seventh to ninth centuries – it was impossible to recognize earlier local and regional ceramics, and Glazed White Wares that appeared there did not do so prior to the tenth century (François 2003: 289). Further along the north coast, the Cide Survey did not distinguish Early Byzantine sites by era, but the Roman/Byzantine material (BC 85–330 for Roman; Byzantine = AD 330–1435) included several forts or fortified farmhouses and a possible flint-working site for the manufacture of threshing sledges (Düring and Glatz 2010). Dark Age material is not noted. Likewise, further east along the coast at Sinope, Doonan (1998, 2002, 2004) noted the hinterland of the city was intensively developed in the Roman imperial period and at least through the sixth century, 'a trend which was reversed toward the end of the first millennium AD' (Doonan 2000: 24). Behind the Black Sea coast, Project Paphlagonia surveyed an 8,500 square metre area and catalogued 330 sites, some 165 of which were categorized broadly as Late Roman/Byzantine in date.

For Lycia, Foss framed the debate in his multi-dimensional study of the coastlands (Foss 1994). While noting that activity may have continued into the Dark Ages, he concluded that there was widespread abandonment of many Lycian cities as well as their hinterlands in the seventh century. Foss also noted major building work at a handful of sites such as the fortress at Dereağzı (Foss 1994: 33) and posited reoccupation of others in later centuries.

Beyond Xanthus (Demargne et al. 1958: 22–27) and Limyra (Rasch and Seyer 1997), there has been scant excavation. At Limyra, which was a bishopric until the end of the ninth century, there is evidence of a seventh-century building installed in the Theatre Baths and imported pottery demonstrating connections with the Levantine coast (Vroom 2007). In neighbouring Pisidia, surveyors have mapped production sites for Late Roman D red ware ceramics that promise to alter our understanding of the dating of the end of the production of these types.

Work throughout Lycia has also challenged conventional views of the use of space during antiquity and the Middle Ages (Harrison 2001), and survey done by Coulton and Armstrong at Balboura (Çölkayiği) on the frontier between Lycia and Phrygia runs counter to the seventh-century decline thesis one sees applied to much of Asia Minor (Armstrong 2006; Coulton and Armstrong 2012). Rural sites near the city in the main continue to be occupied into the eighth century, according to the survey work done there (Coulton and Armstrong 2012: 170–71). As nearly all of the some 700 square kilometres of the territory of Balboura is above 1200 m in elevation, the relatively common use of pottery in this highland environment contrasts with the absence of ceramics in the uplands of certain parts of Greece noted above. Clearly, considerable work needs to be done for us to understand these differences in ceramic distributions and their persistence in some regions. Balboura and its rural landscape are, by traditional measures, disadvantaged – the sea lies over 50 km distant as the crow flies and with little open tilth suitable for cereal cultivation. Nonetheless, the present evidence suggests both a connectedness to the wider Mediterranean attested by finds of fifth- to eighth-century imported ceramics and well resilience beyond the traditional seventh-century threshold of decline.

The environs of Sagalassos in Pisidia have been studied via long-term excavation and survey (Vanhaverbeke et al. 2004, 2009; Waelkens et al. 2006) that included extensive as well as intensive survey (Martens 2004). The city and its surrounding landscapes began to alter considerably from the fifth century onward. From the century spanning roughly 550–650 AD, the change was acute: the monumental public core of the city began to be abandoned or re-purposed from its civic and religious functions. An earthquake of the mid seventh century ended most activity in the city. In this way, Sagalassos seems to share in the apparent fate of many other cities of Asia Minor. Outside Sagalassos, though, this same century witnessed an increase in sites and a rise in the ratio of villages to farms. In the seventh century and later, the lack of sites and the disappearance of the city of Sagalassos as a central place does not imply a decline in the population of the region, rather it reflects a more natural dynamic that prevailed for centuries before the intrusion of Graeco-Roman urbanism (Vanhaverbeke et al. 2009). In part, this sanguine view of the Dark Age landscape of Pisidia is bolstered by the ceramic assemblage, which indicates continued regional production and exchange of domestic wares (Commito 2014: 295–300) (on which, see Chapter 5).

As at Sagalassos, long-term work at Aphrodisias has revealed the persistence of activity within the intramural area of the late antique city well into the Middle Ages, even if the end seventh-century population was reduced to a 'skeleton crew' of a handful of clergy and local civilians (Baeten et al. 2012). The advantage of long-term excavation of a site paired with field survey is obvious at Aphrodisias, where surveyors benefited from a well-established local ceramic profile and had a firm grasp of the dynamics of the city population through time. Interestingly, present data suggest that Aphrodisias did not partake of the great expansion of rural sites witnessed in many other parts of the empire. Once again, field survey indicates that the seventh century was crucial. The surveyors of the Aphrodisian hinterland found no increase in rural population that coincided with decreasing urban population – in other words, the explanation of people emigrating from the town to the country is not a viable one on the current evidence. Ratté and De Staebler (2012: 36) note:

> On this evidence, the large-scale abandonment of Aphrodisias in the early seventh century does not seem to represent simply a dramatic change in settlement pattern, in which a constant regional population redistributed itself differently across the landscape. Rather, it appears to mark a real and significant reduction in population.

At Aizanoi in northern Phrygia, the urban and literary focus of epigraphic survey undoubtedly biases the record towards the late antique period (most inscriptions cease in the seventh century). The population of Aizanoi declined in the seventh century when the inhabitants possibly trickled into the countryside (Rheidt 2003; Niewöhner 2006). Nor is much insight gained from the best of the published survey work from Galatia. On the Konya Plain, Baird (2004) noted evidence for an increase in settlement density from the fifth to seventh centuries ('Early Byzantine'); material was found on 85 sites, an increase from the prior Roman period. Site size also expanded considerably from the Roman/Early Byzantine period. Extensive survey work has also been conducted by members of the Japanese Institute of Anatolia (which also covers part of Cappadocia – see below). Anderson (2008) examined material from 200 sites recorded by this mission and dated 58 of them to the Early Byzantine (AD 330–630) and 35 to the Middle Byzantine (AD 630–1100). Although Anderson acknowledges the lack of diagnostic sherds for Middle Byzantine sites, he also maintains the widely held view that overall site numbers fell across the region during this period. Site size also expanded considerably from the Roman/Early Byzantine period. The excavations at Çadır Höyük have revealed Dark Age occupation and have recorded remnants of an agricultural complex that may have been continuously occupied from the fifth century through the end of the eleventh century, at which time the settlement was apparently destroyed by Seljuk attacks.

Allcock and Roberts (2014) have incorporated results from the Central Anatolian Survey, a project aimed at investigating the Neolithic period in central Anatolia. This was an early, extensive survey that covered territory ranging from Ankara to as far east as Niğde and Nevşehir (Todd 1980). The focus of the Kaman-Kalehöyük general regional survey, directed since 1986 by Sachihiro Omura (1998, 2007, 2008), has evolved over the years to include not only a special interest in tel sites (höyüks) but also other features in the landscape. Byzantium is nonetheless not the principal concern of the investigators who, to date, have catalogued 1,500 sites. The third project noted by TAY (Türkiye Arkeolojik Yerleşmeleri Projesi) for the Byzantine period aims at recording architectural remains. This tremendously mixed bag, none of which focuses on the Byzantine era presents tough methodological problems. One of them is periodization, which Allcock and Roberts work out via a true *longue durée* approach by grouping together sites of the Roman and Byzantine period (AD 395–1071). While such methods may be appropriate for the Neolithic, which at its shortest range extends over millennia, its efficacy for historical periods is debatable. Nonetheless, it is helpful to see other differences ironed out by ignoring other forms of periodization. The resulting comparisons based on adjusted site counts weighted by time and survey area are instructive: 'from ~AD 670, site numbers fell by 61% and reached low values (105 sites) not recorded since the Late Bronze Age' (Allcock and Roberts 2014: 50).

One of the challenges of archaeological survey is often a lack of pottery finds or the inability of surveyors to locate and identify ceramic materials useful in delineating and dating human activity. This problem is especially pronounced in Cappadocia, where there is a distinct lack of surviving pottery in many areas and few other clear markers of past human activity. This probably has much to do with considerable erosion, especially in the area of Rocky Cappadocia, where underground churches, monasteries, and settlements were cut into volcanic tuff. These underground dwellings were a normal feature of early medieval life there (Cooper and Decker 2012). In fact, the unique challenges that these broken, compartmentalized landscapes with their blind valleys and microenvironments carved by the action of wind and water (Fig. 14) present to archaeologist calls for a new plan of attack entirely. Churches are a sure indicator of settlement from the fourth century AD onwards, but in order to place these within their environmental context and thereby understand changes over time, we need tools with which to accurately date rock-cut elements. The pervasiveness of underground dwellings and other architectural forms (Bixio et al. 2012) in regions formerly part of Byzantium should give pause and requires us to consider that our failure to recognize and integrate such loci into the archaeological

Fig. 14 Cappadocia, tuff cones and gardens (photo J. Eric Cooper).

record has likely led to a substantial underestimation of human activity in certain places and times.

While detailed traces of farming and animal husbandry from the Byzantine Mediterranean and Anatolia is somewhat sparse, a range of approaches has helped to colour the picture somewhat. Skeletal material from the sixth- to seventh-century Greece has been closely studied. From Sourtara in northern Greece, isotopic analysis indicates fish was a major component of the diet alongside wheat and barley (Bourbou et al. 2011). Tooth decay representative of a carbohydrate-rich diet was in evidence at Sourtara but the people of Messene in the Peloponnese and Eleutherna on Crete had better teeth due in large part to a plant-rich diet low in carbohydrates (Bourbou 2010). At Eleutherna, traces of scurvy indicate a lack of vitamin C in some instances, while anaemia probably signifies a lack of meat (Bourbou 2004; Bourbou and Tsilipakou 2009). This contrasts with the interpretations of data from the seventh century at Gortyn, where investigators posited high levels of meat and milk consumption (Fornaciari et al. 1988). These peasants were often undernourished and under significant physiological strain from heavy labour and an array of bodily ailments; death around age forty was quite common.

The Dark Age environment: change for the worse?

Was the world of Dark Age Byzantium colder than prior centuries? Were weather patterns less stable with more unseasonable frosts, unusual dryness or wetness, or other disruptive characteristics that could have damaged crops, eroded the landscape or triggered other slow and sudden disasters?

To date, the debate here is rather one-sided, with scholars building up a complicated profile of the past environment which indicates the

Dark Age countryside of Anatolia did indeed suffer from falling temperatures and rainfall. Recently, Haldon and colleagues (2014) have made a pioneering effort to approach the problem in an interdisciplinary and thorough manner. Their study noted that a major solar minimum occurred in the seventh century and that over much of Asia Minor the climate of the late sixth to late seventh centuries was cooler and wetter. Prior to this the bulk of Anatolia experienced environmental conditions characterizing the Beyşehir Occupation Phase (BOP), named from the site where this pollen sequence was first noted (Eastwood et al. 1998). The century of tougher environmental conditions beginning at the close of the sixth century ended the BOP over the bulk of Anatolia: eleven of the twenty-one sites with pollen indicate an end to this era of intensive farming by the sixth or seventh century (Haldon et al. 2014: table 2). In the vicinity of Sagalassos, for example, the BOP seems to have ended *c.* AD 300 at Bereket, *c.* 600–700 at Gravgaz, and *c.* 1000 at Ağlasun (Bakker et al. 2012, 2013). The effect of frost and harsher winters posited for Dark Age Anatolia may have indeed wrought havoc on a range of activities.

While in some instances the authors downplay the role of environmental change and merely one of any number of possible agents of change, in others they afford environmental conditions a greater role in history. One such case is Balboura: 'As the microclimate of this highland became drier and colder during the course of the eighth century, agriculture in such a relatively marginal area became impractical and cost-ineffective, especially with such crops as olives and vines' (Haldon et al. 2014: 147). Certainly, cold and altitude would have rendered Balboura a difficult environment in which to grow olives in the best of times and there is no certain evidence that they ever did grow there. But olives and vines were not the only agricultural products of such a landscape – far from it. Excavation and flotation are required in order to establish what role these plants had in the local regime and if they were so vital that without them the inhabitants of the area would have perished or moved.

Despite the confidence that the authors demonstrate in these data, it is difficult to sustain statements like 'As a whole, Anatolia in this period evinces a much simplified agro-pastoral regime and a reduced level of activity' (Haldon et al. 2014: 139). This cannot be so confidently stated. In one cited instance, that of the Konya Plain, the authors note that the 'hitherto dense settlement relying on extensive seasonal irrigation vanished in the late seventh/eight century' (Haldon et al. 2014: 139). In fact, the above-noted survey of the Konya Plain by Baird published no data from the medieval epoch while the synthesis of Anderson (2008) implies a certain level of continuity in habitation on the Konya Plain through the Dark Ages.

Do the palynological data support a broad decrease in the cereal-centric intensive farming regime of late antiquity? They appear to, but again we must be cautious. Dating remains too imprecise for a truly fine-grained perspective. It is risky to place too much confidence in these proxy data as reflecting local conditions without allowing perhaps a half-century margin for error. Among current data there is wide regional variance in the timing of the end of the BOP: ten of twenty-one sampled areas yielded end dates of the BOP ranging anywhere from the second century BC (!) to the eleventh century AD (Haldon et al. 2014: table 2). In some regions, there was apparently a retreat of the BOP before its return in the tenth or eleventh centuries during the 'Medieval Climate Anomaly' (formerly the Medieval Climate Optimum) of 900–1200 AD.

Another problem with interpreting the precise meaning of the pollen data as proxy for agriculture is in the representation of the plants themselves. An increase in cereals may in part be due to other grasses or wild progenitors indistinguishable from cultivated types in the record (Bottema 1995). In addition, alterations over time in the relative percentages of herbaceous plants, pine, and oak indicate environmental variation for sure, but one should not assume that decreases in synanthropic plant pollen must indicate an *overall* decline in human activity. Instead, we must look to signs of other ways in which people were likely to have exploited their surroundings, especially to strategies in which herding played a preponderant role in local subsistence, something that palynological evidence alone is unable to detail. For example, from AD 450 to AD 700, the faunal assemblage at Sagalassos indicates ovicaprines (sheep/goats) gained increasing importance, a husbandry strategy that meshes well with the rise of pine and oak pollen as goats, in particular, are well-adapted to live in degraded, shrubby, and wooded environments (Vanhaverbeke et al. 2011). Over the same period of time at Sagalassos, cattle too decreased in number. This evidence also supports the notion that people there gradually shifted from an arable-farming regime to a more sylvan system at the end of late antiquity. Unfortunately, an awareness of this possibility has not led to greater recognition of ephemeral sites such as seasonal encampments, sheepcotes, and other features associated with pastoralism. Thus the environmental data are vital but they essentially nest within a range of other evidence.

Other environmental data can be helpful in understanding many facets of this debate. Do these support the view proffered by Haldon et al. (2014: 150) that 'important and largely overlooked historical data suggest that farmers reacted to perceived environmental changes by introducing new crops'? At Sagalassos, the archaeobotanical record of AD 450–600 indicates the appearance of millet and dramatic (doubling) of barley in the aggregate samples (Baeten et al. 2012; Fuller et al. 2012). These shifts are possible indicators of local adaptation to changing growing conditions. In Anatolia, millet was a summer crop. Though there were spring-sown barley varieties, most barley at Sagalassos probably remained an autumn-sown winter crop harvested in early summer. Presumably, this grain was afforded a more prominent role in place of certain wheat varieties recovered at the site in diminishing numbers from the Late Imperial (AD 300–450) period onward. Relative to other crops, the overall percentage of wheat recovered from Sagalassos declined from the Late Imperial to Early Byzantine era. Although the precise site chronology is not entirely certain, preliminary archaeobotanical finds from Çadır Höyük (Smith 2007) are nonetheless essential in this discussion in part because of the rarity of such study from Byzantine contexts in Anatolia. Cereals are the main crop plants recovered and among these are free-threshing wheats (without a glume that needed additional processing to free the kernel), including bread or 'macaroni' wheat (types indeterminate and thus categorized *Triticum aestivum/ T. durum*) – the first of these is noted for its palatability and quality of bread and the second for its drought tolerance and long-term storage qualities. Barley was also present in the Byzantine sample analysed. At Amorium, the archaeobotanical finds are more intriguing still. Bread wheat or other free-threshing wheat types, commonly associated with Hellenistic- and Roman-improved agricultural techniques and 'imperial' palates due to the quality of the bread they rendered, were present in many late antique and Dark Age contexts. Evidence for barley came mostly from a storage pit with probable ninth-century remains, as the charred deposits seem to belong to the sack of the city in 838. Millet was identified from a late fifth-century deposit but not for later periods (the small size of millet grains can make it challenging to recover these seeds). Amorium, which has the best dated Dark Age plant remains, unfortunately shows no indication for the introduction of new crops such as those proposed above (Giorgi 2012).

Environmental data from Cappadocia are also noteworthy. At Lake Nar in Cappadocia, the depth of the lake (26 m) and the anoxic nature of its deepest waters offer a unique window into past land use via pollen coring. Study of pollen from these laminated sediments has allowed a macroscopic view of regional pollen through time (Eastwood et al. 2007; Haldon 2007; England et al. 2008; Haldon et al.

2014). The era of intensive arable farming and dramatic human impact on the land in Anatolia is characterized by cereal cultivation and the pervasiveness of synanthropic plants such as chestnut, vine, olive, and other fruit-bearing trees. According to the Lake Nar record, the BOP ends abruptly in Cappadocia around AD 670. For the span AD 670 to AD 950, the Lake Nar samples exhibit a pronounced decrease in olive and cereal pollen and an increase in grass, pine, and oak. Pine is a pioneer species and indicates the abandonment of arable ground and a return to steppe or forest conditions. The results of the pollen analysis and survey site data, combined with the evidence of historical texts that record widespread Arab raiding, have led scholars to assume that the seventh to ninth centuries were difficult times indeed for the Cappadocians (Haldon 2007). There was no wholesale abandonment of the countryside, however, and evidence to the contrary is not difficult to find. While Caesarea (Kayseri) probably contracted in size from the seventh century, the small city of Mokissos shows signs of continued vitality and settlement, and there are indications of the exploitation of the surrounding area after late antiquity (Berger 1995, 1996, 1998).

As noted above, however, one of the major ways in which Cappadocians adapted to the colder environment was to move underground, into cave homes and complexes that helped keep them warm and safe even if we should be careful not to exaggerate the comfort of such spartan abodes. For example, the rock-cut villages of Ovaören and Filiktepe appear to have developed during the seventh or eighth centuries into sizeable troglodytic settlements where there is considerable evidence for religious and economic activity in the form of churches and stables, as well as defensive features, notably the heavy 'millstone doors' that allowed passages to be sealed to block the ingress of would-be attackers (Cooper and Decker 2012). Rock-cut towns could cover a considerable area and host populations of over 1,000 people. Among the most famous of these is Derinkuyu, 2,500 square metres in area and which may have been home to as many as 20,000 people. Due to the limitations of conventional survey and the specialist skills required to explore such dwellings, it is very likely we have missed evidence of considerable Dark Age activity from Crimea to Cappadocia to Italy (Crescenzi and Caprara 2012). A thorough re-evaluation of this evidence will help to alter our picture of the seventh- to ninth-century population, and consequently provide a clearer view of the extent of change in Byzantium of the seventh to ninth centuries.

5

The Dark Age Economy

The ultimate framer of the debate on the Dark Age economy is Henri Pirenne (1862–1935), whose posthumous work *Mahomet et Charlemagne* (1937) discussed evidence for a flourishing political economy in Western Europe in the sixth century. In this he was far ahead of his day, as the now common view of late antiquity in the eastern Mediterranean as a time of considerable vitality was still decades away. But Pirenne went beyond this; he also claimed that the decline in the European economy came not with the sixth century but with the arrival of Islam in the seventh century when the sea lanes were closed to trade. Although in historical and archaeological circles these arguments, known collectively as the 'Pirenne Thesis', are widely studied, many of the claims have been rejected or modified. Pirenne's work remains nonetheless a fundamental starting point and is even today no mere straw man. In fact, recent decades have revealed certain material trends that some have used to draw renewed attention to aspects of the Pirenne Thesis even while disagreeing with him on issues of timing and other areas. For example, Georges Tchalenko (1953–1958), who spent decades studying the deserted late antique villages of the limestone hills of northern Syria, argued that the Persian Wars of the seventh century, rather than the later Arab conquest, led to the end of a prosperous rural life there. As noted in Chapter 3, some scholars such as Liebeschuetz and Kennedy also find the model of economic decline of the eastern Mediterranean prior to Islam compelling. In fact, much evidence points to a gradual decoupling of the pan-Mediterranean economy after a peak in the mid sixth century (Morrisson 2002: 955). As one reviewer of Hodges and Whitehouse (1983) noted, when it came to Pirenne, 'One modifies *ad nauseam*; one never dislodges' (Scanlon 1986: 545).

A number of studies have greatly expanded the parameters and depth of our understanding of the Dark Age economy. Beginning with Hodges and Whitehouse's *Mohammed, Charlemagne and the Origins of Europe* (1983), archaeologists or archaeological materials have weighed heavily on the debate. In contradistinction to notions of backwardness and decline, Hodges and Whitehouse argued for considerable economic vitality in 'Dark Age' life and commerce. Their study greatly expanded the reach of archaeology within discussions of distinctive forms of urbanism, communications, and exchange to which subsequent generations have owed a considerable debt. Over the past decade and a half, the Transformation of the Roman World series occasionally turned its eyes towards matters of communication, trade, and farming (Chrysos and Wood 1999; Hansen and Wickham 2000; Barceló et al. 2004). Michael McCormick's *Origins of the European Economy* (2001) deals with much of the period and many of the major problems to which scholars are currently devoting their attention. McCormick's view includes Byzantium but tends to place more emphasis on Western Europe and the lands that would form the traditional heart of Western Europe. Wickham's *Framing the Early Middle Ages* (2005) devotes much of its space to discussions of land tenure and management and the ways in which power was exercised by medieval elites and fundamental to debate about the early medieval economy. By contrast, in *The Fall of Rome and the End of Civilization* (2005), Ward-Perkins cast a rather gloomy picture of post-Roman Britain in which many facets of material sophistication failed (e.g. wheel-thrown pottery) and were not immediately replaced; sometimes Roman standards were not re-attained until centuries later. In exploring the evidence and interpretations of the facets of this debate, I will focus predominantly on the evidence of specialized production and regional and long-distance exchange of goods.

Works like the above have framed the debate – for example, there is recognition of a sharp drop in Mediterranean traffic and especially in large-scale seaborne commerce, which the textual and archaeological record suggests was especially prominent in the sixth century. Did this trade in bulk goods, notably grain, wine and olive oil, as well as a host of ancillary products like papyrus continue into the seventh century? What about the routes themselves and the nodes that these links served? These and many other questions present themselves for which time does not permit exploration. Instead, I will attempt to trace some of the major features of the debate about the Dark Age economy in light of the most recent material evidence.

'The seventh century does not look to have been very attractive for high-volume, low-value movements of goods. The eighth and ninth centuries probably did not innovate here' (McCormick 2001: 569). Compared with the massive rush of goods throughout the Mediterranean of the sixth century, this statement seems presently unassailable. But the evidence for bulk transport of goods is feeble but growing, as noted below. McCormick furthermore notes that the shipping links of the eighth and ninth centuries tied together many of the major trading spurs of medieval Europe with those of the former late Roman Empire in Africa, Egypt, and the Levantine coast. It is a potent image. Byzantium has waned. The caliphate has replaced the empire as the economic sun of Eurasia around which the Mediterranean merchants, ships, and caravans orbited. Indeed, the image of Byzantium reduced from powerhouse to pauper emerges in many ways through McCormick's work, nowhere more tellingly than in the comparison of the size of the economy of the empire with that of the caliphate (McCormick 2001: 582). In the tenth and eleventh centuries, the caliphate had roughly twice the inhabited area and population of Byzantium and this at a time in which the empire had made up considerable ground beyond its Dark Age nadir. While this is not new, the expansiveness of McCormick's work has essentially cast Byzantium into a tertiary role in the Mediterranean economy – a galaxy distant from the caliphate and even, it seems, far from the vitality of the western states.

Coins and the Dark Age economy

Although coins have been discussed above in the context of urbanism and changes in settlement patterns of the seventh to ninth centuries, it is useful to discuss the economic implications of the Dark Age coin evidence here. In the seventh century, Byzantine issues of gold coinage receded from the west. Whether the flood of coins in the fifth and sixth centuries west noted by Pirenne was due to market forces, state interventions or some combination thereof, there can be little doubt that the seventh-century picture looks drastically different. Likewise, over most of the empire, the seventh century brought sweeping changes in the lower tiers of exchange of silver and bronze. The emergencies in the reign of Heraclius meant that copper (bronze) issues were frequently produced by peripatetic mints accompanying the emperor on campaign. Heraclius, however, due to the war emergency, issued about twice the number of coins annually as was the peacetime norm. Since coins often remained in circulation for considerable periods, the torrent of Heraclian issues alone would probably have kept levels of monetization fairly high. A major reorganization occurred with the abolition of the sacred *largesse*, which had to that point controlled the money supply. It was replaced by the *archon tes charages* (master of the mint) under the authority of the *eidikon*, though the latter is not certain until the late ninth century by which time its functioning as the state treasury is clear. In any case, Constantinople was the major mint that supplied the Balkans and Asia Minor with specie: it was joined by mints in Macedonia from 824 and Cherson from around 832. Both of the latter only minted bronze coins. These of course formed the 'black money', the utilitarian forms of currency in small everyday transactions. In the West, the fragmented nature of Byzantine political authority in Italy led to the minting of coins at Rome, Ravenna, Naples, and Syracuse (the latter eventually transferred to Reggio), which continued until the peninsula and Sicily were gradually lost to local princes and the Arabs. Metrology varied somewhat depending on the region, but the economic differences of these were not great (Morrisson 2002).

In Chapter 2, we noted that after the seventh-century coinage issued by Heraclius, finds of coins drop precipitously on nearly every excavated site in the empire. Hendy (1985: 620) has estimated that the loss of the eastern provinces and Balkans in the seventh century represented, in the worst case, a loss of 75 per cent of state revenues whose effects were 'truly shattering'. Since state taxation represented 57 per cent of coins in circulation and 38 per cent of the total money supply (the rest being hoarded), there can be little doubt that the overall number of coins in circulation diminished. Not only did the money supply contract, the whole economy shrank, as state expenditure was both a siphon of the overall wealth of the empire and a pump that primed the economy with coins through taxation and payments of salaries and state expenses. Some have attempted to explain the consistent decline in coins found in excavated sites as the result of selection bias or the intentional destruction of coinage of the Iconoclast emperors by later rulers or the subsequent withdrawal of coins due to coinage reforms, like that of Theophilus. However, as Morrisson has noted, the precipitous drop in coinage in the provinces indicated in the archaeological record for the years 668–874 is a real one; although more thorough collection and analysis of materials would help 'improve the general picture in important ways, it would not fundamentally alter it' (Morrisson 2002: 956).

In later Byzantium, documentary evidence indicates that only 20 per cent of expenses among institutions whose basis of wealth was farming (Morrison 2002). Laiou posits that for the twelfth century, agricultural production was monetized at 35 per cent – a rate from an economic peak that therefore was likely far more similar to the sixth rather than the seventh century. Therefore, about one in every five nomismata worth of business was likely conducted in coins in the seventh century, and probably much less than this in the countryside, which was less monetized than Constantinople. The next question of course is what do the coins – or their absence – tell us about the functioning of the economy? To what degree did things change? What ways did people feel these changes on a daily basis? Was change slow or sudden? Was the absence of coins really a major hindrance? After all, the Bronze Age Aegean functioned at a comparatively high level without any coinage whatsoever, as have other traditional economies. Even in times with the highest monetization, barter remained a prominent part of the economy. Certainly coinage allows smoother transactions and the easier flow of wealth. One has to reach a far more advanced stage of economic development, though, to supersede the notional limits that money imposes, and this is something Byzantium never lost. For example, bookkeeping and reckoning of the value of objects in the denominations of coin continued, even if these goods were not exchanged for actual specie. This is a small but important and often-overlooked point, as this sort of reckoning would have allowed credit transactions to continue in centres where a sufficiently literate and interested trading community existed to use them. It appears that such communities did carry on; certainly in Constantinople they did, and even in some provincial areas such as Classe and Comacchio in northern Italy the level of economic activity indicated from excavation suggests that relics of the old late Roman economic frameworks continued to function for some time. The northern Adriatic has become a focal point for students of the Dark Age economy, since a number of sites discovered there indicate a certain degree of economic vibrancy in the seventh to ninth centuries.

Off the record: ephemeral and hard-to-track goods

There are many challenges in rendering a full picture of the Dark Age economy. The Iconoclast controversy, for example, undoubtedly led to the widespread destruction of icons and other religious works of art, many of which would have otherwise survived. For example, the stark image of the Church of Hagia Eirene, where the space of the apse with its spartan black cross surprises the viewer today, as it no doubt did in the eighth century (Mango 1976). Although scholars dispute the toll of destruction, there is little doubt that relatively few works of sacred art securely dated to the period under consideration remain. The same is true, in general, for organic materials that comprised the bulk of material culture. Wood, plant fibre, wool, sinew, horn, and foodstuffs, to take but a few examples, simply break down over time. I have already mentioned the severe challenges resulting from the predominant focus of archaeologists on classical city spaces and their cascading effects on the formation of the archaeological record, and so I will not dwell on it here. But even assuming that the output in craftsmanship and commodities of the empire dropped in quantity and quality – both suggested in the problematic sources – it seems clear that issues of recovery, recognition, and dating remain core problems within Byzantine archaeology of the Dark Ages.

Thus far I have generally avoided relying on textual sources because the focus here is on archaeological data. However, a few examples from written evidence may help illustrate both the possibility that we are missing most markers of early medieval trade in the east. One of the most frequently cited texts for the seventh-century economy is the *Vita* of John the Almsgiver, Chalcedonian patriarch of Alexandria (606–616) (Festugière and Ryden 1974), which attests to long-distance exchange in the first decades of the seventh century, during which time the church at Alexandria and its merchant associates were involved in a brisk trade in the Aegean, the Adriatic, and even as far west as Britain where they sought tin and other local products. Some of this trade was at the pinnacle of the luxury market and included precious metals as well as spices and eastern aromatics. Material evidence supporting what seems like an otherwise fanciful text includes the finds at Tintagel in Cornwall of eastern pottery sherds, including numerous fragments of Phocaean red slip fine wares and transport amphorae from the eastern Mediterranean. Chief among the business ventures of the church under John seems to have been a traffic in silver and other precious metals, apparently bullion, plate or perhaps worked vessels (Mundell Mango 2001) intended for elite consumption. The trading expeditions mentioned in the vita apparently occurred around the time of the Persian invasions of the eastern Mediterranean but, apart from the refugees who arrived in number from conquered Palestine, there is little sense of impending economic crisis caused by the rolling Sasanian advance that contradicts the traditional narrative of decline. Stories like these and the evidence from shipwrecks (discussed below) seem to imply a 'business as usual' attitude among the merchants and shippers of the early seventh-century Mediterranean, even in areas where the coastlands were closest to enemy action. Did this kind of activity prevail through the next five decades and more when the Byzantines successfully counterattacked against Persia but ultimately lost their richest prizes, Egypt and the Levant, to the Arabs? Unfortunately, the texts offer little help on this question, although McCormick's (2001: appendix 4) impressive catalogue of communications 700–900 is a wonderful resource that clearly illustrates future analysis is possible: from the 305 entries spanning the first decade of the seventh century to the first decade of the tenth century, many involve Constantinople and the eastern Mediterranean. Travel obviously did not cease; clerics, ambassadors, merchants, and pilgrims were all on the move.

What textual sources do illuminate, however, is the persistence of certain forms of economic activity, such as monumental building (mostly at the capital) and trade in prestige goods. There was, we know, a brisk movement of holy relics from the east. Among the specialist items mentioned in texts is an organ sent in 757 to Pepin by Constantine V along with the technicians and musicians to show the Franks how to use it, a clear example of the Byzantines demonstrating their technical sophistication and (to their minds) cultural superiority (Brubaker 2004). In 803, Frankish sources record rich presents from the emperor Nikephoros I to Charlemagne, among them two wonderfully executed ivory carvings (Schreiner 2004). John Synkellos carried more than forty *kentenaria* (each *kentenarion* was 100 Byzantine pounds) of gold on his 829–830 embassy to the caliph al-Ma'mun (813–833); this sum alone was to be scattered to the crowd in Baghdad and did not include many other precious gifts reserved for the caliph and his favourites. Obviously such diplomatic exchanges between the uppermost echelons of the elites do not represent trade in a modern sense, but there was often a commercial element to such encounters, as in the case of the meeting between the Kievan ruler Olga (945–963) and her numerous retainers, among them forty-four merchants who had made the journey with her (Cutler 2001). Sumptuous objects included the ivories on the so-called Grado Chair, which may be as early as the fifth century or as late as the seventh (one ivory piece, Metropolitan Museum of Art isl 170, was radiocarbon dated to 440–670 with 95 per cent probability).

Other textual references allude to continued regular shipping activity. In the early eighth century, Justinian II (685–695/705–711) conscripted ships and crews from the capital to launch his punitive attack on Cherson, and Nikephoros I (802–811) demanded extraordinary taxes from shippers in the capital. By the mid ninth century at the latest, there was apparently considerable sailing activity in the Gulf of Corinth, as attested by the Life of St. Gregory the Decapolite, who took ship there in 831–833. Forty years later, the widow Danelis and her retinue travelled at least part of the way to

Constantinople and back – in this case by land. Just beyond our period, in 903, St. Elias travelled to Naupaktos on the northern shores of the Gulf of Corinth en route to Constantinople (McCormick 2001: 533–44). Slender as they are, these textual examples permit some regional perspective, in this case the presumed axis of contact among Sicily, peninsular Italy, the southern Adriatic, and the western Peloponnese.

The case of the widow Danelis is well known but worth noting in more detail, as it offers vital textual testimony. Around 877, as an aged woman, Danelis journeyed to Constantinople, where she offered stupendous gifts to the emperor: 300 male and 100 female slaves, a hundred each of finely brocaded garments and wool cloths, and hundreds of pieces of various grades of linen in addition to gold and silver vessels (Runciman 1940). Upon her return home, the widow had a wondrous carpet woven and adorned with precious stones that she gifted to the emperor Basil I (867–886). Acknowledging the likely exaggerations, one point that this vignette conveys was that the ninth-century Peloponnese was home to at least one fabulously wealthy landowner who possessed legions of slaves and a large stash of portable wealth. Unsurprisingly, most of the surplus is in the form of cloth. Given the evidence in Chapter 4 for the preponderance of sheep and goat in the farms of the region, it is unsurprising that Danelis possessed a great quantity of wool cloth. Flax is not terribly well represented in the archaeological record but it is interesting to note that a scrap of carbonized linen was recovered during excavation at Pyrgouthi (Hjohlman et al. 2005: 164, 246) and flax cloth was likewise recovered in excavation at Amorium (see Chapter 2).

The story of the widow Danelis is useful in illustrating what Byzantines viewed as the fruits or symbols of wealth. Land of course was ultimately the basis of most fortunes in the pre-industrial world. While the land was never commodified in the capitalistic sense in the Byzantine period, it should be understood as the foundation of nearly all riches. It was the basis of the economy and generated directly 70–80 per cent of the emperor's tax revenue (Hendy 1985: 158). Turning to Danelis' portable goods, we find luxury cloths, slaves, and ornate vessels among her valuables. Interestingly, this list differs not at all from past signifiers of ostentation.

Archaeologically, traces of some of these goods are easier to find than others. Luxury cloth, especially brocades and other finely worked pieces in wool, linen, and silk rarely survive in the archaeological record. The empire overcame the loss of the famous textile-producing regions of the empire first to the Persians and then the Arabs in the seventh century. Falling to foreign invasion were the rich coastal cities of the Levant from Cilicia to Palestine with their uniquely skilled workers and developed networks of exchange. The centre of gravity of Byzantine silk production shifted to Constantinople sometime in the seventh or eighth century. This can be partly inferred from the continued export of Byzantine silks to the west during the Dark Ages. Caution is of course advised in relying on style in attributing precise provenance to objects, and it is doubtful that silk production in the Levant faded under Islam: certainly trade connections with the east continued beyond the seventh century. More interesting for Byzantinists and having considerable implications for Dark Age trade is the sixth- to seventh-century 'Elephant' silk fragment from the tomb of Charlemagne. This piece is adorned with an elephant and 'candelabra tree' whose Greek inscription in the border has led scholars to argue for its Constantinopolitan origin (Thomas 2012: 130). Whatever the precise date of the preponderance of Constantinople in silk weaving, its role was long established by the time the *Book of the Eparch* (Koder 1991) was compiled in the early tenth century. By the eighth century, silks were being exported to Italy, apparently in substantial quantity and Byzantine silks were also shipped to the Muslim East and elsewhere (Jacoby 2004). Indeed, McCormick (2001: 722) has argued based on data compiled by Muthesius (1997: 163–203) that the number of silks imported to the west increased from the seventh to eighth centuries and only decreased slightly thereafter. In addition to the rare examples from the empire noted above (Chapter 2), we can add eighth- to ninth-century silk wrappings of the relics of St. Victor, other silks of eighth- or ninth-century date recovered in the nineteenth century at the shrine of St. Servatius, Maastricht (Netherlands), and the charioteer design silk from the shrine of the emperor Charlemagne. A small silk purse from Viking Age York may well be of Byzantine origin and have originally contained relics (Muthesius 1989). These silks clearly represent a tiny portion of the original quantity of the imports. Linen and wool stuffs are much more difficult to find in the record, being commonly produced in the west and thus less rare and luxurious than silk and more prone to loss.

Among the least visible emblems of wealth is slaves. Slavery was commonplace in the seventh to ninth centuries and beyond in the Byzantine and Mediterranean worlds. In addition to the Danelis notice, there are ample attestations to slaves, though many of these from Greece and surrounding regions belong to the tenth century (Curta 2011: 245). Their commerce is known primarily from texts; to my knowledge no clear archaeological evidence of the slave trade in Byzantium survives. During the seventh to ninth centuries, there was a slave market in Constantinople and due to the capital's location between the rest of Europe and the wealthy caliphate, the superpower of the day, Byzantium was well-positioned to benefit from the slave trade. Michael McCormick has provided a detailed overview of this trade in which Byzantium does not feature prominently (McCormick 2001, 2002). While Rotman (2009) does not believe that the principal slave routes of the Dark Ages passed through Constantinople, he notes that the Byzantines took a special interest in levying a tax on slaves and other goods that passed through their realm and attempted to maintain a tight control on the routes via which people were trafficked to the caliphate.

Despite there being few medieval texts that detail them, scholars view the so-called *Radhaniyya* Jewish merchants of the tenth century as playing a pivotal role in the movement of human chattel from Europe to the caliphate. A letter from Pope Adrian I of 776 mentions competition between the Byzantines and Arabs for slaves sold in Italy. In this they were joined by the ever-grasping Venetians, who traded slaves from Central and Eastern Europe. Those trafficked by the Venetians were often Christian despite Carolingian and Byzantine prohibitions upon the practice. There are numerous dimensions to the slave trade that cannot unfortunately be discussed here, and at present the debate of the nature of this early medieval trade in Byzantium and the Near East is malformed and the material evidence scant.

One interesting facet of the debate is the role of the Byzantine state in the sale of slaves, especially in relation to the Slavs. According to the chronicler Theophanes (Mango and Scott 1997: 507–11) writing in about 842, in 688–689 the emperor Justinian II campaigned against the Bulgars and Slavs, taking many captive and settling some of these in Bithynia. A proportion of these Slavs were later formed into an army, which Justinian sent against the Muslim caliphate but they deserted en masse in 692 at the Battle of Sebastopolis. According to Theophanes, the families of these deserters were either killed or uprooted. A group of lead seals used to certify official correspondence and goods has been linked by Oikonomides (1986: appendix 2) to the handling by the Byzantine state of Slav families of the deserters punished by Justinian. These dated lead seals are nearly all from 694–695, and are linked to one another (with one exception) by their mention of an official named George, the *kommerkiarios*. The *kommerkiarios* was an official whose precise functions are in dispute but whose responsibilities apparently derived from those assigned late Roman customs officers. The *kommerkiarios* thus may have been a tax or customs agent (Kazhdan and Oikonomides 1991). Some of the seals mention 'slaves' (*andrapoda*). Oikonomides connects this fragmentary evidence to argue that the seals of George represent the punishment of the families of the Slav deserters at Sebastopolis by their being sold as slaves (*andrapoda*) by the thousands under the supervision and organization of the imperial authorities represented by the *kommerkiarios* George. Thus he raises the intriguing but controversial possibility that the *kommerkiarioi* and thus the Byzantine state were at least some of the time actively engaged in the slave trade and not merely taxing it. This interpretation of the evidence is disputed, with a range of alternative possibilities being invoked (Brandes 2002: 351–65). Whatever the specifics of the Slav episode, the Byzantines were aggressive in drawing revenues from the traffic in thralls across their horizons. In 809, the emperor Nikephoros I restored a previously revoked tax on slaves and added to it a special levy on slaves whose sellers attempted to bypass the empire to avoid tax. This special duty was two *nomismata* each or 10 per cent of the typical value of a slave. The Jewish *Rhadhaniyya* merchants involved in the slave trade seem to have been among those trying to avoid Byzantine territory to escape such onerous customs fees (Rotman 2009).

Turning to the third major category mentioned among the movable wealth of Danelis, sumptuous vessels, there is some material evidence. Imported metal wares from Byzantium survive in considerable numbers in the west, although the bulk of the finds as currently dated belong to the sixth to seventh centuries. At the highest level of elite consumption was the traffic in precious metal objects, especially silver, in which Byzantium attained an extremely high level of technical and artistic sophistication during late antiquity (Mango 1976). One of the best examples of the circulation of Byzantine forms and the allure of imperial exports or tribute among neighbouring peoples are Avar hoards usually dated to the eighth century. Among these is the sumptuous hoard of silver and gold objects from Albania of the 'Avar Treasure' (also called the 'Albanian' or 'Vrap' Treasure: Bálint 2000; Garam 2000), which includes several stunning pieces (although some consider such works crude and ugly: Holcomb 2008). Among the Vrap Treasure are several unfinished items and pieces showing various states of wear, some from Byzantine workshops, whereas others reflect Avar forms and workmanship. The collection of the hoard must postdate 700 to which the last objects are dated. Similarly, the so-called 'Avar Hoard' auctioned by Sotheby's in 1981 and of unknown provenance with objects manufactured *c*. 700 included works of seventh-century Byzantine silversmiths. Like the silver goblet of the Grand Zhupan Sivin of Bulgaria from Preslav and made around 865, and the silver cup from Gotland, Sweden of similar date, these objects can only represent economic activity broadly rather than trade specifically, as they may have been gifted or plundered or come to their find locations by some other means (Mundell Mango 2009b).

Copper objects of Byzantine manufacture, including cast copper alloys, and hammered pieces in copper and various alloys such as brass and tinned copper continued many of the traditions of late antiquity. Polycandela, such as the probable eighth-century example from Anatolia and a whole range of domestic objects, such as jugs, cauldrons, samovars, flasks, and basins of seventh-century date are known from Sardis and were part of Byzantine vernacular in the Levant under Umayyad rule as well, as evidenced in finds at places like Hippos-Sussita and Jerash. One point worth stressing is the conservative nature of many metal vessel shapes: a flask from the seventh-century Yassi Ada shipwreck finds parallels centuries later in a container used in the eleventh century to hoard coins (Mundell Mango 2009b). These copper utensils, while not available to the poorest strata of society, do not represent the highest level of elite consumption within Byzantium, though they may when found outside of imperial bounds. Cast-drop handled basins, for example, were noted above from Pella and Amorium and, though not as common as late antique examples, these types were distributed fairly widely, with Italy and Sicily being centres of export or even local production. These are the so-called Coptic wares whose survival in the archaeological record is mainly tied to their interment with the bodies of high-status individuals. Scores of such objects are known from cemeteries throughout Western Europe, with notable concentrations along the Upper and Middle Rhine, southern Gaul, Spain, and in southern England. 'Coptic' bowls are present, for example, at the rich burial at Sutton Hoo of *c.* 625, but on present evidence these 'Coptic' bowls do not seem to have circulated much beyond 630, although Richards sees the main range of deposition falling between 600 and 675 (Richards 1980: 128). An interesting feature of the 'Coptic' bowls is their high lead content, which ranges from 15 to 20 per cent, a high figure and especially high when compared with examples of certain Egyptian provenance. This discrepancy cannot alone eliminate (Harris et al. 2006) Egypt as a location of manufacture but it should cause scholars to look elsewhere, namely to Italy and Constantinople, or possibly even Asia Minor, for the workshops that produced these objects. Excavations from Sicily, Amorium, and Pella provide securely dated medieval bronze bowls of this kind, but a thorough re-examination of the earlier material is needed in order to determine if earlier work, much of it belonging to the early twentieth century, is in fact valid in light of new methodologies. As discussed in Chapter 2, disentangling the exact place(s) of manufacture of these bronze wares is at present not possible and the 'Coptic' label remains attached to these bowls. This situation prevails across a range of higher-status items.

Seventh-century bronze buckles, for example, were found in excavations at Classe, a site that also yielded finds of Byzantine-type brooches and buckles imported from Constantinople or perhaps representing regional copies manufactured in Sicily (Christie 2010); metal production is also attested from Classe. Additional materials from Olbia underscore a phenomenon that many scholars stress: the persistence of an elite in the Balkans and Mediterranean who, through personal adornment, displayed a preference for Constantinopolitan fashion and the survival of an imperial cultural *koine* known through a variety of artistic forms and objects. At the same time, kidney-shaped, openwork buckles from Crecchio, a Byzantine fort built over a former Roman villa in Abruzzo near the eastern coast of central Italy, are also assigned to the seventh century; these are of types more commonly associated with Lombard graves, indicating that these buckles were accessible to both citizens of the empire and their Lombard foes. In addition to buckles, weapon burials and inhumations have yielded Byzantine style jewellery on Sardinia (Christie 2010). From Sicily, Corinth-type buckles date to the seventh century while D-shaped buckles with animal motifs (Metaxas 2012) are of seventh- or eighth-century origin. Even if we accept the view that buckles were not traded but produced at regional production sites (Schulze-Dörrlamm 2010), they were based on more local as well as cosmopolitan influences. Among the Dark Age Sicily finds analysed by Metaxas (2012) are finger rings, earrings, locks and keys, *hystera* amulets with a 'Medusa' motif, and weights, all of which bear strong resemblance to examples within the empire. At a minimum, these items are good indicators of vectors of cultural exchange and sustained contacts between Sicily and the rest of the Byzantine world. Some may indicate trade. But for pieces like these, mostly of a banal variety and not the opulent styles of the rich, we await full discovery and discussion of their places of manufacture. Tied to the whereabouts of their manufacture are questions of their circulation and meaning within the societies that used them.

The proof is in the potting: ceramic production and regional patterns of exchange

To date, the preponderance of evidence indicates that specialized ceramic production and trade was not even remotely maintained at sixth-century levels. This is not to say that some forms of this economy did not persist – there is growing evidence that in certain places and at certain times the professional (or at least semi-professional) potter-making ceramics on the wheel survived. In most instances, though, non-specialists made the vessels needed for domestic consumption by hand, sometimes with modest local surpluses and circulation of these goods. Handmade ceramics never left the landscapes of the Roman Empire but they assumed a significantly greater role in life in the seventh to ninth centuries. Unlike late antique mass-scale manufacture of ceramics like ARS, production in the Dark Ages was everywhere and nowhere – each locale continued its own pre-seventh-century coarse ware traditions and fine ware production lingered on in some spots, but there was nothing even remotely to rival the potteries of ARS and Late Roman D beyond the seventh or possibly the eighth century at the latest. But as we noted Chapter 2, a new vernacular in some pottery forms indicates fundamental economic and social change. Changing diet and economic conditions, perhaps influenced by climate and the arrivals of new groups from outside the empire, influenced the ceramic traditions within Byzantium and beyond. Paul Arthur noted the strong correlation between certain archaeologically recovered dietary markers (namely animals used for meat) and broad patterns of cookwares. Within the Balkans, Mediterranean, and the Anatolian heartlands of the empire, the choice of ceramics seems to have been predominantly determined by foodways (Curta 2001; Arthur 2007). Arthur (2007) observed, for example, that the prevalence of the closed cooking form was commonly associated with cooler climes and often with the pork or cattle on which populations there depended for protein, and stews and other brothy mixtures were desirable. Open forms can be linked to an ovicaprine (sheep/goat) diet over much of the southern Mediterranean and Levant whereby water content is reduced through cooking. Although there is little doubt that Arthur did not intend to be rigid in this theory, his work has quickly become a framework for fruitful debate. Joanita Vroom (2008) has added to the discussion by noting that in places like Butrint, both open and closed forms were found in Dark Age contexts. Interestingly, although early medieval contexts from the Triconch Palace excavations at Butrint yielded 96 per cent closed shapes, open pots were also found there. In addition, the faunal remains from the site indicate that, as over much of the southern Balkans, ovicaprids predominated in the diet with pork rarely consumed. At Amorium, ceramics from the ninth-century destruction layers indicate a similar situation. As with all known medieval Byzantine sites on the Anatolian plateau, sheep and goat dominate the faunal record. But, as observed for Butrint, both open and closed cooking pots have been found in excavation (Böhlendorf-Arslan 2012).

Another characteristic of the Amorium assemblages of the 838 destruction of the city is the variety of ceramic forms and fabrics attesting that the city drew its pots from a number of different locales. Residual sixth- to seventh-century pottery in these layers included modest quantities of PRS, ARS, and grey fabric pottery with a red-brown slip as well as Cilician wares known as 'Piecrust Rim Ware', the latter indicating seventh-century contacts with the cities of the Cilician coast. Early medieval Amorium exhibits the pattern of localization observed elsewhere within Byzantium. Ceramic forms there appear to be broadly analogous to other regional forms in the empire. One example of this is the production of globular cooking pots with steep sides and slightly flared rims, while at the same time exhibiting considerable local variations in form and, of course, in their fabric. Böhlendorf-Arslan (2012) notes the presence of locally produced coarse ware ceramics of various types, as well as locally produced fine wares, including 'Amorium Glazed Ware' (AGW) imitating CGW I pottery. AGW was made in red rather than the white clay of CGW I but Amorium potters imitated metropolitan forms. In addition, after the sixth century Late Roman ceramic traditions continued in grey wares, which the people of Amorium altered in terms of fabric, form, and surface treatment. A reminder of our present lack of understanding is the peculiar 'jug' with openings at both top and bottom. The use for such a vessel continues to elude us, although inventive solutions such as a samovar, as an aid to yogurt making or for Greek fire can be safely ruled out (Böhlendorf-Arslan et al. 2007). This regionalism or, perhaps better put, localism, has been noted above and is repeated on excavated sites. Good evidence from long-term projects on sites that remained lively in the Dark Ages, such as Gortyn and Amorium, are beginning to reshape perceptions of the manufacture and circulation of pottery. It is nonetheless important to stress that although there is good evidence from a site like Amorium, there is not a vast difference in the variety of vessels available, or in their functionality, from late antiquity to the Dark Ages. Lamps are a notable exception; at Amorium their diminished presence indicates that candles often replaced them. Amorium does possess a few examples of imported pottery, including Günsenin Type 1 amphora of the ninth or tenth century (Böhlendorf-Arslan 2012: 155).

During surveys and excavations, the encounter of archaeologists with red slipped fine wares such as ARS, PRS, and Late Roman D (CRS), sometimes in quantities that appear to carpet the landscape, continue to conjure images of prosperity, buoyant trade, and stalls filled with cheap but eye-pleasing goods. A sizeable part of the image of economic prosperity assigned to late antiquity in the eastern Mediterranean is derived from large-scale trade and specialization the trafficking of bulk goods entailed. Understandably, scholars are equally troubled by the apparent absence of ARS and its relatives beginning in the seventh century (McCormick 2001). Thus the discovery of seven kilns along the borders of the former regions of Pisidia and Pamphylia producing Late Roman D wares reinforces the fact that regionalization of production was well underway in late antiquity and challenges the view of Hayes (2008) that these types were in fact made on Cyprus. Similarly, the relatively recent discovery of Sagalassos Red Slip Ware, which nonetheless faded out of production in the sixth century (Poblome 1999), forces us to look for more dispersed manufacture and a larger number of sites than previous models might indicate. Certainly, pottery consumption at Aphrodisias had become more localized even prior to the sixth century (Hudson 2008). Likewise, the survival of red slipped fine ware production in southern Asia Minor casts doubt on whether we have missed similar data from elsewhere. In addition, if Late Roman D does not belong to Cyprus, at least in its later iterations, then presumed contacts between the island and other regions based on these ceramic types need to be reassessed.

Moreover, alongside a great deal of change, such as the absence of fine wares or imports outside of towns, one can find continuity in some areas of the economy. As with jewellery and other crafts, there was interplay of pottery forms within the empire. Evidence for continued pottery production is increasingly evident in several regions. From Sicily there is proof of local production and wide distribution throughout the island of a group of well-made grey wares whose scratched decoration does not have ready Roman parallels (Arcifa 2010). Throughout Byzantine Italy, local manufacture of cooking wares and amphorae (Arthur 1993) certainly persisted, although not without alterations in their volume as well as changes in style and distribution. On the whole, the current material record supports the view that, apart from population nodes like Constantinople and the small but still active cities of Rome and Naples, we might do better to speak of 'potter-farmers' rather than specialized professional artisans and, along with this, a general 'ruralization' of ceramic methods (Vroom 2008).

One anchor point in the continuity versus cessation debate within pottery studies is the fate of specialized amphorae production. Amphorae, largely standardized and mass-produced transport vessels for liquid and dry bulk goods, are one of our best sources of data for reconstructing the medieval economy. Like red slipped fine wares, several distinct transport vessels of late antiquity are highly visible in the archaeological record. Following Riley's (1979) characterization of the most common of these as a 'package' of wares, archaeologists have produced a great deal of evidence that has generally reinforced the notion of the dominant place of a handful of eastern Late Roman Amphorae (LR types 1–6) in Mediterranean exchange of the fifth to sixth centuries (Reynolds 1995, 2010b). Like ARS and other tablewares, LR 1, LR 2, and LR 5/6 have been taken to support the view of exchange of considerable scope and scale, with cargoes passing from the Levant to as far afield as the southern coast of Britain and the Black and Red Seas (Golofast 2003: Tomber 2000, 2008). In the seventh century, there were notable variations in the vessels themselves and their distribution.

Unlike fine wares, it has long been understood that the various LR amphorae types belong not to one specific city or hinterland, but to disparate regional manufacturers. As new data emerge, such as stamped examples from Kos (Diamanti 2010), this view is reinforced. Among the major makers of many of the LR 1 types, however, were potters in Egypt, Syria-Palestine, Cyprus, and southeast Asia Minor. LR 2, a globular transport jar of Aegean manufacture, was prominent in the provision of troops on the Danube and widely distributed outside the bounds of the empire as well. Whether these wares represent 'trade' in the sense of exchange based on market forces of one kind or another, state-organized supply (or exchange), or some combination thereof, remains an open question. A sheer drop after 550 in the number of findspots and relative quantities within sites seems to indicate marked deceleration of trade. Late versions of LR 1 from Kos were stamped before firing; these were imperial control stamps like those applied to silver or other goods and offer an interesting glimpse of the intervention of the imperial authorities in production. In dispute, however, is the precise dating of the production of these LR 1 types from excavations at Halasarna (modern Kardamaina) on Kos. Most of the amphorae output of the kiln was a local variant of LR 1 but there was also substantial evidence for manufacture of Byzantine Globular Amphorae, a version comparable to LR 13 (Riley 1979: 231–32) (Figs. 15 and 16) and LR 2. Are these amphorae sixth- to early seventh-century as argued (specifically for the LR 1 stamped types) by the excavator Diamanti (2010), or do they belong to the seventh to eighth centuries as argued by ceramicists Poulou-Papadimitriou and Didioumi (2010)? Of course, the precise dating matters, since the later chronology would put this sort of production of an item intended for seaborne export in the midst of the putative Dark Age recession of exchange. Poulou-Papadimitriou and Didioumi assign a late date, for example, to an unguentarium type produced in the sixth or seventh century. But there are several other comparable sites and vessels on which a comparative chronological framework could be constructed for the Kos finds. Indeed, the LR 1 amphora derivatives fired in the Kos kiln belong to a broad category of such jars manufactured widely from Egypt to North

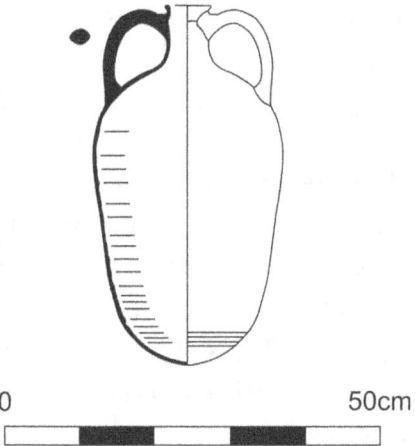

Fig. 15 Complete LR 13 type amphora (Archaeological Data Service).

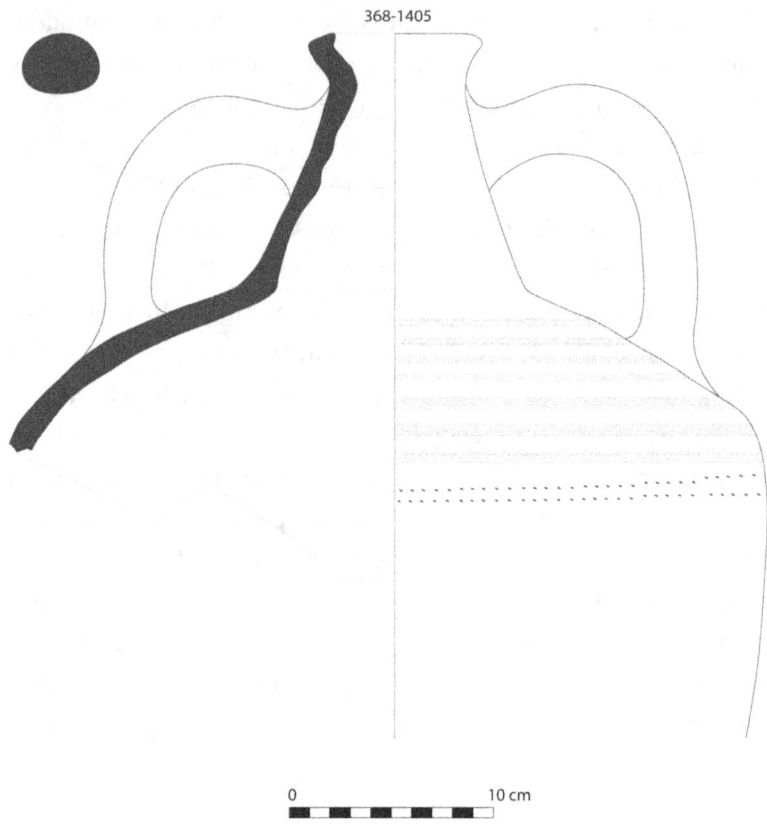

Fig. 16 LR 13 type amphora from Kos (courtesy of Charikleia Diamanti).

Africa in the sixth through early eighth centuries. Elsewhere in the Dodecanese, on the island of Leipsoi a workshop dated to the eighth century produced LR 1 type amphorae (Papavasileiou et al. 2014) and a kiln on the island of Karpathos is assigned a probable ninth-century date (Didioumi 2014). In turn, various forms of Byzantine Globular Amphorae are known from Knossos on Crete and elsewhere in the Aegean, from Egypt at Kellia, North Syria, Cyprus, North Africa, Naples, Rome, and Otranto (Poulos-Papadimitriou and Didioumi 2010). This list is by no means exhaustive and the study of many of these wares is in its early stages. Nonetheless, if the dating of these types is correct, the horizons of Dark Age trade extend beyond their oft-assumed boundaries and frequencies.

On this and other material evidence, much of it surveyed in this volume, one can paint in broad strokes a picture of more compact, regional exchange patterns (Wickham 2005: 169; Pieri 2012). Examples of containers derived from the late Roman repertoire of forms are especially prominent on Crete and in the Aegean and Italy. On the islands and in places like Otranto and settlements in southern Italy, Mediterranean amphorae traditions continued to evolve, as did their range of production, exchange, and the types of wares that were transported in them.

Scholars now recognize numerous major amphora types and subtypes and can trace to some extent the evolution of these vessels (Pieri 2012). Excavated amphorae and kilns of the seventh through ninth century have allowed archaeologists to argue for continuity of specialized production and trade but these discoveries also raise other questions of chronology and scale. Over what timeframe were these vessels made, what did they carry, how far, and why? These are but a few of the issues that remain unresolved.

Some later evidence helps flesh out the picture of regional and long-distance contacts. Finds of Günsenin type 1 amphorae (Fig. 17), some of which were apparently made in the Marmara region by the tenth century, although early prototypes may be from Aegina (see below). Günsenin type 1 seems to have been mainly a wine vessel but, like other jars, it carried a range of goods and would have been reused frequently. Without attempting to be exhaustive, amphorae of this kind have been found at Amorium (Böhlendorf-Arslan 2012), Izmir (Smyrna), Çanakkale, the Marmara shipwreck at Erdek-Marmara, the Mangana Palace area excavation in Istanbul (Constantinople), Sinope, Samsun (Amisos), Svichtov in Bulgaria, Dinogetia in Romania, and as far as Sarkel in South Russia (Günsenin 1989) and Kerch in the southeastern Crimea (Sazanov 1996). Some of these contexts have

Fig. 17 Günsenin type 1 amphora (courtesy of Nergis Günsenin).

ninth-century dates attached to them but Professor Günsenin dates type 1 now to the tenth century (Günsenin, personal communication, 2015). Recently, late analogues to imitations of LR 2, LR 13, and Günsenin type 1 amphorae have been excavated at Kolonna (ancient Aegina); these vessels were probably local products and date from sometime within the seventh through ninth centuries. The Aegina finds are exciting, adding as they do to the growing material of interest for scholars of the early medieval Byzantine economy, while reminding us that we remain in the very early days of our exploration of Dark Age material culture in the eastern Mediterranean.

Saints and seafarers: Dark Age trade

Owing to the faster travel time and the general safety and comfort of sea travel compared with overland transit, the ship was always the preferred means of travel in the pre-industrial Mediterranean, Adriatic, Aegean, and Black Sea. Although little research has been done on the state of the land routes throughout the empire in the seventh to ninth centuries, dwindling political influence and a kind of no-man's land in the northern Balkans complicated overland journeys. The main east–west trunk road across the Balkans, the Via Egnatia, connected the capital to the city of Dyrrachium (modern Durrës in Albania) but it is likely that at some points during the Dark Ages important branches of this route would have been difficult to traverse, such as the leg that connected the Via Egnatia with Thessaloniki (McCormick 2001: 69–73).

In general, sea travel prevailed. When around 830–831 Gregory the Decapolite travelled from his home town of Eirenopolis (near modern Kazancı) to Rome, he did so by way of Ephesus and Proconnesus (modern-day Marmara). He changed his mind about seeking martyrdom under the Iconoclast emperor Theophilus (829–842) and instead travelled to Ainos in Thrace (today Enez), then to Thessaloniki. He arrived in Reggio in Calabria after quelling the fear of Arab pirates among the sailors whom he persuaded to ferry him from Corinth (McCormick 2002).

Some of these movements can be traced through those vessels that were less fortunate and wound up on the seafloor. Since the pioneering work of Parker (1992), knowledge of shipwrecks has increased substantially. In the ten years that followed, a sizeable increase in published information was made available: McCormick (2012) noted a 27 per cent increase in the number of known Mediterranean shipwrecks (Kingsley forthcoming a) (Map 3). Of the sunken vessels belonging to our period, one of the most famous and well studied is the Yassi Ada wreck, which sank off the coast of Bodrum in southwest Turkey (Bass and Van Doorninck 1982). This wreck was excavated in the 1960s by Frederick van Doorninck and J.R. Steffy and is of interest on many fronts, not least because she went down around the year 625

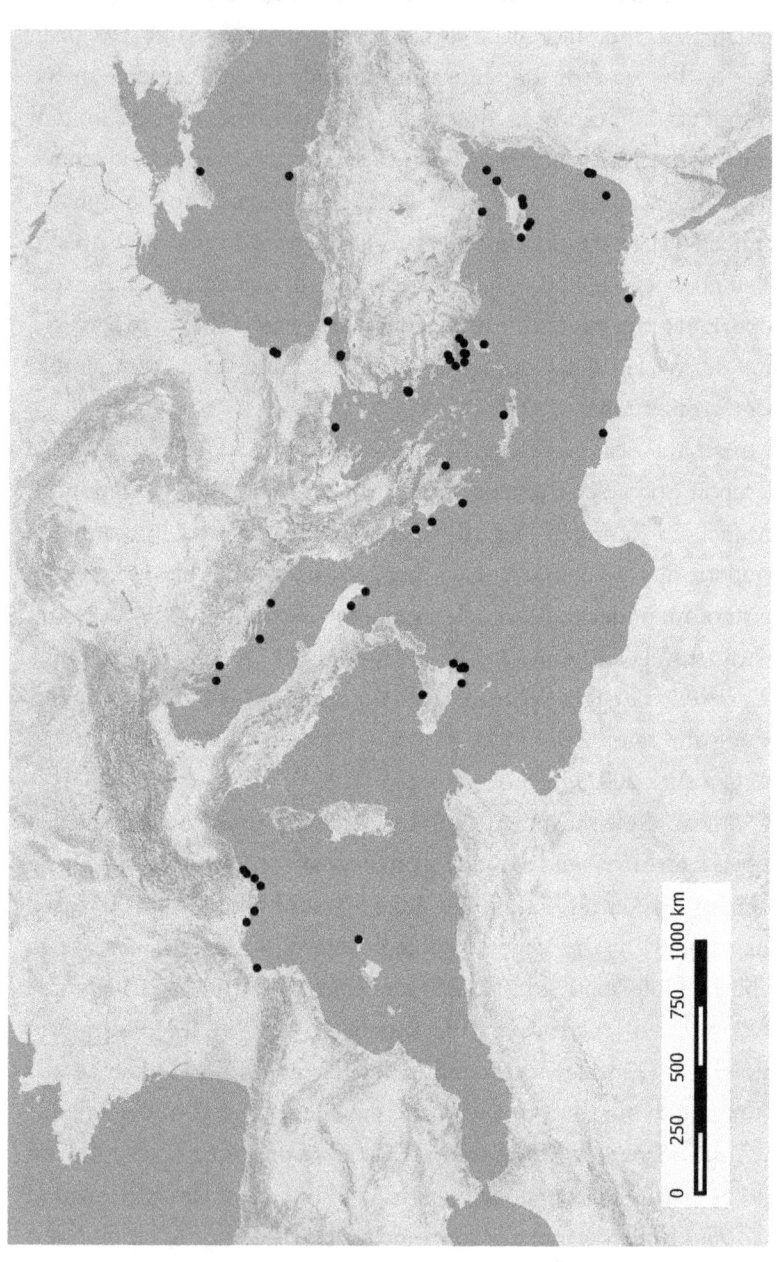

Map 3 Shipwrecks of the medieval period (Michael J. Decker).

in the midst of the Byzantine–Persian Wars. Yassi Ada was a medium-sized vessel of 60 tons burden; she was 70 tons when fully loaded (Hocker and Ward 2004) and her cargo was relatively well preserved. The ship carried 822 amphorae, 710 of LR 2 type and 103 of LR 1 type. LR 2 often carried oil and LR 1 often contained wine; since each type and its variants were made across considerable swaths of the empire, not all contents can be known for certain. The recovery of grape pips indicates wine filled at least a portion of the LR 1 jars.

By the time McCormick tallied his data, the number of Mediterranean wrecks had again increased. In 2004, the discovery of the Theodosian Harbour of Constantinople at Yenikapı in Istanbul and the excavations that followed have increased exponentially the data on early Byzantine shipping, seafaring technologies, harbours, and the natural environment of the city and port from late antiquity through the Middle Byzantine era (Kingsley forthcoming a, forthcoming b). Over the centuries, storms and silting of the small Lycus River that ran through the city slowly filled in the harbour and activity gradually shifted to the eastern end after the eleventh century by which time the port had ceased to serve all but small local vessels. Thirty-seven shipwrecks dating from the fifth through the eleventh centuries have been excavated at Yenikapı, the largest concentration of wrecks from this period ever discovered. The Yenikapı ships allow unprecedented views of ship construction, maritime technology, organic materials in maritime contexts, moorings, and environmental data, as well as shipboard assemblages of small finds, ceramics, seeds, and fauna. The publication of these data is far from complete and only four of the thirty-seven wrecks contained their cargo. Despite this and the nature of the excavation – a salvage project intended only to record and safeguard some material in the midst of a subway expansion – work at Yenikapı has added to our knowledge of Dark Age shipping in Byzantium as well as the environmental and social space of the empire.

Among some of the interesting finds from Yenikapı are the medium merchantmen YK 3 yielding a C14 date of AD 668–987, and six other examples of ships of similar make. YK 3 contained bricks with stamps of fifth- to sixth-century date, perhaps earlier ballast or re-used cargo, or an indication that the C14 dating is incorrect. Marble fragments recovered from inside YK 3 help to reconstruct its possible route to Marmara Island, site of the famous quarries supplying Proconnesian marble (Kocabaş 2015). A more precise dating of this vessel may shed light on the marble trade in the empire. The construction of YK 12, dated by C14 to AD 690–876, makes it one of the more intriguing vessels from the Dark Age period discovered at Yenikapı. The vessel was wide bowed, about 9.6 m long and 2.6 m wide. YK 12 was solidly constructed with a keel of hornbeam (*Carpinus* L.), chestnut (*Castanea* L.) planking, oak (*Quercus* L.) floor timbers (Akkemik and Kocabaş 2014), and ash-wood (*Fraxinus* L.) futtocks (curved sections joined together to form the lower portion of the ribs) (Özsait-Kocabaş and Kocabaş 2008). Ultimately, these hardwood timbers probably came from nearby woodlands, the Belgrade Forest to the north of the city being a prime candidate (Akkemik 2008). Personal effects likely belonging to the captain were preserved and include a cooking stove, pot, and fragments of a wine glass. The bulk of the cargo of YK 12 comprised Günsenin type 1 amphorae dated to the ninth century; these vessels were from Crimea (Kocabaş 2015) or possibly were wine jars made on the Marmara island of Ganos (Özsait-Kocabaş and Kocabaş 2008). If its point of origin is correct, the Black Sea, YK 12 represents further proof that the Black Sea, an area of intensive contacts and exchange in late antiquity, maintained a prominent role in the trade of Dark Age Byzantium.

Changes in the types of wood preferred for shipbuilding is suggested by a general transition from construction in conifer components (mainly pine) used in fifth- to sixth-century ships. By the ninth to eleventh centuries, hardwoods from broadleaf trees typically made up large portions of Byzantine vessels. The use of hardwood planking, including chestnut and white oak, in the seventh- to ninth-century merchant ships sampled indicates that these changes evolved throughout the Dark Ages. YK 12 was built of especially durable woods, with chestnut planking and ash-wood futtocks. Different timbers represented by the increased prominence of hardwoods may indicate a change in forest resources or a preference for more durable materials (Akkemik and Kocabaş 2014). These alterations in shipbuilding may also imply a transformation in the ways Byzantine peoples exploited their woods, or the kinds of species available in the reduced territories of Asia Minor and the Balkans.

The ships noted above are not the only Dark Age vessels excavated at Yenikapı or throughout the Mediterranean. As research advances, some of the darkness will lift. Whether such finds will drastically alter the present picture of a decline in shipping following the sixth century remains an open question.

The evidence reviewed here offers up a perspective that modifies somewhat the Pirenniste vista of Dark Age trade. As has long been known, trade clearly continued. What is new in this debate is the relatively recent discovery of centres of production and trade indicating the movement of bulk goods around the eastern Mediterranean and Black Sea from more locations and seemingly with more intensity than previously thought. Scholars have yet to digest this evidence and work it into the narrative of early medieval Europe. If the debate about exchange among historians and archaeologists presently lacks a certain verve, the academic separation of specialized fields is partly to blame. Historians and archaeologists talk to one another only infrequently and too rarely collaborate on large issues like the Dark Age economy. As the late Roman era has finally emerged from the dustbin where it was once relegated based on scholarly constructions of 'barbarism' and backwardness, so too scholars will increasingly turn their focus to the world after late antiquity. But what will they find? Even those like Michael McCormick (2001) and Chris Wickham (2005) note that Mediterranean communications and trade, though persisting, hit bottom sometime between 650 and 780.

Researchers have not been blind to long-distance exchange and specialized production, and the past thirty years have brought to light material that will support more intensive links than previously presumed. We should be attuned to the presence of the rare, though noteworthy objects, such as amethyst in the necklaces most likely worn by the cream of European elites, because they tell us something about connectivity and the far horizons of European exchange in ways that we miss entirely if we focus on pottery and other markers of a trade in commodities. Amethyst beads and fine jewellery alert us not only to this otherwise hidden web of connections but also to the existence of greater specialization and overall economic activity throughout the three centuries under review. It is certain that the eighth and ninth centuries are much less well represented than the seventh and this problem should not be underplayed. Our ability to identify and date artefacts certainly plays a part in this and there is little doubt that the sundry fields involved in studying material culture will witness substantial revision in the coming decades. It is uncertain, however, whether new discoveries and recalibrated dating standards will drastically alter the picture of the recession in trade that can be pushed back as far as the late seventh century but not much later. Nonetheless, new discoveries and interpretations of the past three decades have indicated a greater volume in trade than has been hitherto generally acknowledged. To state that all regions and all times were equal in their economic activity and connectedness is of course false and this is not the intention here. Rather, my intention is to reveal, via selected examples, the possibility of greater diversity than is usually associated with the 'Dark Ages'.

6

New Directions

The story of Dark Age Byzantium is an exciting one and remains in many ways unwritten. Here I wish to highlight salient points that have emerged, I hope, in the course of preceding chapters. I raise these not for the purpose of bringing closure to the discussion on any particular point but to note potential paths of exploration; indeed this series aims to explain, frame, and foster debates rather than resolve them. Throughout this work I have attempted to demonstrate aspects of the major types of material evidence and debates around them, some fully formed, others nascent within scholarly discourse. By design, I have privileged here the discussion of archaeological data. This is in part because of the dearth of textual evidence, but also because the weaving of text into the framework I established at the start would otherwise be awkward and not of the depth that would satisfy historians, archaeologists or others working in Byzantine Studies. Although I think it has become plain to the reader, it is worth noting that the 'Dark Ages' represents in Byzantium an increasingly problematic term. It is profitable, though, to draw attention to the lack of documentary evidence and juxtapose this with the growing body of archaeological material of seventh- to ninth-century date. For students of the medieval west, the term Dark Ages is applied more rarely than ever before.

Even the use of Dark Ages in popular culture has waned: a quick search of Google trends or Google NGram viewer will show that the use of the phrase Dark Ages peaked in the early years of the Second World War. Interestingly, among news and other materials of recent date, the 1980s represented a low point for the concept, at least in the media and popular culture, with some revival of interest since 2000. But the term seems nowhere near as pervasive compared with the early twentieth century. The point of emphasis in all of this is to note that the Dark Ages is a term that is both powerful and problematic and which both attracts and repels. Historians and archaeologists, however, are themselves shaped by various discourses, some more, some less engaged with the sources of this trend. For scholars interested in Byzantium, as I stressed at the outset, the utility of the label is in its descriptive power to convey the lack of textual sources and the present lack of knowledge, and in doing so provoke scholars to action to seek alternative ways of engaging these centuries, which are virtually absent from the narrative of Europe, the Middle East, and North Africa. This is unfortunate. One cannot help but think of the common view of the later centuries of the Roman Empire prior to the birth of 'late antiquity' as a scholarly sub-discipline, and before an interest in engaging with the people of these eras more on their own terms than previously possible.

It is critical to stress the important place of the Dark Ages within the history and material culture of the Byzantine Empire, a millennial civilization whose study is almost absent from the teaching and study of history around the world. The centuries of the Dark Ages are the 'in-between spaces' of history, grey shaded regions of our understanding. Though coloured differently from scholarship of the late antique era before it, as well as the 'Macedonian Renaissance' that followed, the early middle ages are no less vital. In these fraught centuries, after all, we strain to see through the cloudy lens of meagre sources the tides of momentous change. After all, depending on individual perspective, the seventh to ninth centuries brought either tragedy or triumph. These were the years of Rome's agony in the East, the end of Hellenistic civilization and its subsumption by Christianity. For Gibbon and Enlightenment humanists, the Dark Ages are dark indeed. But this perspective is blind to the civilization that we can see and appreciate after the light of the sources return in the ninth century. Medieval Byzantium of the tenth to twelfth centuries is certainly not honey on the tongue of humanists with its autocratic government, trappings of Christianity, and mandarins of state, which have been more the objects of caricature rather than serious, reasoned study. But, lest we forget, the branches of all that was 'new' in this strange hybridity of East and West, of Rome and Greece, of ancient and medieval, were not really new at all. Most were pruned from the trees of their ancient traditions in the winter of the Dark Ages; we only see the flowers in the Macedonian spring.

Of course, compared to late antiquity, the study of the seventh to ninth centuries has a long way to go. In terms of textual discovery and analysis, historians have yet to make available many early medieval hagiographic texts, there is no full epigraphic, nor a comprehensive prosopography (the study of names) corpus. Alongside this, sigillography (the study of seals) for the period is missing. These specialist disciplines bridge the chasm between text and object and as such they demand the attention of specialists in both, preferably simultaneously. Indeed, if we consider this carefully, many disciplines should challenge themselves to undermine these neat binaries (e.g. text/non-text; object/non-object) and think about ways of approaching material culture without discarding quite useful traditional categories.

An online, international collaborative database and other digital humanities projects seem the way to go. Projects like the Prosopography of the Byzantine World (http://blog.pbw.cch.kcl.ac.uk/) and others like it demonstrate what is possible with such work. Although it lay outside the boundaries of the empire by the mid seventh century, Egypt also has the potential to inform us a great deal about Mediterranean agriculture and trade. Egypt of the seventh, eighth, and ninth centuries has yet to be fully integrated into the early medieval narratives of lands beyond the Dar al-Islam, but it certainly has a place there. The later Greek, Coptic, and Arabic papyrus documents from Egypt are a wealth of untapped knowledge that would no doubt richly repay our efforts.

Beyond the 'textual evidence' noted above, art historians, archaeologists, and other academics have much work to do in terms of theoretical and methodological approaches. Periodization, as noted in the Introduction, presents serious problems and this is unlikely to be resolved anytime soon. The solution favoured by many archaeologists of assigning 'Byzantine' to the period 500–1000 over Greece and Asia Minor has something to commend it but also happens to disregard the nearly five centuries in many regions where Byzantine political control or at least cultural norms continued. Should historical questions of this kind even enter the discussion? By its very nature, the half millennium periodization noted above serves to mask the issue of 'breaks', 'decline', 'transition' or 'transformation' by its transgression of the notional boundary between late antiquity and the medieval world as conceived by historians. By their very structure, such conceptions eliminate the Dark Ages as a distinct era within Byzantine archaeology and history. Whether such efforts are useful or not will likely be negotiated through subtle shifts in perception and scholarly presentation, rather than in fora of open, conscious debate.

All the material evidence noted above requires serious effort. Amphorae and imported regional ceramics have begun to receive some treatment. Most pressing, as is the case for nearly all periods and places, is work that will increase our understanding of locally produced wares. As with other areas where 'big data' are involved, it seems that an online collaborative database project would be the most productive way forward so that the impossible task of assessing such a massive array of materials does not fall on one individual or even one team of scholars. The plain wares, and indeed utilitarian objects generally, also deserve much closer and more widespread study. It seems to me that in the case of the workaday objects usually lumped under 'small finds' on site reports, there are many lifetimes of work to be done on classifying and comprehending the nature of their manufacture and use. Some of these items, though not many, circulated beyond the local level and these could hold keys to expanding considerably our knowledge of trade and networks. Coins as markers of trade and sources of raw material have been subjected to precious little analysis. The tools to begin a preliminary exploration of this are now relatively inexpensive and accessible to archaeologists. Fairly recent technologies or applications within archaeology include 3D scanning, terrain modelling, luminescence dating, and isotope analysis. The use of unmanned aerial vehicles (UAVs or drones) and their pairing with terrain and architectural modelling software means that mapping and remote sensing of sites can be done with a precision previously unattainable by the average scholar. DNA analysis, which is currently expensive and infrequently employed, offers considerable promise in identifying populations – especially microbial ones – and understanding their movements. Although this list is far from comprehensive, it suffices to demonstrate that the potential of the archaeological sciences to contribute to the study of materials and to specific, more general research questions is vast.

Crucial, too, is further understanding of the role of urbanism within complex societies. For classical scholars, and many students of late antiquity as well, the expression of civic life exemplified by Hellenism could not exist without the *polis*. Already in the fifth century BC, Sophocles had grasped the tensions of private versus civic life and the contrasts of the domestic space (*oikos*) with its feminine presence if not preeminence, with the public sphere of the polis, where male elites dominated the public spaces of the classical city (Segal 1981). The agora, stoas, and gymnasia of the Greek and Roman city were competitive spaces for masculine elites and the culture that they represented; this had foundered under the hammer blows of Christianity and the imperial court. The former rejected the trappings of human vanity while the latter sought to gather all of them into its possession and thereby enhance their own prestige and power. With the passing of the hundreds of urban centres from the landscape of the East, the principal physical embodiment of classical Hellenism ceased to exist. Without cities, the world of the Dark Ages looked markedly different. It is doubtful that even excavation of major classical city sites that specifically sought to explore these questions would drastically alter the present picture: by the end of the seventh century the articulation of space in its Hellenized form of the Roman Empire was dead. We may argue about degrees of survival, the pace of change, the lingering of certain features of certain sites, but the renovation was total. There can be no underestimating the consequences that led to this situation or those that resulted from it. Medieval urbanism over much of the Mediterranean and Middle East was, like its Iron Age and Bronze Age predecessors, a much more organic and pragmatic expression of space, more compressed, and with quite different emphases on the way space was used, organized, and managed to articulate power.

Elites, of course, remained. There is plenty of evidence of their continued presence and domination of politics and life in Constantinople. They make their appearance in the countryside and in the provincial towns, often in the guise of saints or among the families of saints. They appear, as if by accident, in stories like those of Danelis. They are, however, sometimes absent, as in the so-called *Farmer's Law* (*Nomos Georgikos*) of the eighth century. The absence of elites in the text has led scholars, especially in the Soviet Union, to consider it as evidence of their absence. This seems, however, somewhat unlikely. Even if it were the case that the peasants mentioned in the text were independent, such a situation was undoubtedly short-lived. With the first or second bad harvest, the initial major disparity in the wealth of a peasant community was likely to be the last, with the powerful asserting themselves over the poor. Such is the narrative of Byzantium in the Middle Byzantine period. In fact, one can speculate that events of the Dark Ages and the retreat of Constantinople from many of its provinces does seem to have disrupted traditional systems of power and patronage and thrown the peasants and petty artisans back into relationships that were kith- and kin-dominated. Future discussion among scholars will settle the question of whether we are witnessing landscapes, which, for some reason, became depopulated by the end of the seventh century or whether we simply have not looked for Dark Age inhabitants in the right ways. In order to address these questions, the methodological obstacles currently hindering general agreement about survey praxis will have to be examined and resolved. Without a clear understanding of the way local ceramics were produced (or not) and used (or not), efforts in other areas will be largely negated by our inability to control chronology and numerous other factors, such as 'clutter' in the landscape.

The Dark Age economy is far less dim than it was just a decade ago. Determined investigators have added a great deal of data from European museum collections, site discoveries, shipwrecks, and survey. There is now much more evidence of activity from the islands and Asia Minor especially than there was just ten years ago. Work at places such as Amorium, Cyprus, Crete, and Sicily indicates that regional studies remain paramount to advance knowledge of the economy. The discovery of multiple ships of Dark Age date at Yenikapı – certainly unexpected if not quite unimaginable – points to the possibility of rich new finds over the whole of material culture. While it may not yet be time for a general synthetic overview of achievements to date, such an overview would certainly help clarify the state of the field and the areas that could be most fruitfully pursued in the short term. Whether the current picture of Dark Age trade as being rather restrictive – luxuries and slaves appear to have held a central place rather than bulk goods – awaits further study. With the retreat of the Byzantine state from much of the Mediterranean, it seems that many of the structures that underpinned the bulk trade of the sixth century were corroded and collapsed sometime in the seventh century.

As noted in Chapter 1, the term Dark Ages is both accurate and useful. Its accuracy lies less in its ability to encapsulate living conditions or the state of culture at the time, rather Dark Ages more appropriately labels the state of the evidence through which we attempt to access and formulate knowledge of these conditions. This shift in emphasis from the thing viewed to the viewer has largely overtaken, but not replaced, traditional decline and fall models of the Roman Empire. Part of the utility of the term Dark Ages is the way that it typically galvanizes scholarly opinion. For those who view the Dark Ages as defined by loss, backwardness, and barbarism, the Dark Ages label excites intellectual resistance. For those who see in the successors of Rome fascinating and vibrant societies equal to Rome in their worthiness of our attention, the Dark Ages label is offensive as it is taken to imply cultural inferiority and an unbalanced privileging of classical history and archaeology from which we have suffered too long. Controversy exposes deep suppositions required to engage in honest, healthy debate. Controversy likewise generates interest – I hold this to be true among scholars as much as the general public. Scholars who find the label Dark Ages unacceptable based on assumptions that its use always portrays the early medieval world in a negative way are hopefully encouraged to act, just as scholars of late antiquity acted decades ago, to paint a very different picture of the age which then prevailed. If the lessons from late antique studies offer one insight, it is the prospect of the appearance of a rich vein of scholarship of the Dark Ages in the coming years.

Bibliography

Adams, R.McC. (1965), *Land Behind Baghdad: A history of settlement on the Diyala Plains* (Chicago, IL: University of Chicago Press).

Akkemik, Ü. (2008), 'Identification of timbers from Yenikapı shipwreck', in U. Kocabaş (ed.), *The Old Ships of the 'New Gate'* (Istanbul: Ege Yayınları): 201–12.

Akkemik, Ü. and Kocabaş, U. (2014), 'Woods of Byzantine trade ships of Yenikapı (Istanbul) and changes in wood use from 6th to 11th century', *Mediterranean Archaeology and Archaeometry* 14: 317–27.

Alcock, S. (1993), *Graecia Capta: The landscapes of Roman Greece* (Cambridge: Cambridge University Press).

Allcock, S.L. and Roberts, N. (2014), 'Changes in regional settlement patterns in Cappadocia (central Turkey) since the Neolithic: A combined site survey perspective', *Anatolian Studies* 64: 33–57.

Anderson, W. (2008), 'Settlement change in Byzantine Galatia: An assessment of finds from the General Survey of Central Anatolia', *Anatolian Archaeological Studies: Kaman-Kalehöyük* 17: 233–40.

Andréadès, A.M. (1924), 'De la monnaie et de la puissance d'achat des métaux précieux dans l'Empire byzantine', *Byzantion* 1: 75–115.

Andréadès, A.M. (1948), 'The economic life of the Byzantine empire: Population, agriculture, industry, commerce', in N.H. Baynes and H. Moss (eds), *Byzantium: An introduction to East Roman civilization* (Oxford: Clarendon Press): 51–70.

Antonaras, A.C. (2010), 'Early Christian and Byzantine glass vessels: Forms and uses', in F. Daim and J. Drauschke (eds), *Byzanz – das Römerreich im Mittelalter* (Mainz: Römerreich im Mittelalter): 383–430.

Arcifa, L. (2010), 'Nuove ipotesi a partire dalla rilettura dei dati archeologici: la Sicilia orientale', in A. Nef and V. Prigent (eds), *La Sicile de Byzance à l'Islam* (Paris: De Boccard): 15–49.

Arık, R. (2007), 'Architectural tiles from the Kubad-Abad excavations', in B. Böhlendorf-Arslan, A. Uysal and J. Witte-Orr (eds), *Çanak: Late antique and medieval pottery and tiles in Mediterranean archaeological contexts* (Istanbul: Ege Yayınları): 489–500.

Armstrong, P. (2001), 'From Constantinople to Lakedaimon: Impressed white wares', *British School at Athens Studies* 8: 57–67.

Armstrong, P. (2006), 'Rural settlement in Lycia in the eighth century: New evidence', in K. Dörtlük (ed.), *Proceedings of the IIIrd Symposium on Lycia*, 7–10 November 2005, Antalya (Antalya: Suna & Inan Kiraç Akdeniz Medeniyetleri Arastirma Enstitüsü): 19–29.

Armstrong, P. (2009), 'Trade in the east Mediterranean in the 8th century', in M. Mundell Mango (ed.), *Byzantine Trade, 4th–12th Centuries: The archaeology of local, regional, and international exchange* (Farnham: Ashgate): 157–78.

Armstrong, P. and Günsenin, N. (1995), 'Glazed pottery production at Ganos', *Anatolia Antiqua* 3: 179–201.

Arthur, P. (1993), 'Early medieval amphorae, the Duchy of Naples and the food supply of Rome', *Papers of the British School at Rome* 61: 231–44.

Arthur, P. (2005), 'La Chiesa di Santa Maria della Strada, Taurisano (Lecce). Scavi 2004', *Archeologia Medievale* 32: 173–205.

Arthur, P. (2007), 'Pots and boundaries: On cultural and economic areas between Late Antiquity and the early Middle Ages', in M. Bonifay and J.-C. Tréglia (eds), *LRCW 2: Late Roman coarse wares, cooking wares and amphorae in the Mediterranean: Archaeology and archaeometry* (Oxford: Archaeopress): 15–27.

Arthur, P. (2008), 'Form, function and technology in pottery production from Late Antiquity to the Early Middle Ages', *Late Antique Archaeology* 4: 159–86.

Arthur, P. (2012), 'Hierapolis of Phrygia: The drawn-out demise of an Anatolian city', in N. Christie and A. Augenti (eds), *Vrbes Extinctae: Archaeologies of abandoned classical towns* (Burlington, VT: Ashgate): 277–305.

Arthur, P. (forthcoming), 'The Byzantine West to the Pillars of Hercules', in M.J. Decker (ed.) *The Cambridge handbook to Byzantine archaeology* (Cambridge: Cambridge University Press).

Arthur, P., Caggia, M.P., Ciongoli, G.P., Melissano, V., Patterson, H. and Roberts, P. (1992), 'Fornaci altomedievali ad Otranto'. Nota preliminaire. *Archeologia Medievale* 19: 91–122.

Arthur, P., Fiorentino, G. and Imperiale, M.L. (2008), 'L'insediamento in Loc. Scorpo (Supersano, LE) nel VII–VIII secolo. La scoperta di un paesaggio di èta altomedievale, *Archeologia Medievale* 35: 365–80.

Arthur, P., Fiorentino, G. and Grasso, A.M. (2012), 'Roads to recovery: An investigation of early medieval agrarian strategies in Byzantine Italy in and around the eighth century', *Antiquity* 86: 444–55.

Aupert, P. (1980), 'Céramique slave à Argos (585 ap. J.-C.)', *Bulletin de correspondance hellénique (suppl. VI: Études argiennes)*: 373–94.

Aupert, P. (1989), 'Les Slaves à Argos', *Bulletin de correspondance hellénique* 113: 417–19.

Avner, U. and Magness, J. (1998), 'Early Islamic settlement in the southern Negev', *Bulletin of the American Schools of Oriental Research* 310: 39–57.

Avni, G. (2010), 'The Persian conquest of Jerusalem (614 c.e.): An archaeological assessment', *Bulletin of the American Schools of Oriental Research* 357: 35–48.

Avni, G. (2011), 'Continuity and change in the cities of Palestine during the Early Islamic period', in K.G. Holum and H. Lapin (eds), *Shaping the Middle East: Jews, Christians, and Muslims in an age of transition, 400–800 C.E.* (Bethesda, MD: University Press of Maryland): 115–33.

Avni, G. (2014), *The Byzantine–Islamic Transition in Palestine: An archaeological approach* (Oxford: Oxford University Press).

Avramea, A. (1997), *Le Peloponnèse du IVe au VIIIe siècle. Changements et persistances* (Paris: Publications de la Sorbonne).

Baeten, J., Marinova, E., De Laet, V., Degryse, P., De Vos, K. and Waelkens, M. (2012), 'Faecal biomarker and archaeobotanical analyses of sediments from a public latrine shed new light on ruralisation in Sagalassos, Turkey', *Journal of Archaeological Science* 39: 1143–59.

Baird, D. (2004), 'Settlement expansion on the Konya Plain, Anatolia: 5th–7th centuries AD', in W. Bowden, L. Lavan and C. Machado (eds), *Recent Research on the Late Antique Countryside* (Leiden: Brill): 219–46.

Bakker, J., Paulissen, E., Kaniewski, D., De Laet, V., Verstraeten, G., Waelkens, M. (2012), 'Man, vegetation and climate during the Holocene in the territory of Sagalassos, Western Taurus Mountains, SW Turkey', *Vegetation History and Archaeobotany* 21: 249–66.

Bakker, J., Paulissen, E., Kaniewski, D., Poblome, J., De Laet, V., Verstraeten, G. and Waelkens, M. (2013), 'Climate, people, fire and vegetation: New insights into vegetation dynamics in the Eastern Mediterranean since the 1st century AD', *Climate of the Past* 9: 57–87.

Baldini, I., Cosentino, S., Marsili, G., Sgarzi, E. and Lippolis, E. (2013), 'Gortina, Mitropolis e il suo episcopato nel VII e nell'VIII secolo. Ricerche preliminari', *Annuario della Scuola Archeologica di Atene e delle Missioni Italiane in Oriente* 90: 239–308.

Baldwin, B. (1991), 'Simokattes, Theophylaktos', in A.P. Kazhdan and A.-M. Talbot (eds), *The Oxford Dictionary of Byzantium* (New York: Oxford University Press): 1900–1.

Bálint, C. (2000), 'Some Avar and Balkan connections of the Vrap Treasure', in K.R. Brown, D. Kidd and C.T. Little (eds), *From Attila to Charlemagne: Arts of the early medieval period in the Metropolitan Museum of Art* (New York: The Metropolitan Museum of Art): 180–87.

Ballance, M. (1989), *Excavations in Chios 1952–55: Byzantine Emporio* (Athens: British School of Archaeology at Athens).

Barceló, M., Sigaut, F. and Barcels, M. (2004), *The Making of Feudal Agriculture?* (Leiden: Brill).

Bardill, J. (1999), 'The Great Palace of the Byzantine emperors and the Walker Trust excavations', *Journal of Roman Archaeology* 12: 216–30.

Barnett, H.G. (1948), 'On science and human rights', *American Anthropologist* 50: 352–55.

Bass, G. and Van Doorninck, F.H. (1982), *Yassı Ada: A seventh century Byzantine shipwreck*, Vol. 1 (College Station, TX: Texas A&M University Press).

Bates, M.L. and Kovacs, F.L. (1996), 'A hoard of large Byzantine and Arab-Byzantine coppers', *Numismatic Chronicle* 156: 165–73.

Bauer, F.A. and Klein, H.A. (2006), 'The church of Hagia Sophia in Bizye (Vize): Results of the fieldwork seasons 2003 and 2004', *Dumbarton Oaks Papers* 60: 249–70.

Baumgarten, Y. (2004), *Map of Shivta* (Jerusalem: Israel Antiquities Authority).

Bavant, B. (2007), 'Caričin Grad and the changes in the nature of urbanism in the Central Balkans in the sixth century', in A.G. Poulter (ed.), *The*

Transition to Late Antiquity: On the Danube and beyond (Oxford: British Academy): 337–74.

Baynes, N.H. and Moss, H. (eds) (1948), *Byzantium: An introduction to East Roman civilization* (Oxford: Clarendon Press).

Beckwith, J. (1970), *Early Christian and Byzantine Art* (Harmondsworth: Penguin Books).

Bénazeth, D. (1991), 'Metalwork, Coptic', in A.S. Atiyah (ed.), *Coptic Encyclopaedia* (New York: Macmillan), Vol. 5: 1601–2.

Benndorf, O. (1898), 'Vorläufige Berichte über die Ausgrabungen in Ephesos', *Jahreshefte des Österreichischen Archäologischen Institutes* 1: 53–82.

Berger, A. (1995), 'Survey in Viranşehir (Mokisos)', *Araştırma Sonuçları Toplantısı* XIII: 109–29.

Berger, A. (1996), 'Survey in Viranşehir (Mokisos)', *Araştırma Sonuçları Toplantısı* XIV: 27–41.

Berger, A. (1998), 'Viranşehir (Mokisos), eine byzantinische Stadt in Kappadokien', *Istanbuler Mitteilungen* 48: 349–429.

Bevan, A. and Conolly, J. (2004), 'GIS, archaeological survey, and landscape archaeology on the island of Kythera, Greece', *Journal of Field Archaeology* 29: 123–38.

Biers, J.C. (1985), *The Great Bath on the Lechaion Road* (Princeton, NJ: The American School of Classical Studies at Athens).

Bintliff, J. (1999), *Reconstructing Past Population Trends in Mediterranean Europe* (Oxford: Oxbow).

Bintliff, J. (2000), 'Reconstructing the Byzantine countryside: New approaches from landscape archaeology', in K. Blekle, F. Hild, J. Koder and P. Soustal (eds), *Byzanz als Raum* (Vienna: Verlag der Österreichischen Akademie der Wissenschaften): 37–63.

Bintliff, J. (2013), 'The contribution of regional surface survey to Byzantine landscape history in Greece', in J. Poblome and M. Waelkens (eds), *Exempli Gratia: Sagalassaos, Marc Waelkens and interdisciplinary archaeology* (Leuven: Leuven University Press): 127–40.

Bintliff, J., Howard, P. and Snodgrass, A. (2007), *Testing the Hinterland: The work of the Boeotia Survey (1989–1991) in the southern approaches to the city of Thespiai* (Cambridge: McDonald Institute for Archaeological Research).

Bixio, R., Caloi, V. and De Pascale, A. (2012), *Cappadocia: schede dei siti sotterranei = records of the underground sites* (Oxford: Archaeopress).

Blanchet, A. (1936), 'Les rapports entre les dépots monétaires et les événements militaires, politiques et économiques', *Revue numismatique* 39: 1–70, 205–69.

Böhlendorf-Arslan, B. (2004), *Glasierte byzantinische Keramik aus der Türkei* (Istanbul: Ege Yayınları).

Böhlendorf-Arslan, B. (2012), 'The pottery from the destruction contexts in the enclosure', in C.S. Lightfoot and E.A. Ivison (eds), *Amorium Reports 3: The lower city enclosure finds reports and technical studies* (Istanbul: Ege Yayınları): 153–79.

Böhlendorf-Arslan, B., Uysal, A. and Witte-Orr, J. (eds) (2007), *Çanak: Late antique and medieval pottery and tiles in Mediterranean archaeological contexts* (Istanbul: Ege Yayınları).

Bommeljé, S. and Doorn, P.K. (1987), *Aetolia and the Aetolians: Towards the interdisciplinary study of a Greek region* (Utrecht: Parnassus Press).

Bonifay, M. and Tréglia, J.-C. (eds) (2007), *LRCW 2: Late Roman coarse wares, cooking wares and amphorae in the Mediterranean: Archaeology and archaeometry* (Oxford: Archaeopress).

Borchhardt, J., Konecny, A., Rasch, B., Kuban, Z., Blakolmer, F., Kucher, S., Stanzl, G., Krickl, A., Alanyali, H., Peschlow, U., Mader, I., Eisenmenger, U., Knötig, M., Raslagg, A., Großschmidt, K. and Forstenpointner, G. (1997), 'Grabungen und Forschungen in Limyra aus den Jahren 1991–1996', *Jahreshefte des Österreichischen Archäologischen Institutes in Wien* 66: 321–426.

Bottema, S. (1995), 'Holocene vegetation of the Van area: Palynological and chronological evidence from Söğütlü, Turkey', *Vegetation History and Archaeobotany* 4: 187–93.

Bourbou, C. (2004), *The People of Early Byzantine Eleutherna and Messene, 6th–7th Centuries A.D.: A bioarchaeological approach* (Athens: University of Crete).

Bourbou, C. (2010), *Health and Disease in Byzantine Crete (7th–12th Centuries AD)* (Burlington, VT: Ashgate).

Bourbou, C. and Tsilipakou, A. (2009), 'Investigating the human past of Greece during the 6th–7th centuries A.D.', in L.A. Schepartz, S. Fox and

C. Bourbou (eds), *New Directions in the Skeletal Biology of Greece* (Princeton, NJ: American School of Classical Study at Athens): 121–36.

Bourbou, C., Fuller, B.T., Garvie-Lok, S.J. and Richards, M.P. (2011), 'Reconstructing the diets of Greek Byzantine populations (6th–15th centuries AD) using carbon and nitrogen stable isotope ratios', *American Journal of Physical Anthropology* 146: 569–81.

Bowden, W. (2011a), 'The *domus* and the Triconch Palace', in W. Bowden and R. Hodges (eds), *Butrint 3: Excavations at the Triconch Palace* (Oxford: Butrint Foundation): 277–302.

Bowden, W. (2011b), 'The 5th–mid 7th-century occupation', in W. Bowden and R. Hodges (eds), *Butrint 3: Excavations at the Triconch Palace* (Oxford: Butrint Foundation): 56–117.

Bowden, W. (2011c), 'The *domus* and Triconch palace as aristocratic residences', in W. Bowden and R. Hodges (eds), *Butrint 3: Excavations at the Triconch Palace* (Oxford: Butrint Foundation): 277–302.

Bowden, W. (2011d), 'Urban change and the Triconch Palace site in the 5th to 7th centuries', in W. Bowden and R. Hodges (eds), *Butrint 3: Excavations at the Triconch Palace* (Oxford: Butrint Foundation): 303–18.

Bowden, W. and Hodges, R. (eds) (2011), *Butrint 3: Excavations at the Triconch Palace* (Oxford: Butrint Foundation).

Brandes, W. (2002), *Finanzverwaltung in Krisenzeiten: Untersuchungen zur byzantinischen Administration im 6.–9. Jahrhundert* (Frankfurt: Löwenklau- Gesellschaft).

Brentano, L. (1917), 'Die byzantinische Volkswirtschaft: ein Kapitel aus Vorlesungen über Wirtschaftsgeschichte', *Schmollers Jahrbuch* 41: 569–614.

Brentano, L. and Plotnikov, I. (1924), *Narodnoe khoziaistvo Vizantii* (Leningrad: Put' k Znaniiu Publishing).

Brown, A.R. (2010), 'Islands in a sea of change? Continuity and abandonment in Dark Age Corinth and Thessaloniki', *International Journal of Historical Archaeology* 14: 230–40.

Brown, K.R., Kidd, D. and Little, C.T. (eds) (2000), *From Attila to Charlemagne: Arts of the early medieval period in the Metropolitan Museum of Art* (New York: Metropolitan Museum of Art).

Brown, P. (1978), *The Making of Late Antiquity* (Cambridge, MA: Harvard University Press).

Brubaker, L. (2004), 'The elephant and the ark: Cultural and material interchange across the Mediterranean in the eighth and ninth centuries', *Dumbarton Oaks Papers* 58: 175–95.

Bulle, H. (1934), 'Ausgrabungen bei Aphiona auf Korfu', *Mitteiungen des Deutschen Archäologischen Instituts. Athenische Abteilung* 39: 147–240.

Burger, A. (1966), 'The late Roman cemetery at Ságvár', *Acta Archaeologica Academiae Scientiarum Hungaricae* 18: 99–234.

Bury, J.B. (1913), *The Cambridge Medieval History, Vol. II: The rise of the Saracens and the foundation of Western Europe* (Cambridge: Cambridge University Press).

Cameron, Alan (1969), 'The last days of the Academy at Athens', *Proceedings of the Cambridge Philological Society (NS)* 15: 7–29.

Cameron, Averil (2001), 'Reponses', in L. Lavan (ed.), *Recent Research in Late-Antique Urbanism* (Portsmouth, RI: JRA Supplementary Series No. 42): 233–45.

Cameron, Averil (2014), *Byzantine Matters* (Princeton, NJ: Princeton University Press).

Caraher, W., Nakassis, D. and Pettigrew, D.K. (2007), 'Siteless survey and intensive data collection in an artifact-rich environment: Case studies from the eastern Corinthia, Greece', *Journal of Mediterranean Archaeology* 19: 7–43.

Caraher, W., Moore, R.S., Olson, B.R. and Papalexandrou, A. (2013), 'The South Basilica at Arsinoe (Polis-Tes-Chrysochou): Change and innovation in an early Christian basilica on Cyprus, *Cahiers du Centre d'Études Chypriotes* 43: 79–92.

Caramessini-Oeconomides, M. and Drossoyianni, Ph. (1989), 'A hoard of gold Byzantine coins from Samos', *Revue numismatique* 31: 142–82.

Carretta, M.-C. (1982), *Il catalogo del vasellame bronzeo italiano altomedievale* (Florence: All'insegna del Gigglio).

Casson, S., Rice, D.T., Jones, A.H.M. and Hudson, G.F. (1928), *Preliminary Report upon the Excavations Carried Out in the Hippodrome of Constantinople* (London: H. Milford).

Catling, H. (1972), 'An early Byzantine pottery factory at Dhiorios in Cyprus', *Levant* 4: 1–85.

Catling, H. and Dikigoropoulos, A. (1970), 'The Kornos Cave: An early Byzantine site in Cyprus', *Levant* 2: 37–62.

Cesnola, L. (1877), *Cyprus: Its ancient cities, tombs, and temples* (London: John Murray).

Charanis, P. (1952), 'On the capture of Corinth by the Onogurs and its recapture by the Byzantines', *Speculum* 27: 343–50.

Charanis, P. (1955), 'The significance of coins as evidence for the history of Athens and Corinth in the seventh and eighth centuries', in K. Weitzmann (ed.), *Late Classical and Medieval Studies in Honor of Albert Mathias Friend, Jr.* (Princeton, NJ: Princeton University Press): 163–72.

Cherry, J.F., Davis, J.L. and Mantzourane, E. (1991), *Landscape Archaeology as Long-term History: Northern Keos in the Cycladic Islands from earliest settlement until Modern times* (Los Angeles, CA: Cotsen Institute of Archaeology).

Cheynet, J.-C. and Sode, C. (2003), *Studies in Byzantine Sigillography* (Münich: K.G. Saur).

Chrysos, E.K. and Wood, I. (1999), *East and West: Modes of communication. Proceedings of the First Plenary Conference at Merida* (Leiden: Brill).

Clapham, J.H. and Power, E. (eds) (1941), *The Cambridge Economic History: The agrarian life of the Middle Ages* (Cambridge: Cambridge University Press).

Commito, A.R. (2014), *Southwest Asia Minor and Northwest Syria at the end of Antiquity: A view from the countryside* (PhD dissertation, University of Michigan, Ann Arbor, MI).

Conrad, S. (2006), 'Archaeological survey on the Lower Danube: Results and perspectives', in P.G. Bilder and V.F. Stolbe (eds), *Surveying the Greek Chora: The Black Sea region in a comparative perspective* (Aarhus: Danish National Research Foundation's Centre for Black Sea Studies): 309–31.

Cooper, J.E. and Decker, M.J. (2012), *Life and Society in Byzantine Cappadocia* (London: Palgrave).

Cormack, R. (1991), 'The wall-painting of St. Michael in the theatre', in R.R.R. Smith and K.T. Erim (eds), *Aphrodisias Papers 2: The theatre, a sculptor's workshop, philosophers, and coin types* (Ann Arbor, MI: JRA Supplementary Series No. 2), 109–22.

Coulton, J.J. and Armstrong, P. (2012), *The Balboura Survey and Settlement in Highland Southwest Anatolia* (London: British Institute at Ankara).
Cresceni, C. and Caprara, R. (2012), *The Rupestrian Settlements in the Circum-Mediterranean* (Florence: Università degli studi di Firenze).
Curta, F. (2001), 'The Prague type: A critical approach to pottery classification', *Archaeologia Bulgarica* 5: 73–106.
Curta, F. (ed.) (2005), *Borders, Barriers, and Ethnogenesis: Frontiers in Late Antiquity and the Middle Ages* (Turnhout: Brepols).
Curta, F. (2009), 'The early Slavs in Bohemia and Moravia: A response to my critics', *Archeologické rozhledy* 61: 725–54.
Curta, F. (2010), 'Still waiting for the barbarians? The making of the Slavs in "Dark-Age" Greece', in F. Curta (ed.), *Neglected Barbarians* (Turnhout: Brepols): 403–78.
Curta, F. (2011), *The Edinburgh History of the Greeks* (Edinburgh: Edinburgh University Press).
Curta, F. (2013a), 'Seventh-century fibulae with bent stems in the Balkans', *Archaeologia Bulgarica* 17: 49–70.
Curta, F. (2013b), 'The beginning of the Middle Ages in the Balkans', *Millennium* 10: 145–214.
Curta, F. (2014), 'Coins and burials in Dark-Age Greece: Archaeological remarks on the Byzantine "Reconquista"', in R. Kostova (ed.), *Medieval Man and His World: Studies in honor of the 70th anniversary of Prof. Dr. Habil Kazimir Popkonstantinov* (Velko Trnovo: Faber): 55–86.
Cutler, A. (2001), 'Gifts and gift exchange as aspects of the Byzantine, Arab, and related economies', *Dumbarton Oaks Papers* 55: 247–78.
D'Andria, F. (2001), 'Hierapolis of Phrygia: Its evolution in Hellenistic and Roman times', in D. Parrish (ed.), *Urbanism in Western Asia Minor* (Portsmouth, RI: JRA Supplementary Series No. 45): 96–115.
D'Andria, F. (2006), 'Hierapolis of Phrygia', in W. Radt (ed.), *Stadtgrabungen und Stadtforschung in westlichen Kleinasien*, Byzas 3: 113–24.
D'Andria, F. and Caggia, P. (2007), *Hierapolis di Frigia I, Le attività delle campagne di scavo e restauro 2000–2003* (Istanbul: Ege Yayınları).
Dark, K. (2010), 'Pottery production and use in Byzantine Constantinople', *Byzantinoslavica* 1/2: 115–28.

Davidson, G. (1952), *Corinth, Vol. XII: The minor objects* (Princeton, NJ: American School of Classical Studies at Athens).

Davidson, G. (1974), 'A wandering soldier's grave in Corinth', *Hesperia* 43: 512–21.

De Bernardi Ferrero, D. and Verzone, P. (2002), *Hierapolis, Scavi e ricerche IV, Saggi in onore di Paolo Verzone* (Rome: Bretschneider).

Di Berardino, A. (2006), *I canoni dei concili della chiesa antica* (Rome: Institutum Patristicum Augustinianum).

Decker, M.J. (2009), *Tilling the Hateful Earth: Agricultural production and trade in the late antique east* (Oxford: Oxford University Press).

Decker, M.J. (forthcoming), *The Cambridge Handbook to Byzantine Archaeology* (Cambridge: Cambridge University Press).

De Goeje, M. (1889), *Bibliotheca geographorum Arabicorum, 6: Kitab al-masalik wa'l-mamalik, auctore Abu'l-Kasim Obaidallah ibn Abdallah ibn Khordadhbeh. Accedunt excerpta e Kitab al-kharâdj, auctore Kodama ibn Dja'far* (Leiden: Brill).

Demargne, P., Coupel, P. and Prunet, P. (1958), *Fouilles de Xanthos. Tome 1, Les piliers funéraires* (Paris: C. Klinsksieck).

Diamanti, C. (2010), 'Stamped late Roman/proto-Byzantine amphoras from Halasarna of Kos', *Rei Cretariae Romanae Fautorum Acta* 41: 1–8.

Diamond, J. (1997), *Guns, Germs, and Steel: The fates of human societies* (New York: W.W. Norton).

Diamond, J. (2005), *Collapse: How societies choose to fail or succeed* (New York: Viking).

Didioumi, S. (2014), 'Local pottery production in the island of Cos, Greece from the early Byzantine period: A preliminary report', in N. Poulou-Papadimitriou, E. Nodarou and V. Kilikoglou (eds), *LRCW 4: Late Roman coarse wares, cooking wares and amphorae in the Mediterranean: Archaeology and archaeometry. The Mediterranean: A market without frontiers* (Oxford: Archaeopress): 169–80.

Di Vita, A. (1985), 'Contributi alla conoscenza di Gortina bizantina', *Pepragmena tou e diethnous Kretologikou synedriou* (Heraklion, Crete: Hetairia Kretikon Historikon Meleton): 137–43.

Di Vita, A. (1996), 'Earthquakes and civil life at Gortyn (Crete) in the period between Justinian and Constant II (6–7th century AD)', in S. Stiros and

R.E. Jones (eds), *Archaeoseismology* (Athens: Institute of Geology & Mineral Exploration/British School at Athens): 45–50.

Doonan, O. (1998), 'Survey of the hinterland of Sinop, Turkey', *Near Eastern Archaeology* 61: 178–79.

Doonan, O. (2000), 'Gerna Dere: Roman and Byzantine settlement along the coast of Sinope', *Talanta* 32/33: 17–26.

Doonan, O. (2002), 'Production in a Pontic landscape: The hinterland of Greek and Roman Sinope', in M. Faudot, A. Fraysse and É. Geny (eds), *Pont-Euxin et Commerce: Actes du IXe Symposium de Vani* (Besançon: Presses universitaires franc-comtoises): 185–98.

Doonan, O. (2004), *Sinop Landscapes: Exploring connection in a Black Sea hinterland* (Philadelphia, PA: University of Pennsylvania Museum of Archaeology and Anthropology).

Donner, F. (2012), *Muhammad and the Believers* (Cambridge, MA: Harvard University Press).

Drandakis, N.V. (1977), 'Erevnai eis ten Manen', *Praktika tes en Athenais Archaiologikes Hetaireias* 132: 200–8.

Drandakis, N.V. and Gkioles, N. (1980), 'Anaskaphe sto Tigani Manis', *Praktika tes en Athenais Archaeiologikes Hetaireias* 135: 247–58.

Drandakis, N.V., Gkioles, N. and Konstantinidi, C. (1981), 'Anaskaphe sto Tigani Manis', *Praktika tes en Athenais Archaiologiskes Hetaireias* 136: 241–53.

Dunn, A. (1997), 'Stages in the transition from the late antique to the Middle Byzantine urban centre in S. Macedonia and Thrace', in K. Babuskos and N.G.L. Hammond (eds), *Aphierooma ston N.G.L. Hammond* (Thessalonike: Hetaireia Makedonikon Spudon): 137–51.

Dunn, A. (1999), 'From polis to kastron in southern Macedonia: Amphiopolis, Khrysoupolis, and the Strymon Delta', *Collection de l'École française de Rome* 105: 399–413.

Düring, B.S. and Glatz, C. (2010), 'The Cide archaeological Project 2009: First results', *Anatolia Antiqua* 18: 202–13.

Eastwood, W.J., Roberts, N. and Lamb, H.F. (1998), 'Palaeoecological and archaeological evidence for human occupance in Southwest Turkey: The Beyşehir Occupation Phase', *Anatolian Studies* 48: 69–86.

Eastwood, W.J., Leng, M.J., Roberts, N. and Davis, B. (2007), 'Holocene climate change in the eastern Mediterranean region: A comparison of stable isotope and pollen data from Lake Gölhisar, southwest Turkey', *Journal of Quaternary Science* 22: 327–41.

Eger, A. (2012), *The Spaces Between the Teeth: A gazetteer of towns on the Islamic-Byzantine frontier* (Istanbul: Yayınları).

El-Cheikh, N. (2004), *Byzantium Viewed by the Arabs* (Cambridge, MA: Harvard University Press).

England, A., Eastwood, W.J., Roberts, C.N., Turner, R. and Haldon, J.F. (2008), 'Historical landscape change in Cappadocia (central Turkey): A palaeoecological investigation of annually laminated sediments from Nar Lake', *The Holocene* 18: 1229–45.

Evans, H. and Wixom, W.D. (1997), *The Glory of Byzantium: Art and culture of the Middle Byzantine era, AD 843–1261* (New York: Metropolitan Museum of Art).

Fagan, B. (1996), *The Oxford Companion to Archaeology* (Oxford: Oxford University Press).

Fagan, B. (2008), *The Great Warming: Climate change and the rise and fall of civilizations* (New York: Bloomsbury Press).

Fairclough, G. (2006), 'Large scale, long duration and broad perceptions: Scale issues in historic landscape characterisation', in G. Lock and B. Molyneaux (eds), *Confronting Scale in Archaeology* (New York: Springer): 203–15.

Festugière, A.J. and Ryden, L. (1974), *Léontios de Neapolis. Vie de Syméon le Fou et Vie de Jean de Chypre* (Paris: P. Geuthner).

Forbes, H. (2013), 'Off-site scatters and the manuring hypothesis in Greek survey archaeology', *Hesperia* 82: 551–94.

Fornaciari, G., Ceccanti, B. and Menicagli, E. (1988), 'Ricerca degli elementi guida della nutrizione e di alcuni metalli pesanti mediante spettroscopia ad assorbimento atomico', in A. Di Vita (ed.), *Gortina I* (Rome: L'Erma di Bretschneider).

Foss, C. (1977), 'Archaeology and the "Twenty Cities" of Asia Minor', *American Journal of Archaeology* 81: 469–86.

Foss, C. (1994), 'The Lycian coast in the Byzantine age', *Dumbarton Oaks Papers* 48: 1–52.

Foss, C., and Winfield, D. (1986), *Byzantine Fortifications: An introduction* (Pretoria: University of South Africa).

François, V. (2003), 'La céramique byzantine et ottomane en Bithynie', in B. Geyer and J. Lefort (eds), *La Bithynie au Moyen Âge* (Paris: Lethielleux): 287–308.

Freestone, I.C., Greenwood, R. and Gorin-Rosen, Y. (2002), 'Byzantine and early Islamic glassmaking in the eastern Mediterranean: Production and distribution of primary glass', in G. Kordas (ed.), *Hyalos = Vitrum = Glass: History, technology and conservation of glass and vitreous materials in the Hellenic world* (Athens: Glasnet): 167–74.

Fulghum, M.M. (2001–2002), 'Under wraps: Byzantine textiles as major and minor arts', *Studies in the Decorative Arts* 9: 13–33.

Fuller, B.T., De Cupere, B., Marinova, E., Van Neer, W., Waelkens, M. and Richards, M.P. (2012), 'Isotopic reconstruction of human diet and animal husbandry practices during the Classical-Hellenistic, Imperial, and Byzantine periods at Sagalassos, Turkey', *American Journal of Physical Anthropology* 149: 157–71.

Gabrieli, R.S., Jackson, M.P.C. and Kardelli, A. (2007), 'Stumbling into the darkness: Trade and life in post-Roman Cyprus', in M. Bonifay and J.-C. Tréglia (eds), *LRCW 2: Late Roman coarse wares, cooking wares and amphorae in the Mediterranean: Archaeology and archaeometry* (Oxford: Archaeopress): 791–801.

Gândilă, A. (2009), 'Early Byzantine coin circulation in the Eastern provinces: A comparative statistical approach', *American Journal of Numismatics* 21: 151–226.

Garam, E. (2000), 'The Vrap Treasure', in K.R. Brown, D. Kidd and C.T. Little (eds), *From Attila to Charlemagne: Arts of the early Medieval period in the Metropolitan Museum of Art* (New York: The Metropolitan Museum of Art): 170–79.

Garvie-Lok, S. (2010), 'A possible witness to the sixth century Slavic invasion of Greece from the stadium tunnel at ancient Nemea', *International Journal of Historical Archaeology* 14: 271–84.

Gibbon, E. (1776), *The History of the Decline and Fall of the Roman Empire* (London: Strahan & Cadell).

Gibbon, E. and Bury, J.B. (1906), *The History of the Decline and Fall of the Roman Empire* (New York: F. DeFau).

Gill, M.A.V. (2003), 'Middle Byzantine terracotta lamps with a discussion and two appendices by C.S. Lightfoot', in C.S. Lightfoot (ed.), *Amorium Reports II: Research papers and technical reports* (Oxford: Archaeopress): 65–71.

Giorgi, J. (2012), 'The plant remains', in C.S. Lightfoot and E.A. Ivison (eds), *Amorium Reports 3: The lower city enclosure finds reports and technical studies* (Istanbul: Ege Yayınları): 395–418.

Given, M., Knapp, A.B., Noller, J.S., Sollars, L. and Kassianidou, V. (2013), *Landscape and Interaction: The Troodos Archaeological and Environmental Survey Project, Cyprus* (Oxford: Oxbow).

Golofast, L.A. (2003), 'Cherson in the 7th century AD: The archaeological aspect', *Ancient West & East* 2: 96–115.

Gordus, A.A. and Metcalf, D.M. (1970), 'The alloy of the Byzantine miliaresion and the question of reminting of Islamic silver', *Hamburger Beiträge zur Numismatik* 24: 9–36.

Grabar, A. (1928), *Recherches sur les influences orientales dans l'art balkanique* (Paris: Les Belles Lettres).

Grandi, E. (2007), 'Late antique and early medieval (5th–7th cent. A.D.) fine pottery from archaeological contexts in Venice's Lagoon', in B. Böhlendorf-Arslan, A. Uysal and J. Witte-Orr (eds), *Çanak: Late antique and medieval pottery and tiles in Mediterranean archaeological contexts* (Istanbul: Ege Yayınları):1–24.

Greene, K. (2007), 'Late Hellenistic and early Roman invention and innovation: The case of lead-glazed pottery', *American Journal of Archaeology* 111: 653–71.

Greenslade, S. (2013), 'The Vrina Plain settlement between the 1st–13th centuries', in I.L. Hansen, R. Hodges and S. Leppard (eds), *Butrint 4: The archaeology and histories of an Ionian town* (Oxford: Oxbow Books): 123–64.

Greenslade, S. and Hodges, R. (2013), 'The aristocratic oikos on the Vrina Plain, Butrint c. A.D. 830–1200', *Byzantine and Modern Greek Studies* 37: 1–19.

Greenslade, S., Leppard, S. and Logue, M. (2013), 'The acropolis of Butrint reassessed', in I.L. Hansen, R. Hodges and S. Leppard (eds), *Butrint 4: The archaeology and histories of an Ionian town* (Oxford: Oxbow Books): 47–76.

Gregory, T.E. (1979), 'The late Roman wall at Corinth', *Hesperia* 48: 264–80.
Gregory, T.E. (1993), 'An early Byzantine (Dark Age) settlement at Isthmia: A preliminary report', in T.E. Gregory (ed.), *The Corinthia in the Roman Period* (Ann Arbor, MI: JRA Supplementary Series No. 8): 149–60.
Gregory, T.E. (1994), 'Archaeology and theoretical considerations on the transition from Antiquity to the Middle Ages in the Aegean area', in P.N. Kardulias (ed.), *Beyond the Site: Regional studies in the Aegean area* (Lanham, MD: University Press of America): 137–59.
Gregory, T.E. (2004), 'Less is better: The quality of ceramic evidence from archaeological survey and practical proposals for low-impact survey in a Mediterranean context', in E. Athanassopoulos and L. Wandsnider (eds), *Mediterranean Archaeological Landscapes: Current issues* (Philadelphia, PA: University of Pennsylvania Museum Publications): 15–36.
Grierson, P. (1968), *Catalogue of the Byzantine Coins in the Dumbarton Oaks Collection and in the Whittemore Collection: Vol. 2. Phocas to Theodosius III 602–717. Part I: Phocas and Heraclius (602–641)* (Washington, DC: Dumbarton Oaks).
Guerreau, A. (1986), [Review of] 'Morrisson, C., Brenot, C., Callu, J-P., Bar-Randon, J.-N., Porier, J., Halleux, R., *L'or monayé*, *Histoire & Mesure* 1: 254–60.
Günsenin, N. (1989), 'Recherches sur les amphores byzantines dans les musées turcs', in V. Déroche and J.-M. Spieser (eds), *Recherches sur la céramique byzantine* (Athens: École française d'Athènes): 267–76.
Günsenin, N. (1995), 'Ganos: resultats des campagnes de 1992 et 1993', *Anatolia Antiqua* 3: 167–78.
Günsenin, N. (1998), 'Récentes découvertes sur l'île de Marmara (Proconnèse) à l'époque byzantine', *Archaeonautica* 14: 309–16.
Günsenin, N. (2001), 'L'épave de Çamalti Burnu I (Ile de Marmara, Proconnese): Resultats des campagnes 1998–2000', *Anatolia Antiqua* 9: 117–33.
Haggis, D.C. (1996), 'Archaeological survey at Kavousi, East Crete: Preliminary report', *Hesperia* 65: 373–432.
Hahn, M. (1996), 'The early Byzantine to Modern periods', in B. Wells and C. Runnels (eds), *The Berbati-Limnes Archaeological Survey 1988–1990* (Stockholm: Paul P. Åströms): 345–452.

Haldon, J.F. (1993), 'Military service, military lands, and the status of soldiers: Current problems and interpretations', *Dumbarton Oaks Papers* 47: 1–67.

Haldon, J.F. (1999), 'The idea of the town in the Byzantine Empire', in G.P. Brogiolo and B. Ward-Perkins (eds), *The Idea and Ideal of the Town Between Late Antiquity and the Early Middle Ages* (Leiden: Brill): 1–24.

Haldon, J. (2007), 'Cappadocia will be given over to ruin and become a desert: Environmental evidence for historically-attested events in the 7th–10th centuries', in J. Koder and K. Belke (eds), *Byzantina Mediterranea: Festschrift für Johannes Koder zum 65. Geburstag* (Vienna: Böhlau): 215–30.

Haldon, J.F., Roberts, N., Izdebski, A., Fleitmann, D., McCormick, M., Cassis, M., Doonan, O., Eastwood, W., Elton, H. and Ladstätter, S. (2014), 'The climate and environment of Byzantine Anatolia: Integrating science, history, and archaeology', *Journal of Interdisciplinary History* 45: 113–61.

Hansen, I.L. and Wickham, C. (2000), *The Long Eighth Century* (Leiden: Brill).

Hansen, I.L., Hodges, R. and Leppard, S. (eds) (2013), *Butrint 4: The archaeology and histories of an Ionian town* (Oxford: Oxbow).

Harris, A., Blinkhorn, P., Evison, V., Gilmour, B. and Riddler, I. (2006), *Early Anglo-Saxon Vessels and Containers from Saltwood Tunnel, Kent* (London: London and Continental Railways).

Harrison, R.M. (2001), *Mountain and Plain: From the Lycian coast to the Phrygian plateau in the late Roman and early Byzantine period* (Ann Arbor, MI: University of Michigan Press).

Harrison, R.M. and Christie, N. (1993), 'Excavations at Amorium: 1992 interim report', *Anatolian Studies* 43: 147–62.

Harrison, R.M., Firatli, N. and Hayes, J. (1968), 'Excavations at Saraçhane in Istanbul: Fifth preliminary report, with a contribution on a seventh-century pottery group', *Dumbarton Oaks Papers* 22: 195–216.

Hayes, J. (1972), *Late Roman Pottery: A catalogue of Roman fine wares* (London: British School at Rome).

Hayes, J. (1980), *A Supplement to Late Roman Pottery* (London: British School at Rome).

Hayes, J. (1992), *Excavations at Saraçhane in Istanbul. Vol. 2, The pottery* (Princeton, NJ: Princeton University Press).

Hayes, J.W. (2008), *Roman Pottery: Fine-ware imports* (Princeton, NJ: American School of Classical Studies at Athens).

Hendy, M. (1985), *Studies in the Byzantine Monetary Economy, c. 300–1450* (Cambridge: Cambridge University Press).

Hillman, G. (2001), 'Archaeology, Percival, and the problems of identifying wheat remains', in P.D.S. Caligari and P.E. Brandham (eds), *Wheat Taxonomy: The legacy of John Percival* (London: Linnean Society): 27–36.

Hirschfeld, Y. (2004), 'A climatic change in the Early Byzantine period? Some archaeological evidence', *Palestine Exploration Quarterly* 136: 133–49.

Hjohlman, J., Penttinen, A., Wells, B. and Basiakos, I. (2005), *Pyrgouthi: A rural site in the Berbati Valley from the Early Iron Age to Late Antiquity. Excavations by the Swedish Institute at Athens, 1995 and 1997* (Stockholm: Swedish Institute at Athens).

Hocker, F. and Ward, C. (eds.) (2004), *The Philosophy of Shipbuilding* (College Station, TX: Texas A&M University Press).

Hodder, I. (1982a), *Symbols in Action: Ethnoarcheological studies of material culture* (Cambridge: Cambridge University Press).

Hodder, I. (1982b), *The Present Past: An introduction to anthropology for archaeologists* (London: Batsford).

Hodges, R. (1997), *Light in the Dark Ages: The rise and fall of San Vincenzo al Volturno* (Ithaca, NY: Cornell University Press).

Hodges, R. (2011): 'From Roman *insula* to medieval quarter?', in W. Bowden and R. Hodges (eds), *Butrint 3: Excavations at the Triconch Palace* (Oxford: Butrint Foundation): 319–26.

Hodges, R. (2012), *Dark Age Economics: A new audit* (London: Bristol Classical Press).

Hodges, R. (2013), 'Excavating away the "poison": The topographic history of Butrint, ancient *Buthrotum*', in I.L. Hansen, R. Hodges and S. Leppard (eds), *Butrint 4: The archaeology and histories of an Ionian town* (Oxford: Oxbow Books): 1–21.

Hodges, R. and Whitehouse, D. (1983), *Mohammed, Charlemagne and the Origins of Europe: Archaeology and the Pirenne thesis* (Ithaca, NY: Cornell University Press).

Hodges, R., Gibson, S. and Mitchell, J. (1997), 'The making of a monastic city: The architecture of San Vincenzo al Volturno in the ninth century', *Papers of the British School at Rome* 65: 233–86.

Holcomb, M. (2008), 'Ugly but ... important: The Albanian Hoard and the making of the archaeological treasure in the early twentieth century' *Early Medieval Europe* 16: 3–22.

Howard-Johnston, J.D. (1999), 'Heraclius' Persian campaigns and the revival of the East Roman Empire, 622–30', *War in History* 6: 1–44.

Hoyland, R. (2011), *Theophilus of Edessa's Chronicle and the Circulation of Historical Knowledge in Late Antiquity and Early Islam* (Liverpool: Liverpool University Press).

Hudson, N. (2008), 'Three centuries of Late Roman pottery', in C. Ratté and R.R.R. Smith (eds), *Aphrodisias Papers 4: New research on the city and its monuments* (Portsmouth, RI: JRA Supplementary Series No. 70): 318–45.

Isler, H.P. (1969), 'Heraion von Samos: eine frühbyzantinische Zisterne', *Mitteilungen des Deutschen Archäologischen Instituts Athenische Abteilung* 84: 202–30.

Ivison, E. (2007), 'Amorium in the Byzantine Dark Ages (seventh to ninth centuries)', in J. Henning (ed.), *Post-Roman Towns, Trade and Settlement in Europe and Byzantium*, Vol. 2 (New York: Walter de Gruyter): 25–59.

Jackson, M., Zelle, M., Vandeput, L. and Köse, V. (2012), 'Primary evidence for Late Roman D Ware production in southern Asia Minor: A challenge to "Cypriot Red Slip Ware"', *Anatolian Studies* 62: 89–114.

Jacobs, I. (2014), *Production and Prosperity in the Theodosian Period* (Leuven: Peeters).

Jacoby, D. (2004), 'Silk economics and cross-cultural artistic interaction: Byzantium, the Muslim World, and the Christian West', *Dumbarton Oaks Papers* 58: 197–240.

James, L. (1996), *Light and Colour in Byzantine Art* (Oxford: Oxford University Press).

Jameson, M.H., Runnels, C.N. and Van Andel, T.H. (eds) (1994), *A Greek Countryside: The Southern Argolid from prehistory to the present day* (Stanford, CA: Stanford University Press).

Jones, A.H.M. (1937), *Cities of the eastern Roman provinces* (Oxford: Clarendon Press).

Jones, A.H.M. (1964), *The Later Roman Empire, 284–602: A social, economic and administrative survey* (London: Blackwell).

Jones, R.E. and Boardman, J. (1986), *Greek and Cypriot Pottery: A review of scientific studies* (Athens: British School at Athens).

Kaegi, W. (1998), 'Egypt on the eve of the Muslim conquest', in C.F. Petry (ed.), *The Cambridge History of Egypt*, Vol. 1 (Cambridge: Cambridge University Press): 34–61.

Kaegi, W. (2010), *Heraclius: Emperor of Byzantium* (Cambridge: Cambridge University Press).

Kamani, S. (2013), 'The western defences', in I.L. Hansen, R. Hodges and S. Leppard (eds), *Butrint 4: The archaeology and histories of an Ionian town* (Oxford: Oxbow Books): 245–56.

Kaplan, M. (1992), *Les hommes et la terre à Byzance du VIe au XIe siècle: propriété et exploitation du sol* (Paris: Sorbonne).

Karagiorgou, O. (2001), 'LR2: A container for the military annona on the Danubian border', in S. Kingsley and M. Decker (eds), *Economy and Exchange in the East Mediterranean during Late Antiquity*. Proceedings of a conference at Somerville College, Oxford, 29 May 1999 (Oxford: Oxbow Books): 129–66.

Kazhdan, A.P. and Oikonomides, N. (1991), 'Kommerkiarios', in A.P. Kazhdan and A.-M. Talbot (eds), *The Oxford Dictionary of Byzantium* (New York: Oxford University Press): 1141.

Kazhdan, A.P. and Talbot, A.-M. (eds) (1991), *The Oxford Dictionary of Byzantium* (New York: Oxford University Press).

Kennedy, H. (1985), 'From *polis* to *madina*: Urban change in late antique and early Islamic Syria, *Past & Present* 106: 3–27.

Kennedy, H. (2007), *The Great Arab Conquests: How the spread of Islam changed the world we live in* (Philadelphia, PA: Da Capo).

Keys, D. (1999), *Catastrophe: An investigation into the origins of the modern world* (London: Century).

Kingsley, S.A. (forthcoming a), 'Revival and revolution: Byzantine shipwrecks of the Greater Mediterranean World', in M.J. Decker (ed.), *The Cambridge Handbook to Byzantine Archaeology* (Cambridge: Cambridge University Press).

Kingsley, S.A. (forthcoming b), 'Byzantine ports and harbourless seas', in M.J. Decker (ed.), *The Cambridge Handbook to Byzantine Archaeology* (Cambridge: Cambridge University Press).

Kocabaş, U. (2015), 'The Yenikapı Byzantine- era shipwrecks, Istanbul, Turkey: A preliminary report and inventory of the 27 wrecks studied by Istanbul University', *International Journal of Nautical Archaeology* 44: 5–38.

Koder, J. (1973), *Negroponte. Untersuchungen zur Topographie und Siedlungsgeschichte der Insel Euboia während der Zeit der Venezianerherrschaft* (Vienna: Österreichische Akademie der Wissenschaften).

Koder, J. (1991), *Das Eparchenbuch Leons des Weisen* (Vienna: Das Eparchenbuch Leons des Weisen).

Koder, J. (1996), 'Climatic change in the fifth and sixth centuries?' in P. Allen and E. Jeffreys (eds), *The Sixth century, End or Beginning?* (Brisbane: Australian Association for Byzantine Studies): 270–86.

Koebner, R. (1941), 'The settlement and colonization of Europe', in J.H. Clapham and E. Power (eds.), *The Cambridge Economic History: The agrarian life of the Middle Ages* (Cambridge: Cambridge University Press): 1–88.

Kosso, C. (2003), *The Archaeology of Public Policy in Late Roman Greece* (Oxford: Archaeopress).

Kostova, R. (2009), 'Polychrome ceramics in Preslav, 9th to 11th centuries: Where were they produced and used?', in M. Mundell Mango (ed.), *Byzantine Trade, 4th–12th Centuries: The archaeology of local, regional, and international exchange* (Farnham: Ashgate): 97–117.

Kourelis, K. (2003), *Monuments of Rural Archaeology: Medieval settlements in the northwestern Peloponnese* (PhD Dissertation, University of Pennsylvania).

Kourelis, K. (2007), 'Byzantium and the avant-garde: Excavations at Corinth, 1920's–1930's', *Hesperia* 76: 391–442.

Laiou, A. (2002), 'Exchange and trade, seventh–twelfth centuries', in A. Laiou (ed.), *The Economic History of Byzantium*, Vol. 2 (Washington, DC: Dumbarton Oaks): 697–770.

Landon, M.E. (1994), *Contributions to the Study of the Water Supply of Ancient Corinth* (PhD dissertation, University of California Berkeley).

Lauffray, J. (1983–1991), *Halabiyya-Zenobia, place forte du limes oriental et la Haute-Mésopotamie au VIe siècle* (Paris: P. Geuthner).

Lavan, L. (ed.) (2001), *Recent Research in Late-Antique Urbanism* (Portsmouth, RI: JRA Supplementary Series No. 42).

Lavan, L. (2009), 'What killed the ancient city? Chronology, causation, and traces of continuity', *Journal of Roman Archaeology* 22: 803–12.

Lawson, J. (1996), 'The Roman pottery', in W.G. Cavanagh and P. Armstrong (eds), *The Laconia Survey: Continuity and change in a Greek rural landscape* (London: British School at Athens): 111–23.

Lemerle, P. (1979, *The Agrarian History of Byzantium from the Origins to the Twelfth Century: The sources and problems* (Galway: Galway University Press).

Lemerle, P. (1979–1981), *Les plus anciens recueils des miracles de Saint Démétrius et la pénétration des Slaves dans les Balkans* (Paris: Éditions du Centre national de la recherche scientifique).

Leone, A. (2003), 'Late antique North Africa', *Al-Masaq: Islam in the Medieval Mediterranean* 15: 21–33.

Leone, A. (2013), *The End of the Pagan City: Religion, economy, and urbanism in late antique North Africa* (Oxford: Oxford University Press).

Lewit, T. (2011), 'Dynamics of fineware production and trade: The puzzle of supra-regional exporters', *Journal of Roman Archaeology* 24: 313–32.

Liebeschuetz, J.H.W.G (2001), *The Decline and Fall of the Roman City* (Oxford: Oxford University Press).

Liebeschuetz, J.H.W.G and Kennedy, H. (1988), 'Antioch and the villages of Northern Syria in the fifth and sixth centuries AD: Trends and problems', *Nottingham Medieval Studies* 32: 65–90.

Lightfoot, C.S. (2002), 'Byzantine Anatolia: Reassessing the numismatic evidence', *Revue numismatique* 158: 229–39.

Lightfoot, C.S. (ed.) (2003), *Amorium Reports II: Research papers and technical reports* (Oxford: Archaeopress).

Lightfoot, C.S. (2005), 'Glass finds at Amorium', *Dumbarton Oaks Papers* 59: 173–81.

Lightfoot, C.S. (2007), 'Trade and industry in Byzantine Anatolia: The evidence from Amorium', *Dumbarton Oaks Papers* 61: 269–86.

Lightfoot, C.S. (2012), 'Middle Byzantine terracotta lamps: 1993–2005', in C.S. Lightfoot and E.A. Ivison (eds), *Amorium Reports 3: The lower city enclosure finds reports and technical studies* (Istanbul: Ege Yayınları): 217–32.

Lightfoot, C.S. and Ivison, E.A. (eds) (2012), *Amorium Reports 3: The lower city enclosure finds reports and technical studies* (Istanbul: Ege Yayınları).

Lightfoot, M. (2003), 'Belt buckles from Amorium and in the Afyon Archaeological Museum', in C.S. Lightfoot (ed.), *Amorium Reports 2: Research papers and technical studies* (Oxford: BAR International Series 1170): 81–103.

Linscheid, P. (2003), 'Textile fragments from the Lower City, Trench AB and Trench LC5', in C.S. Lightfoot (ed.), *Amorium Reports 2: Research papers and technical studies* (Oxford: BAR International Series 1170): 185–92.

Little, L. (2007), *Plague and the End of Antiquity: The pandemic of 541–750* (Cambridge: Cambridge University Press).

Livarda, A. (forthcoming), 'Towards an understanding of the subsistence base at Vrina Plain: The archaeobotanical evidence', in S. Gleenslade and R. Hodges (eds), *Butrint 5: Excavations on the Vrina Plain: The Roman and Byzantine Suburb* (Oxford: Oxbow Books).

MacDowall, D. (1965), 'The Byzantine coin hoard found at Isthmia', *Archaeology* 18: 264–67.

Macri, C.M. (1925), *L'organisation de l'économie urbaine dans Byzance sous la dynastie de Macédoine, 867–1057* (Paris: R. Guillon).

Magness, J. (1993), *Jerusalem Ceramic Chronology: Circa 200–800 C.E.* (Sheffield: JSOT Press).

Magness, J. (2003a), *The Archaeology of the Early Islamic Settlement in Palestine* (Winona Lake, IN: Eisenbrauns).

Magness, J. (2003b), 'Late Roman and Byzantine pottery', in H. Geva (ed.), *Jewish Quarter Excavations in the Old City of Jerusalem*, Vol. II (Jerusalem: Israel Exploration Society): 423–32.

Magness, J. (2010), 'Early Islamic pottery: A revolution in diet and dining habits?', in P. Matthiae and L. Romano (eds), *Proceedings of the 6th International Congress of the Archaeology of the Ancient Near East, 5–10 May 2009, 'La Sapienza', Università di Roma* (Wiesbaden: Harrassowitz): 129–42.

Maguire, H. (1995), *Materials Analysis of Byzantine Pottery* (Washington, DC: Dumbarton Oaks).

Malingoudis, P. (1981), *Studien zu den slawischen Ortsnamen Griechenlands 1. Slawische Flurnamen aus der messenischen Mani*, (Wiesbaden: Franz Steiner).

Mango, C. (1963), 'Antique statuary and the Byzantine beholder', *Dumbarton Oaks Papers* 17: 53–75.

Mango, C. (1972), *The Art of the Byzantine Empire 312–1453: Sources and documents* (Englewood Cliffs, NJ: Prentice-Hall).

Mango, C. (1976), *Byzantine Architecture* (New York: H.N. Abrams).

Mango, C. and Scott, R. (1997), *The Chronicle of Theophanes Confessor* (Oxford: Oxford University Press).

Martens, F. (2004), *Interdisciplinary Research Concerning the Urban Development of Sagalassos: Settlement development, urban layout and infrastructure* (PhD dissertation, Katholieke Universiteit Leuven).

Mastronuzzi, G. and Melissano, V. (2007), 'Le case bizantine sul lato ovest dell'Agorà (Regio I)', in F. D'Andria and M.P. Caggia (eds.), *Hierapolis di Frigia I. Le attività delle campagne di scavo e restauro 2000–2003* (Istanbul: Ege Yayınları): 541–81.

Mattingly, D. (1999), 'Methods of collection, recording and quantification', in R. Francovich and H. Patterson (eds), *Extracting Meaning from Ploughsoil Assemblages: The archaeology of Mediterranean landscapes* (Oxford: Oxbow): 5–15.

McClellan, M., Rautman, M. and Wallace, P. (1995), 'Where have all the farmers gone? The Cypriot countryside in the seventh to tenth centuries', in P.W. Wallace (ed.), *Visitors, Immigrants and Invaders in Cyprus* (Albany, NY: Institute of Cypriot Studies): 85–86.

McCormick, M. (2001), *Origins of the European Economy: Communications and commerce AD 300–900* (Cambridge: Cambridge University Press).

McCormick, M. (2002), 'New light on the "Dark Ages": How the slave trade fuelled the Carolingian economy', *Past & Present* 177: 17–54.

McCormick, M. (2003), 'Rats, communications, and plague: Toward an ecological history', *Journal of Interdisciplinary History* 34: 1–25.

McCormick, M. (2012), 'Climate change during and after the Roman Empire: Reconstructing the past from scientific and historical evidence', *Journal of Interdisciplinary History* 43: 169–220.

McCormick, M., Dutton, P.E. and Mayewski, P.A. (2007), 'Volcanoes and the climate forcing of Carolingian Europe, A.D. 750 to 950', *Speculum* 82: 865–95.

McDonald, W.A. and Hope Simpson, R. (1961), 'Prehistoric habitation in southwest Peloponnese', *American Journal of Archaeology* 65: 221–60.

McDonald, W.A. and Hope Simpson, R. (1964), 'Further exploration in southwestern Peloponnese: 1962–1963', *American Journal of Archaeology* 68: 229–45.

McDonald, W.A. and Hope Simpson, R. (1969), 'Further exploration in southwestern Peloponnese: 1964–1968', *American Journal of Archaeology* 73: 123–78.

McDonald, W.A., Coulson, W. and Rosser, J. (1983), *Excavations at Nichoria in Southwest Greece, Vol. III: Dark Age and Byzantine occupation* (Minneapolis, MN: University of Minnesota Press).

McNicoll, A. and Smith, R.H. (1982), *Pella in Jordan 1: An interim report on the joint University of Sydney and the College of Wooster excavations at Pella 1979–1981* (Canberra: Australian National Gallery).

Megaw, A. (1975), 'An early thirteenth-century Aegean glazed ware', in G. Robertson and G. Henderson (eds), *Studies in Memory of David Talbot Rice* (Edinburgh: Edinburgh University Press): 34–45.

Megaw, A. (1986), 'Betwixt Greeks and Saracens', in V. Karageorghis (ed.), *Acts of the International Symposium 'Cyprus between the Orient and the Occident'* (Nicosia: Department of Antiquities): 505–19.

Meritt, B.D. (1931), *Corinth VIII: Greek inscriptions, 1896–1927* (Cambridge, MA: American School of Classical Studies at Athens).

Messina, A. and Di Stefano, G. (1997), 'I villaggi bizantini degli Iblei (Sicilia)', in S, Gelichi (ed.), *I Congresso nazionale di archeologia medievale: auditorium del Centro studi della Cassa di risparmio di Pisa (ex Benedettine): Pisa, 29–31 maggio 1997* (Florence: All'insegna del giglio): 116–19.

Metaxas, S. (2012), 'Zur materiellen Kultur des byzantinischen Sizilien', in B. Böhlendorf-Arslan and A. Ricci (eds), *Byzantine Small Finds in Archaeological Contexts* (Istanbul: Ege Yayınları): 39–48.

Metcalf, D.M. (1962), 'The Aegean coastlands under threat: Some coins and coin hoards from the reign of Heraclius', *Annual of the British School at Athens* 57: 14–23.

Metcalf, D.M. (2001), 'Monetary recession in the Middle Byzantine period: The numismatic evidence', *The Numismatic Chronicle* 161: 111–55.

Metcalf, D.M. and Pitsillides, A.G. (1992), 'Studies of the Lusignan coinage IV: The Kormakiti Hoard of 1961', *Epetēris* 19: 66–88.

Meyer, C. (1988), 'Glass from the North Theater Byzantine Church, and soundings at Jerash, Jordan, 1982–1983', in W.E. Rast (ed.), *Preliminary Reports of ASOR-Sponsored Excavations, 1982-85* (Baltimore, MD: BASOR Supplementary Series No. 25): 175–222.

Mijatev, K. (1937), *Preslavskata keramika* (Sofia: Staatsdruckerei).

Millett, M. (1991), 'Pottery: Population or supply patterns? The "Ager Tarraconensis" approach', in C. Haselgrove and M. Millett (eds), *Roman Landscapes: Archaeological survey in the Mediterranean region* (London: British School at Rome): 18–28.

Mirguet, C. (2009), 'Microscanning XRF, XANES, and XRD studies of the decorated surface of Roman terra sigillata ceramics', https://escholarship.org/uc/item/5j79x3c7 [accessed October 18, 2014]

Molinari, A. (1994), 'Il popolamento rurale in Sicilia tra V e x VIII secolo: alcuni spunti di riflessione', in R. Francovich and G. Noyé (eds), *La storia dell'alto Medioevo italiano (VI–X secolo) alla luce dell'archeologia: convegno internazionale (Siena, 2–6 dicembre 1992)* (Florence: All'insegna del giglio): 361–77.

Molla, N., Paris, M.F. and Venturini, F. (2013), 'Material boundaries: The city walls at Butrint', in I.L. Hansen, R. Hodges and S. Leppard (eds), *Butrint 4: The archaeology and histories of an Ionian town* (Oxford: Oxbow Books): 260–79.

Mommsen, Th. (1942), 'Petrarch's conception of the Dark Ages', *Speculum* 17: 226–42.

Morgan, C.H. (1939), 'Excavations at Corinth, 1938', *American Journal of Archaeology* 43: 255–67.

Morgan, C.H. (1942), *Corinth XI: The Byzantine pottery* (Cambridge, MA: American School of Classical Studies at Athens).

Morrisson, C. (1994), *Monnaie et finances à Byzance: Analyses, techniques* (Aldershot: Ashgate).

Morrisson, C. (2002), 'Byzantine money: Its production and circulation', in A. Laiou (ed.), *The Economic History of Byzantium* (Washington, DC: Dumbarton Oaks): 909–66.

Morrisson, C., Popović, V. and Ivanišević, V. (2006), *Les trésors monétaires byzantins des Balkans et d'Asie Mineure (491–713)* (Paris: Lethielleux).

Mundell Mango, M. (2001), 'Beyond the amphora: Non-ceramic evidence for late antique industry and trade', in S. Kingsley and M. Decker (eds), *Economy and Exchange in the East Mediterranean during Late Antiquity* (Oxford: Oxbow): 87–106.

Mundell Mango, M. (ed.) (2009a), *Byzantine Trade, 4th–12th Centuries: The archaeology of local, regional, and international exchange* (Farnham: Ashgate).

Mundell Mango, M. (2009b), 'Tracking Byzantine silver and copper metalware, 4th–12th centuries', in M. Mundell Mango (ed.), *Byzantine Trade, 4th–12th Centuries: The archaeology of local, regional, and international exchange* (Farnham: Ashgate): 221–36.

Mundell Mango, M. and Boyd, S. (1993), *Ecclesiastical Silver Plate in Sixth-century Byzantium* (Washington, DC: Dumbarton Oaks).

Muthesius, A. (1989), 'Silks and saints: The Rider and Peacock silks from the relics of St. Cuthbert', in G. Bonner, D.W. Rollason and C.E. Stancliffe (eds), *St. Cuthbert, His Cult and His Community to AD 1200* (Woodbridge, UK: Boydell Press): 343–66.

Muthesius, A. (1993), 'The Byzantine silk industry: Lopez and beyond', *Journal of Medieval History* 19: 1–67.

Muthesius, A. (1997), *Byzantine Silk Weaving: AD 400 to AD 1200* (Vienna: Fassbaender).

Mylona, D. (2005), 'The animal bones from Pyrgouthi in the Berbati Valley', in J. Hjohlman, A. Penttinen, B. Wells and I. Basiakos (eds), *Pyrgouthi: A rural site in the Berbati Valley from the Early Iron Age to Late Antiquity. Excavations by the Swedish Institute at Athens, 1995 and 1997* (Stockholm: Swedish Institute at Athens): 301–8.

Naylor, J. (2007), 'The circulation of early-medieval European coinage: A case study from Yorkshire, c. 650–c. 867', *Medieval Archaeology* 51: 41–61.

Nesbitt, J., Oikonomidès, N. and McGeer, E. (1991–2009), *Catalogue of Byzantine Seals at Dumbarton Oaks and in the Fogg Museum of Art* (Washington, DC: Dumbarton Oaks).

Niewöhner, P. (2006), 'Aizanoi and Anatolia: Town and countryside in late antiquity', *Millennium* 3: 239–53.

Niewöhner, P., Dikilitaş, G., Erkul, E., Giese, S., Gorecki, J., Prochaska, W., Sarı, D., Stümpel, H., Vardar, A., Waldner, A., Walser, A.V. and Woith, H. (2013), 'Bronze Age höyüks, Iron Age hilltop forts, Roman poleis and Byzantine pilgrimage in Germia and its vicinity: "Connectivity" and a lack of "definite places" on the central Anatolian high plateau', *Anatolian Studies* 63: 97–136.

Noce, C. (2006), *I Canoni dei concili della Chiesa antica: I. I concili Greci* (Rome: Institutum Patristicum Augustinianum).

Nystazopoulou-Pelekidou, M. (1986), 'Les Slaves dans l'Empire byzantin', in *The 17th International Byzantine Congress, major papers*, Dumbarton Oaks/Georgetown University, Washington, DC, 3–8 August 1986 (New Rochelle, NY: Aristide D. Caratzas): 345–67.

Obolensky, D. (1971) *The Byzantine Commonwealth: Eastern Europe, 500–1453* (New York: Praeger).

Oikonomides, N. (1986), 'Silk trade and production in Byzantium from the sixth to the ninth century: The Seals of Kommerkiarioi', *Dumbarton Oaks Papers* 40: 33–53.

Omura, S. (1998), 'An archaeological survey of Central Anatolia (1995)', in M. Takahito (ed.), *Essays on Ancient Anatolia in the Second Millennium B.C.* (Wiesbaden: Harrasowitz): 78–132.

Omura, S. (2007), 'Preliminary report on the general survey in central Anatolia (2006)', *Kaman-Kalehöyuk* 16: 45–84.

Omura, S. (2008), 'Preliminary report of the general survey in central Anatolia (2007)', *Kaman-Kalehöyuk* 17: 45–92.

Orsi, P. (1942), *Sicilia Bizantina* (Catania: Brancato).

Ostrogorsky, G. (1929), 'Die wirtschaftlichen und sozialen Entwicklungsgrundlagen des byzantinischen Reiches', *Vierteljahrschrift für Sozial- und Wirtschaftsgeschichte* 22: 129–43.

Ostrogorsky, G. (1941), 'Agrarian conditions in the Byzantine Empire in the Middle Ages', in J.H. Clapham and E. Power (eds), *The Cambridge*

Economic History: The agrarian life of the Middle Ages (Cambridge: Cambridge University Press): 194–223.

Ostrogorsky, G. (1959), 'Byzantine cities in the Early Middle Ages', *Dumbarton Oaks Papers* 13: 45–66.

Ostrogorsky, G. (1969), *History of the Byzantine State* (New Brunswick, NJ: Rutgers University Press).

Özsait-Kocabaş, I. (2011), 'The Yenikapı 12 shipwreck: A local trading vessel from the Middle Byzantine period', *Skyllis: Zeitschrift für Unterwasserarchäologie* 11: 60–63.

Özsait-Kocabaş, I. and Kocabaş, U. (2008), 'Technological and constructional features of Yenikapı shipwrecks: A preliminary evaluation', in U. Kocabaş (ed.), *The Old Ships of the 'New Gate'* (Istanbul: Ege Yayınları): 97–186.

Özyiğit, Ö. (1989), '1989 yili Phokaia kazi çalişmalari', in *XII Sonuçlari Toplantisi I* (Ankara: Anitlar ve Müzeler Genel Müdürlügü): 127–153.

Özyiğit, Ö. (1992), '1990 yili Phokaia kazi çalişmalari', in *XII Sonuçlari Toplantisi II* (Ankara: Anitlar ve Müzeler Genel Müdürlügü): 99–122.

Pagano, M. (1992), 'Recherches sur l'aqueduc Romain de Gortyne (Crete)', in G. Argoud, L. Marankou, V. Panagiotopoulos and C. Villain-Gandossi (eds), *L' eau et les hommes en Méditerranée et en Mer Noire dans l'antiquité de l'époque mycénienne au règne de Justinien: actes de congrès international, Athénes, 20–24 mai 1988* (Athens: CNRS): 279–92.

Pallas, D.I. (1976), 'Anaskaphike tes basilikes tou Kraneiou en Korintho', *Praktika tes en Athenais Archaiologikes Hetaireias* 131: 163–95.

Pallas, D.I. (1977), *Les monuments paléochrétiens de Grèce découverts de 1959 à 1973* (Vatican City: Pontificio Istituto di archeologia Cristiana).

Papavasileiou, E., Sarantidis, K. and Papanikolaou, E. (2014), 'A ceramic workshop of the early Byzantine period on the island of Lipsi in the Dodecanese (Greece): A preliminary approach', in N. Poulou-Papadimitriou, E. Nodarou and V. Kilikoglou (eds), *LRCW 4: Late Roman coarse wares, cooking wares and amphorae in the Mediterranean: Archaeology and archaeometry. The Mediterranean: A market without frontiers* (Oxford: Archaeopress): 159–68.

Patlagean, E. (1977), *Pauvreté économique et pauvreté sociale à Byzance, 4e–7e siècles* (Paris: Mouton).

Parović-Pešikan, M. (1971), 'Excavations of a Late Roman villa at Sirmium, Part 1', *Sirmium* 2: 15-50.

Pelagatti, P. and Di Stefano, G. (1999), *Kaukana: il chorion bizantino* (Palermo: Regione Siciliana, Assessorato ai beni culturali ed ambientali).

Périn, P. (2005), 'La vaisselle de bronze dit "coptes" dans les royaumes romano-germaniques d'Occident. Etat de la question', *Antiquité Tardive* 13: 85-97.

Petridis, P. (2007a), 'Relations between pottery workshops in the Greek mainland during the Early Byzantine period', in B. Böhlendorf-Arslan, A. Uysal and J. Witte-Orr (eds), *Çanak: Late antique and medieval pottery and tiles in Mediterranean archaeological contexts* (Istanbul: Ege Yayınları): 43-54.

Petridis, P. (2007b), 'Pottery and society in the ceramic production centre of Late Roman Delphi', *Rei Cretariae Romanae Fautorum Acta* 42: 15-22.

Pettegrew, D.K. (2002), 'Chasing the classical farmstead: Assessing the formation and signature of rural settlement in Greek landscape archaeology', *Journal of Mediterranean Archaeology* 14: 189-209.

Pettegrew, D.K. (2006), *Corinth on the Isthmus: Studies of the end of an ancient landscape* (PhD dissertation, The Ohio State University).

Pettegrew, D.K. (2007), 'The busy countryside of Late Roman Corinth: Interpreting ceramic data produced by regional archaeological surveys', *Hesperia* 76: 743-84.

Pieri, D. (2012), 'Regional and interregional exchanges in the Eastern Mediterranean during the early Byzantine period: The evidence of the amphorae', in C. Morrisson (ed.), *Trade and Markets in Byzantium* (Washington, DC: Dumbarton Oaks): 27-49.

Pirenne, H. (1937), *Mahomet et Charlemagne* (Paris: Nouvelle Societé d'éditions).

Poblome, J. (1999), *Sagalassos Red Slip Ware: Typology and chronology* (Turnhout, Belgium: Brepols).

Poblome, J. and Firat, N. (2011), 'Late Roman D: A matter of open(ing) or closed horizons?', in M. Ontiveros, P. Reynolds and M. Bonifay (eds), *LRFW 1: Late Roman fine wares: Solving problems of typology and chronology. A review of the evidence, debate and new contexts* (Oxford: Archaeopress): 49-55.

Poirier, J. (1985), 'Aureus obryziacus', in C. Morrrisson, J.-P. Callu, X. Loriot and C. Brenot (eds), *L'or monnayé 1: Purification et alterations de Rome à Byzance* (Paris: CNRS Editions): 81–96.

Porath, J. (2002), 'The water-supply of Caesarea: A reassessment', in D. Amit, Y. Hirschfeld and J. Patrich (eds), *The Aqueducts of Israel* (Portsmouth, RI: JRA Supplementary Series No. 46): 104–29.

Postan, M. and Rich, E.E. (eds) (1952), *The Cambridge Economic History of Europe from the Decline of the Roman Empire, Vol. II: Trade and industry in the Middle Ages* (Cambridge: Cambridge University Press).

Poulou-Papadimitriou, N. (2001), 'Byzantine keramike apo ton elleniko nesiotiko choro kai apo ten Peloponneso (7os–9 os ai.): mia prote prosengise', in. E. Kountoura-Galake (ed.), *The Dark Centuries of Byzantium (7th–9th c.)* (Athens: Ethniko Hidryma Ereunon): 231–66.

Poulou-Papadimitriou, N. and Didioumi, S. (2010), 'Nouvelles données sur la production de l'atelier céramique protobyzantin à Kardamaina (Cos–Grèce)', in S. Menchelli, S. Santoro, M. Pasquinucci and G. Giuducci (eds), *LRCW 3: Late Roman coarse wares, cooking wares and amphorae in the Mediterranean: Archaeology and archaeometry: Comparison between western and eastern Mediterranean* (Oxford: Archaeopress): 741–49.

Poulou-Papadimitriou, N., Tzavella, E. and Ott, J. (2012), 'Burial practices in Byzantine Greece: Archaeological evidence and methodological problems for its interpretation', in M. Salamon, M. Wołoszyn, A. Musin and P. Špehar (eds), *Rome, Constantinople and Newly-converted Europe: Archaeological and historical evidence* (Krakow: Geisteswissenschaftliches Zentrum Geschichte und Kultur Ostmitteleuropas): 377–428.

Poulou-Papadimitriou, N., Nodarou E. and Kilikoglou, V. (eds) (2014), *LRCW 4: Late Roman coarse wares, cooking wares and amphorae in the Mediterranean: Archaeology and archaeometry. The Mediterranean: A market without frontiers* (Oxford: Archaeopress).

Poulter, A.G. (2002), 'From city to fortress and from town to country: 15 years of Anglo-Bulgarian collaboration', in L. Ruseva-Slokoska, R.T. Ivanov and V. Dinchev (eds), *The Roman and Late Roman City*, The International Conference, Veliko Turnovo, 26–30 July 2000 (Sofia: Prof. Marin Drinov Academic Publishing House): 14–29.

Poulter, A.G. (2007a), 'The transition to late antiquity on the Lower Danube: The city, a fort, and the countryside', in A.G. Poulter (ed.), *The Transition to Late Antiquity: On the Danube and beyond* (Oxford: British Academy): 51–100.

Poulter, A.G. (2007b), 'Site-specific field survey: The methodology', in A.G. Poulter (ed.), *The Transition to Late Antiquity: On the Danube and beyond* (Oxford: British Academy): 583–96.

Poulter, A.G. (ed.) (2007c), *The Transition to Late Antiquity: On the Danube and beyond* (Oxford: British Academy).

Raab, H.A. (2001), *Rural Settlement in Hellenistic and Roman Crete: The Akrotiri Peninsula* (Oxford: Archaeopress).

Rasch, B. and Seyer, M. (1998), 'Die Grabungen in der Nordweststadt', in J. Borchhardt et al. 'Grabungen und Forschungen in Limyra aus den Jahren 1991–1996', *Jahreshefte des Österreichischen Archäologischen Institutes in Wien* 66: 345–48.

Ratté, C.J. and De Staebler, P.D. (2012), *The Aphrodisias Regional Survey* (Darnstadt: Zabern).

Rautman, M. (1998), 'Handmade pottery and social change: The view from Late Roman Cyprus', *Journal of Mediterranean Archaeology* 11: 81–104.

Rautman, M. (2003), *A Cypriot Village of Late Antiquity: Kavalassos-Kopetra in the Vasilikos Valley* (Portsmouth, RI: JRA Supplementary Series No. 52).

Rautman, M. (2005), 'The villages of Byzantine Cyprus', in J. Lefort, C. Morrisson and J.-P. Sodini (eds), *Les villages dans l'empire byzantin, IVe–XVe siècle* (Paris: Lethielleux): 453–63.

Renfrew, C. and Wagstaff, J.M. (eds) (1982), *An Island Polity: The archaeology of exploitation in Melos* (Cambridge: Cambridge University Press).

Reynolds, P. (1995), *Trade in the Western Mediterranean, AD 400–700: The ceramic evidence* (Oxford: Tempus).

Reynolds, P. (2010a), *Hispania in the Roman Mediterranean* (London: Duckworth).

Reynolds, P. (2010b), 'Trade networks of the East, 3rd to 7th centuries: The view from Beirut (Lebanon) and Butrint (Albania) (fine wares, amphorae and kitchen wares)', in S. Menchelli, S. Santoro, M. Pasquinucci and

G. Giuducci (eds), *LRCW3: Late Roman coarse wares, cooking wares and amphorae in the Mediterranean: Archaeology and archaeometry: Comparison between western and eastern Mediterranean* (Oxford: Archaeopress): 89–114.

Rheidt, K. (2003), 'Archäologie und Spätantike in Anatolien. Methoden, Ergebnisse und Probleme der Ausgrabungen in Aizanoi', in G. Brands and H.-G. Severin (eds), *Die spätantike Stadt und ihre Christianisierung* (Wiesebaden: Reichert): 239–47.

Richards, P.M. (1980), *Byzantine Bronze Vessels in England and Europe: The origins of Anglo-Saxon trade* (PhD dissertation, Cambridge University).

Riley, J.A. (1979), 'The coarse pottery from Berenice', in J.A. Lloyd (ed.), *Excavations at Sidi Khrebish, Benghazi (Berenice)* (Tripoli: Supplements to Libya Antiqua No. 5): 91–467.

Rizzo, M.S. (2005), 'L'insediamento rurale nella valle del Platani tra Tardoantico e Altomedioeo', *Insulae Diomedeae* 4: 641–47.

Rose, B.C. (2011), 'Troy and the Granicus River valley in late antiquity', in. O. Dally and C. Ratté (eds), *Archaeology and the Cities of Asia Minor in Late Antiquity* (Ann Arbor, MI: Kelsey Museum): 151–72.

Rose, B.C., Tekkök, B. and Körpe, R. (2007), 'Granicus River Valley Survey Project, 2004–2005', *Studia Troica* 17: 65–150.

Rosen, W. (2007), *Justinian's Flea: Plague, empire, and the birth of Europe* (New York: Viking).

Rotman, Y. (2009), *Byzantine Slavery and the Mediterranean World* (Cambridge, MA: Harvard University Press).

Runciman, S. (1940), 'The widow Danelis', in A.M. Andréadès (ed.), *Études dédiées à la mémoire d'André M. Andréadès* (Athens: Pyrsos): 425–31.

Runciman, S. (1952), 'Byzantine trade and industry', in M. Postan and E.E. Rich (eds), *The Cambridge Economic History of Europe from the Decline of the Roman Empire, Vol. II: Trade and industry in the Middle Ages* (Cambridge: Cambridge University Press): 86–118.

Rupp, D.W. (1986), 'Problems in Byzantine field reconnaissance: A non-specialist's view', *Byzantine Studies* 13: 177–88.

Sams, G.K. (1994), *The Gordion Excavations, 1950–1973: Final Reports, Vol. IV: The early Phrygian pottery* (Philadelphia, PA: University Museum).

Sanders, G. (1995), 'Pottery from medieval levels in the orchestra and lower cavea', *Annual of the British School at Athens* 90: 451–57.

Sanders, G. (2003), 'Recent developments in the chronology of Byzantine Corinth', in C.K. Williams and N. Bookidis (eds), *Corinth, Vol. XX: The centenary 1896–1996* (Princeton, NJ: American School of Classical Studies at Athens): 385–99.

Sanders, G. (2004), 'Problems in interpreting rural and urban settlement in southern Greece, AD 365–700', in N. Christie (ed.), *Landscapes of Change: Rural evolutions in late antiquity and the early Middle Ages* (Aldershot: Ashgate): 163–93.

Sarpaki, A. (2005), 'The archaeobotanical material from the site of Pyrgouthi in the Berbati Valley', in J. Hjolhman, A. Penttinen and B. Wells (eds), *Pyrgouthi: A rural site in the Berbati Valley from the Early Iron Age to Late Antiquity: Excavations by the Swedish Institute at Athens, 1995* and 1997 (Stockholm: Paul Åströms): 313–42.

Sarris, P. (2002), 'The Justinianic plague: Origins and effects', *Continuity and Change* 17: 169–82.

Sarris, P. (2006), *Economy and Society in the Age of Justinian* (Cambridge: Cambridge University Press).

Sazanov, A. (1996), 'Les niveaux de la première moitié du XIe siècle à Kerch (Crimée)', *Anatolia Antiqua* 4: 191–200.

Sbeinati, M.R., Darawcheh, R. and Mouty, M. (2005), 'The historical earthquakes of Syria: An analysis of large and moderate earthquakes from 1365 BC to 1900 AD', *Annals of Geophysics* 48: 347–435.

Scanlon, G.T. (1986), 'Review of Richard Hodges and David Whitehouse, Mohammed, Charlemagne & the Origins of Europe: Archaeology and the Pirenne Thesis', *International Journal of Middle East Studies* 18: 545–47.

Schliemann, H. (1874), *Trojanische Alterthümer: Bericht über die Ausgrabungen in Troja* (Leipzig: Brockhaus).

Schliemann, H. (1884), *Troja. Ergebnisse meiner neuesten Ausgrabungen auf der Baustelle von Troja, in den Heldengräbern, Bunarbaschi und andern Orten der Troas im Jahre 1882* (Leipzig: Brockhaus).

Schreiner, P. (2004), 'Diplomatische Geschenke zwischen Byzanz und dem Westen ca. 800–1200: Eine Analyse der Texte mit Quellenanhang', *Dumbarton Oaks Papers* 58: 251–82.

Schulze-Dörrlamm, M. (2010), 'Ungarneinfälle in die Schweiz im Spiegel archäologischer Funde', *Helvetia archaeologica* 41: 13–29.

Scotton, P.D. (1997), *The Julian Basilica at Corinth: An architectural investigation* (PhD dissertation, University of Pennsylvania).

Scranton, R.L. (1957), *Corinth, Vol. XVI: Medieval architecture in the central area of Corinth* (Princeton, NJ: American School of Classical Studies at Athens).

Segal, C. (1981), *Tragedy and Civilization: An interpretation of Sophocles* (Cambridge, MA: Harvard University Press).

Seibt, W. (2002), *Studies in Byzantine Sigillography 7* (Washington, DC: Dumbarton Oaks).

Setton, K.M. (1950), 'The Bulgars in the Balkans and the occupation of Corinth in the seventh century', *Speculum* 25: 502–43.

Setton, K.M. (1952), 'The Emperor Constans II and the capture of Corinth by the Onogur Bulgars', *Speculum* 27: 351–62.

Smith, A. (2007), 'Plant use at Çadır Höyük, Central Anatolia', *Anatolica* 33: 169–84.

Snodgrass, A.M. (1994), 'Response: The archaeological aspect', in I. Morris (ed.), *Classical Greece: Ancient histories and modern archaeologies* (Cambridge: Cambridge University Press): 197–200.

Stathakopoulos, D. (2004), *Famine and Pestilence in the Late Roman and Early Byzantine Empire: A systematic survey of subsistence crises and epidemics* (Aldershot: Ashgate).

Stein, E. (1923–1925), 'Untersuchungen zur spätbyzantinischen Verfassungs- und Wirtschaftsgeschichte', *Mitteilungen zur osmanischen Geschichte* 2: 1–62.

Stevenson, R. (1947), 'The pottery, 1936–37', in G. Brett, W.J. Macaulay and R.B.K. Stevenson (eds), *The Great Palace of the Byzantine Emperors, First Report* (London: Oxford University Press): 31–63.

Stewart, C.A. (2008), *Domes of Heaven: The domed basilicas of Cyprus* (PhD dissertation, Indiana University).

Stewart, C.A. (2010), 'The first vaulted churches in Cyprus', *Journal of the Society of Architectural Historians* 69: 162–89.

Talbot Rice, D. (1928), *The Byzantine Pottery: Preliminary report upon the excavations carried out in the Hippodrome of Constantinople in 1927 on behalf of the British Academy* (London: H. Milford).

Talbot Rice, D. (ed.) (1958), *The Great Palace of the Byzantine Emperors, Second Report* (Edinburgh: Edinburgh University Press).

Talbot Rice, D., Casson, S., Hudson, G.F. and Gray, B. (1929), *Second Report upon the Excavations Carried Out in the Hippodrome of Constantinople in 1928 on Behalf of the British Academy* (London: H. Milford).

Taxel, I. (2011), 'Egyptian coarse ware in Early Islamic Palestine: Between commerce and migration', *Al-Masaq* 23: 77–97.

Tchalenko, G. (1953–1958), *Villages antiques de la Syrie du Nord: Le massif du Bélus a l'époque romaine* (Paris: P. Geuthner).

Thomas, A. (2007a), 'Inter Moesos et Thraces: A contribution to the studies on the rural hinterland of Novae in Lower Moesia', *Archeologia (Warszawa)* 58: 31–47.

Thomas, A. (2007b), 'Municipium Novensium? Report on the field survey at Ostrite Mogili, Veliko Turnovo District', *Światowit* 47: 11–116.

Thomas, T.K. (2012), '"Ornaments of excellence" from "the miserable gains of commerce": Luxury art and Byzantine culture', in H.C. Evans (ed.), *Byzantium and Islam: Age of transition, 7th–9th century* (New York: Metropolitan Museum of Art): 124–33.

TIB (1976–) = *Tabula Imperii Byzantini* (Vienna: Verlag de Österreichischen Akademie der Wissenschaften).

Tite, M.S., Freestone, I., Mason, R., Molera, J., Vendrell-Saz, M. and Wood, N. (1998), 'Lead glazes in antiquity – methods of production and reasons for use', *Archaeometry* 40: 241–60.

Todd, I.A. (1980), *The Prehistory of Central Anatolia I. The Neolithic period* (Gothenburg: Åström).

Tomber, R. (2000), 'Egyptian amphorae in Britain and the western provinces', *Britannia* 31: 41–54.

Tomber, R. (2008), *Indo-Roman Trade: From pots to pepper* (London: Duckworth).

Tougher, S. (1997), *The Reign of Leo VI (886–912): Politics and people* (Leiden: Brill).

Treadgold, W.T. (1983), 'The military lands and the imperial estates in the Middle Byzantine Empire', *Harvard Ukrainian Studies* 7: 619–31.

Treadgold, W.T. (1997), *A History of Byzantine State and Society* (Stanford, CA: Stanford University Press).

Treadgold, W.T. (2013), *The Middle Byzantine Historians* (London: Palgrave).
Tsounkarakes, D. and Chrysos, E.K. (1988), *Byzantine Crete: From the 5th century to the Venetian conquest* (Athens: St. D. Basilopoulos).
Turner, S. and Crow, J. (2010), 'Unlocking historic landscapes in the eastern Mediterranean: Two pilot studies using Historic Landscape Characterisation', *Antiquity* 84: 216–29.
Vaag, L.E. (2008), 'Medieval pottery', in P.G. Bilde, B. Poulsen, S. Sande, L.E. Vaag and J. Zahle, *The Temple of Castor and Pollux II.1: The finds* (Rome: L'Erma di Bretschneider): 213–24.
Vanhaverbeke, H., Martens, F., Waelkens, M. and Poblome, J. (2004), 'Late antiquity in the territory of Sagalassos', in W. Bowden, L. Lavan and C. Machado (eds), *Recent Research on the Late Antique Countryside* (Leiden: Brill): 611–48.
Vanhaverbeke, H., Martens, F. and Waelkens, M. (2007), 'Another view on late antiquity: Sagalassos (SW Anatolia), its suburbium and its countryside in late antiquity', in A.G. Poulter (ed.), *The Transition to Late Antiquity: On the Danube and beyond* (Oxford: British Academy): 611–48.
Vanhaverbeke, H., Vionis, A.K., Poblome, J. and Waelkens, M. (2009), 'What happened after the 7th century AD? A different perspective on post-Roman rural Anatolia', in T. Vorderstrasse and J.J. Roodenberg (eds), *Archaeology of the Countryside in Medieval Anatolia* (Leiden: Nederlands Instituut voor het Nabije Oosten): 177–90.
Vanhaverbeke, H., Degryse, P., De Cupere, B., Van Neer, W., Waelkens, M. and Muchez, P. (2011), 'Urban–rural integration at ancient Sagalassos (SW Turkey): Archaeological, archaeozoological and geochemical evidence', *Archaeofauna* 20: 73–83.
Veikou, M. (2009), '"Rural towns" and "in-between" or "third" spaces: Settlement patterns in Byzantine Epirus (7th–11th c.) from an interdisciplinary approach', *Archaeologia Medievale* 36: 43–54.
Veikou, M. (2010), 'Urban or rural? Theoretical remarks on the settlement patterns in Byzantine Epirus (7th–11th centuries)', *Byzantinische Zeitschrift* 103: 171–93.
Veikou, M. (2012), *Byzantine Epirus: A topography of transformation. Settlements of the seventh–twelfth centuries in southern Epirus and Aetoloacarnania, Greece* (Leiden: Brill).

Veikou, M. (2013), 'Settlements in the Greek countryside from the 4th to 9th century: Forms and patterns', *Antiquité Tardive* 21: 125–33.

Verzone, P. (1965), 'Hierapolis christiana', *Corsi di cultura sull'arte ravennate e bizantina* 12: 613–27.

Vida, T. and Völling, T. (2000), *Das slawische Brandgräberfeld von Olympia* (Rahden: Marie Leidorf).

Vikatou, O. (2002), 'To christianiko nekrotapheio sten Agia Triada Heleias. Symbole ste melete tes cheiropoietes keramikes', in P.G. Themelis and V. Konti (eds), *Protobyzantine Messene kai Olympia. Aktikos kai agrotikos choros ste Dytike Peloponneso. Praktika tou Deithnous symposiou, Athena, 29–30 maiou 1998* (Athens: Hetaireia Messeniakon Arkhaiologikon Spoudon/Instituoto Byzantinon Ereunon): 238–70.

Vionis, A.K. (2013), 'Pottery and social dynamics in the Mediterranean and beyond in medieval and post-medieval times', in J. Bintliff and M. Caroscio (eds), *Pottery and Social Dynamics in the Mediterranean and Beyond in Medieval and Post-Medieval Times* (Oxford: Archaeopress): 25–40.

Vionis, A.K., Poblome, J. and Waelkens, M. (2009), 'Ceramic continuity and daily life in medieval Sagalassos, SW Anatolia', in T. Vorderstrasse and J.J. Roodenberg (eds), *Archaeology of the Countryside in Medieval Anatolia* (Leiden: Nederlands Instituut voor het Nabije Oosten): 191–213.

Vladkova, P. (2007), 'The late Roman agora and the state of civic organization', in A.G. Poulter (ed.), *The Transition to Late Antiquity: On the Danube and beyond* (Oxford: British Academy): 203–18.

Völling, T. (1995), 'Ein frühbyzantinischer Hortfund aus Olympia', *Mitteilungen des Deutschen Archäologischen Instituts. Athenische Abteilung* 110: 425–59.

Völling, T. (2001), 'The last Christian Greeks and the first pagan Slavs in Olympia', in E. Kountoura-Galake (ed.), *The Dark Centuries of Byzantium (7th–9th c.)* (Athens: Ethniko Hidryma Ereunon): 302–23.

Völling, T. (2002), 'Early Byzantine agricultural implements from Olympia (5th/6th centuries AD)', in P.G. Themelis and V. Konti (eds), *Protobyzantine Messene kai Olympia. Aktikos kai agrotikos choros ste Dytike Peloponneso. Praktika tou Diethnous symposiou* (Athens: Hetaireia Messeniakon Archaiologikon Spudon): 195–207.

von Saldern, A. (1962), 'Glass from Sardis', *American Journal of Archaeology* 66: 5–12.

Vorderstrasse, T. and Roodenberg. J. (eds.) (2009), *Archaeology of the Countryside in Medieval Anatolia* (Leiden: Nederlands Instituut voor het Nabije Oosten).

Vroom, J. (1998), 'Medieval and post-Medieval pottery from a site in Boeotia: A case study example of post-classical archaeology in Greece,' *Annual of the British School at Athens* 93: 513–46.

Vroom, J. (2003), *After Antiquity: Ceramics and society in the Aegean from the 7th to 20th century AC. A case study from Boeotia, Central Greece* (Leiden: Leiden University Press).

Vroom, J. (2004), 'Late antique pottery, settlement and trade in the East Mediterranean: A preliminary comparison of ceramics from Limyra (Lycia) and Boeotia', in W. Bowden, L. Lavan and C. Machado (eds), *Recent Research on the Late Antique Countryside* (Leiden: Brill): 281–331.

Vroom, J. (2005a), *Byzantine to Modern Pottery in the Aegean, 7th–20th Century: An introduction and field guide* (Utrecht: Parnassus Press).

Vroom, J. (2005b), 'New light on "Dark Age" pottery: A note on finds from south-western Turkey', *Rei Cretariae Romanae Fautorum Acta* 39: 249–55.

Vroom, J. (2007), 'Limyra in Lycia: Byzantine/Umayyad pottery finds from excavations in the eastern part of the city', in S. Lemaître (ed.), *Céramiques antiques en Lycie (VIIe S. a.C. – VII S. p.C.) Les produits et les marches* (Bordeaux: Ausonius): 261–92.

Vroom, J. (2008), 'Dishing up history', *Melanges de l'ecole Française de Rome-Serie Moyen Age* 120: 291–305.

Vryonis, S. (1963), 'An attic hoard of Byzantine coins (668–741) from the Thomas Whittemore Collection and the numismatic evidence for the urban history of Byzantium', *Zbornik radova Vizantoloskog instituta* 8: 291–300.

Vryonis, S. (1992), 'The Slavic pottery (jars) from Olympia, Greece', in S. Vryonis, Jr. (ed.), *Byzantine Studies: Essays on the Slavic world and the eleventh century* (New Rochelle: Aristide D. Caratzas): 15–42.

Waelkens, M., Vannhaverbeke, H., Martens, F., Talloen, P., Poblome, J., Kellens, N., Putzeys, T., Degryse, P., Van Thuyne, T. and Van Neer, W. (2006), 'The late antique to early Byzantine city in southwest Anatolia.

Sagalassos and its territory: A case study', in J.-U. Krause and C. Witschel (eds), *Die Stadt in der Spätanike – Niedergang oder Wandel?* (Stuttgart: Franz Steiner): 199–255.

Wagner, D.M., Klunk, J., Harbeck, M., Devault, A., Waglechner, N., Sahl, J.W., Enk, J., Birdsell, D.N., Kuch, M., Lumibao, C., Polnar, D., Pearson, T., Fourment, M., Golding, B., Riehm, J.M., Earn, D.J., Dewitte, S., Rouillard, J.M., Grupe, G., Wiechmann, I., Bliska, J.B., Kelm, P.S., Scholz, H.C., Holmes, E.C. and Poinar, H. (2014), 'Yersinia pestis and the plague of Justinian 541–543 AD: A genomic analysis', *The Lancet Infectious Diseases* 14: 319–26.

Walmsley, A. (2007), *Early Islamic Syria: An archaeological assessment* (London: Duckworth).

Ward-Perkins, B. (2001), 'Reponses', in L. Lavan (ed.), *Recent Research in Late-Antique Urbanism* (Portsmouth, RI: JRA Supplementary Series No. 42): 233–45.

Ward-Perkins, B. (2005), *The Fall of Rome and the End of Civilization* (Oxford: Oxford University Press).

Warner Slane, K. and Sanders, G.D.R. (2005), 'Corinth: Late Roman horizons', *Hesperia* 74: 234–97.

Watson, P.M. (1995), 'Ceramic evidence for Egyptian links with northern Jordan in the 6th–8th centuries AD', in S. Bourke and J.-P. Descoeudres (eds), *Trade, Contact, and the Movements of Peoples in the Eastern Mediterranean* (Sydney: Meditarch): 303–24.

Weinberg, G.D. (1974), 'A wandering soldier's grave in Corinth', *Hesperia* 43: 512–21.

Weiner, A. and Schneider, J. (1989), *Cloth and the Human Experience* (Washington, DC: Smithsonian Institution Press).

Werner, J. (1957), 'Zwei gegossene koptische bronzeflaschen aus salona', *Bulletin d'archéologie et d'histoire dalmate* 59: 115–28.

Werner, J. (1961), 'Fernhandel und Naturalwirtschaft im östlichen Merowingerreich nach archäologischen und numismatischen Zeugnissen', *Bericht der Römisch-Germanischen Kommission* 42: 307–46.

Whitby, M. and Whitby, M. (1986), *The History of Theophylact Simocatta: An English translation with introduction* (Oxford: Oxford University Press).

Whittow, M. (1990), 'Ruling the Late Roman and Early Byzantine city: A continuous history', *Past & Present* 129: 3–29.

Whittow, M. (2001), 'Responses', in L. Lavan (ed.), *Recent Research in Late-Antique Urbanism* (Portsmouth, RI: JRA Supplementary Series No. 42): 233–45.

Wickham, C. (2005), *Framing the Early Middle Ages: Europe and the Mediterranean 400–800* (New York: Oxford University Press).

Wilkinson, T.J. (1982), 'The definition of ancient manured zones by means of extensive sherd-sampling techniques', *Journal of Field Archaeology* 9: 223–33.

Williams, C. (1977), 'A Byzantine well-deposit from Anemurium (Rough Cilicia)', *Anatolian Studies* 27: 175–90.

Williams, C.K. (1993), 'Roman Corinth as a commercial center', in T.E. Gregory (ed.), *The Corinthia in the Roman Period, including the papers given at a symposium held at The Ohio State University on 7–9 March, 1991* (Ann Arbor, MI: JRA).

Wilson, A.I. (2013), 'The aqueduct of Butrint', in I.L. Hansen, R. Hodges and S. Leppard (eds), *Butrint 4: The archaeology and histories of an Ionian town* (Oxford: Oxbow Books): 77–96.

Winther-Jacobsen, K. (2010), 'The classical farmstead revisited: Activity differentiation based on a ceramic use-typology', *Annual of the British School at Athens* 105: 269–90.

Yannopoulos, P. (1978), *L'hexagramme: Un monnayage byzantine en argent du Vie siècle* (Louvain-la-Neuve: Institut supérieur d'archéologie et d'histoire de l'art, Séminaire de numismatique Marcel Hoc).

Zaccaria Ruggiu, A. (2007), 'Regio VIII, insula 104. Le strutture abitative: fase e trasformazioni', in F. D'Andria and M.P. Caggia (eds), *Hierapolis di Frigia I. Le attività delle champagne di scavo e restauro 2000–2003* (Istanbul: Ege Yayınları), 211–56.

Zacos, G., Veglery, A. and Nesbitt, J.W. (1972–1985), *Byzantine Lead Seals* (Basel/Glückstadt: J.J. Augustin).

Zagari, F. (2005), 'Il vasellame bronzeo dell'inizio dell'epoca bizantina: l'Italia: Riflessiono e storia degli studi', *Antiquité Tardive* 13: 105–13.

Zanini, E. (2009), 'La ceramica del Quartiere Bizantino del Pythion di Gortina (Creta): qualche appunto per un approccio riflessivo', *Facta* 3: 75–88.

Zanini, E. and Costa, S. (2011), 'Ceramica e contesti nel Quartiere Bizantino del Pythion di Gortina (Creta): alla ricerca della "complessità" nella datazione', in M. Ontiveros, P. Reynolds and M. Bonifay (eds), *LRFW 1: Late Roman fine wares: Solving problems of typology and chronology. A review of the evidence, debate and new contexts* (Oxford: Archaeopress): 33–44.

Zanini, E., Costa, S., Giorgi, E. and Triolo, E. (2009), 'Indagini archeologiche nell'area del quartiere bizantino del Pythion di Gortyna: quinta relazione preliminare (campagne 2007–2010), *Annuario della Scuola archeologica di Atene e delle missioni italiane in Oriente* 87: 1099–1129.

Zavagno, L. (2009), *Cities in Transition: Urbanism in Byzantium between Late Antiquity and the Early Middle Ages* (Oxford: Archaeopress).

Index

Acropolis Basilica, 93, 95
African red slip ware, 45–7
Agrarian Life of the Middle Ages, 29–30
Aizanoi, 145–6
Albanian Treasure, 168–9
Alexandria, 16
Amorian dynasty, 24
Amorium
  bathhouses, 111–12
  ceramic production, 173–4
  churches, 109, 111
  city walls, 109
  coins, 112
  glazed pottery, 59
  introduction, 108–9
  plan, 110
  resettlement, 113
  sacking by caliph al-Mu'tasim (838–42), 112–13
  water, 112
Amphorae
  Byzantine Globular Amphorae, 177–8
  generally, 175–80
  Günsenin type 1 amphorae, 179–80
Anatolia. *See also* Amorium; Hierapolis
  environment, 149–50
  field surveys, 141–2
Andréadès, 29
Anemurium, 53
Animal bone items, 78
Anthropology, 32–3
Aphrodisias, 144–5
Apollonia, 142
Aqueducts, 84
Archaeology. *See also* Evidence
  anthropology, 32–3

Austrian Academy of Sciences, 35
  Corinth excavation, 33
  excavations, 33–4
  Foss, Clive, 34
  generally, 28, 30–2, 36
  Hendy, Michael, 36
  historiographical and anthropological approaches, 35
  Marxist approaches, 35
  Morrisson, Cécile, 35
  New Archaeology, 36
  Oxford Companion to Archaeology, 34
  Patlagean, Évelyne, 35
  periodization, 37
  Tabula Imperii Byzantinii, 36
  Turkey, 36–7
Armstrong, Pamela, 58–9
Artefacts, 126
Arthur, Paul, 172
Asia Minor. *See* Anatolia
Austrian Academy of Sciences, 35
Avar Treasure, 168–9
Avaro-Slavic Ware, 62–3
Avni, Gideon, 128

Balboura, 149
Balkans. *See also* Butrint; Corinth; Nicopolis ad Istrum
  ceramic production, 172–3
  excavations, 87–8
  field surveys, 129–30
  historical overview, 9, 16–17
Bathhouses, 111–12
Bema church, 106
Beyşehir Occupation Phase, 149–50
Bone items, 78
Brentano, Lujo, 28
Buckles, 170–1
Bulgars, 21, 23

Burials, 103–4. *See also* Coptic wares
Bury's *Cambridge Medieval History*, 28
Butrint
    Acropolis Basilica, 93, 95
    ceramic production, 173
    churches, 93, 95
    city centre, 96
    city walls, 95
    construction, 93
    earthquakes, 93, 95
    evidence, 96–8
    facilities, 92–3
    glazed pottery, 59–60
    introduction, 92–3
    lower city, 96
    maps, 94, 97
    Merchant's House, 96
    St. Elias the Younger, 97–8
    Triconch Palace, 96
Byzantine Globular Amphorae, 177–8
Byzantine studies, 12–14. *See also* Dark Age research
Byzantium, 86–7

Caliphate, 18, 20
Cambridge Economic History, 29–30
Cappadocia, 152–4
Central Anatolian Survey, 146
Ceramic production
    Amorium, 173–4
    amphorae, 175–80
    Arthur, Paul, 172
    Balkans, 172–3
    Butrint, 173
    Byzantine Globular Amphorae, 177–8
    forms, 173–4
    Günsenin type 1 amphorae, 179–80
    handmade ceramics, 172
    introduction, 171–3
    Kos, 176–7
    lamps, 174
    red slip ware, 174–5
    regional exchange patterns, 179
    regional manufacture, 175–6
Ceramics. *See also* Glazed pottery; Red slip ware
    Corinth, 102
    field surveys, 146–7
    introduction, 43–5
Charlemagne, 165–6
Churches and cathedrals
    Amorium, 109, 111
    Bema church, 106
    Butrint, 93, 95
    Corinth, 104–5
    field surveys, 147
    Hierapolis, 116–18
    Nicopolis ad Istrum, 91
    St. Kodratos Church, 105
Cities. *See also* Amorium; Butrint; Corinth; Hierapolis; Nicopolis ad Istrum
    aqueducts, 84
    Byzantium, 86–7
    Constantinople, 87
    elite culture, 82, 84
    facilities, 82–3
    Foss, Clive, 87
    introduction, 81–2
    Kennedy, Hugh, 85–6
    Liebeschuetz, Wolf, 84–5
    Muslims, 86
    religion, 83
    Roman cities, 81–2
    Roman Empire decline, 84–5
    summary, 120–2
    urban decline, 84–6
City walls
    Amorium, 109
    Butrint, 95
Cloth
    evidence, 78–77
    silk, 165–6
Coarse wares, 61–2
Coins
    Amorium, 112
    archaeology, 66–7, 70–2

coin types, 69–70
dating of sites, 67
economic activity, 67–9, 71–2
economy, 158–60
introduction, 65–6
minting locations, 68–9
production and metals, 69–70
Collaboration, 189–91
Constans II, 18
Constantine IV, 18–19
Constantine V, 21
Constantinople
  cities, 87
  hard-to-track goods, 162, 164–5
  historical overview, 10, 20
Constantinopolitan Glazed White
  Ware, 55–7
Copper objects, 169–70
Copper vessels, 75
Coptic wares
  Coptic bowls, 74–6
  hard-to-track goods, 170
Corinth
  archaeology, 33
  Bema church, 106
  burials, 103–4
  ceramic studies, 102
  churches, 104–5
  evidence, 102–3
  fourth/fifth century remodelling, 100
  introduction, 98, 100
  location and size, 98
  maps and plans, 99, 101, 107
  rural areas, 106, 108
  sacking by Slavs (584), 103–4
  Scranton, Robert L., 102–3
  sixth century occupation, 100, 102
  St. Kodratos Church, 105
Countryside
  Aizanoi, 145–6
  Anatolia, 141–2, 149–50
  Aphrodisias, 144–5
  Apollonia, 142
  artefacts, 126

Avni, Gideon, 128
Balboura, 149
Balkans, 129–30
Beyşehir Occupation Phase, 149–50
Cappadocia, 152–4
Central Anatolian Survey, 146
churches, 147
Crete, 140–1
Cyprus, 131, 139–40
data interpretation, 126–7
diet, 148
environment, 148–54
farming, 148
field surveys, 124–48
Foss, Clive, 142–3
Gortyn, 140–1
Greece, 134–6
Haldon, John, 149–50
introduction, 123–4
Israel, 128
Kaukana, 138–9
large-scale surveys, 128–9
Lycia, 142–3
Olympia, 135–6
Orsi, Paolo, 138
Pettigrew, Richard M., 132
Pisidia, 144
pollen analysis, 149–53
pottery, 146–7
Pyrgouthi, 136–7
Sagalassos, 144, 151–2
Sanders, Guy, 133
settlement activity and density, 130–1
Sicily, 138
site classifications, 125–6
Supersano, 137
surface finds, 133
survey methodologies, 127–8
Vrina Plain, 137–8
Vroom, Joanita, 132
Crete, 140–1
Cultural relativism, 38–9
Cypriot cooking pot, 64

Cypriot red slip ware, 47–8, 51
Cyprus, 131, 139–40

Danelis, 164–5
Dark Age research. *See also* Archaeology
   Agrarian Life of the Middle Ages, 29–30
   Andréadès, 29
   Brentano, Lujo, 28
   Bury's *Cambridge Medieval History*, 28
   Byzantine studies, 12–14
   Cambridge Economic History, 29–30
   economy, 28–9
   introduction, 28–9
   Macri, 28
   Ostrogorsky, George, 28–30
   Pirenne, Henri, 28
   Pirenne Thesis, 30
   political economy, 28–9
   Runciman, Steven, 30
Dark Ages of Byzantium (general)
   collaboration, 189–91
   definitions, 1, 194
   economy, 193
   elite culture, 192–3
   historical overview, 24–5
   historical context, 188–9
   periodization, 2–3
   popular culture, 187–8
   studies, 3–7
   summary, 187–94
   transformation vs. decline, 1–3
   urbanism, 191–2
Data interpretation, 126–7
'Decline and fall' model, 41
Diet, 148
Diocletian, 15
Dust-veil (536–7), 11–12

Earthquakes
   Butrint, 93, 95
   Hierapolis, 114–15

Economy
   Amorium, 173–4
   amphorae, 175–80
   Arthur, Paul, 172
   Avar/Albanian Treasure, 168–9
   Balkans, 172–3
   buckles, 170–1
   Butrint, 173
   Byzantine Globular Amphorae, 177–8
   ceramic production, 171–80
   Charlemagne, 165–6
   coins, 158–60
   Constantinople, 162, 164–5
   copper objects, 169–70
   Coptic wares, 170
   Dark Age research, 28–9
   'elephant' silk, 165
   George the kommerkiarios, 167–8
   Günsenin type 1 amphorae, 179–80
   handmade ceramics, 172
   hard-to-track goods, 161–71
   Hodges, Richard, 156
   holy relics, 163
   imported metal wares, 168–9
   introduction, 155–8, 193
   jewellery, 171
   Jewish merchants, 167
   Kos, 176–7
   lamps, 174
   McCormick, Michael, 156, 181, 183
   Morrisson, Cécile, 159–60
   Nicopolis ad Istrum, 91–2
   prestige goods, 163
   production, 185–6
   Radhaniyya, 167
   red slip ware, 174–5
   regional exchange patterns, 179
   regional manufacture, 175–6
   Rotman, Youval, 166
   shipbuilding, 184–5
   shipping activity, 163–4
   shipwrecks, 181–5

silk and luxury cloth, 165–6
Slav slaves, 167–8
Slavery, 166–8
Synkellos, John, 163
Theodosian Harbour, 183
Tintagel, 162
trade, 161–2
trade and sea travel, 180–6
trade routes, 185–6
Vrap Treasure, 168–9
Ward-Perkins, Bryan, 156
Whitehouse, David, 156
widow Danelis, 164–5
Yassi Ada shipwreck, 181, 183
Yenikapı, 183–4
Egypt, 16
'Elephant' silk, 165
Elite culture
    cities, 82, 84
    generally, 192–3
Environment
    Anatolia, 149–50
    Balboura, 149
    Beyşehir Occupation Phase, 149–50
    Cappadocia, 152–4
    Haldon, John, 149–50
    introduction, 148–9
    pollen analysis, 149–53
    Sagalassos, 151–2
Epidemics, 11
Evidence. *See also* Cities; Coins; Glazed pottery; Hard-to-track goods; Red slip ware
    animal bone items, 78
    Butrint, 96–8
    ceramics, 43–9
    cloth, 78–9
    copper vessels, 75
    Coptic bowls, 74–6
    Corinth, 102–3
    glass, 72–3
    historical overview, 26
    introduction, 43
    ivory items, 78
    metalwork, 73–6
    opus sectile, 77
    stone items, 76–7
    textiles, 78–9
Farming, 148
Field surveys
    Aizanoi, 145–6
    Anatolia, 141–2
    Aphrodisias, 144–5
    Apollonia, 142
    artefacts, 126
    Avni, Gideon, 128
    Balkans, 129–30
    Central Anatolian Survey, 146
    churches, 147
    Crete, 140–1
    Cyprus, 131, 139–40
    data interpretation, 126–7
    diet, 148
    farming, 148
    Foss, Clive, 142–3
    Gortyn, 140–1
    Greece, 134–6
    introduction, 124–5
    Israel, 128
    Kaukana, 138–9
    large-scale surveys, 128–9
    limitations and criticisms, 131–4
    Lycia, 142–3
    Olympia, 135–6
    Orsi, Paolo, 138
    Pettigrew, Richard M., 132
    Pisidia, 144
    pottery, 146–7
    Pyrgouthi, 136–7
    Sagalassos, 144
    Sanders, Guy, 133
    settlement activity and density, 130–1
    Sicily, 138
    site classifications, 125–6
    Supersano, 137
    surface finds, 133
    survey methodologies, 127–8

Vrina Plain, 137–8
Vroom, Joanita, 132
Foss, Clive
  archaeology, 34
  cities, 87
  field surveys, 142–3

George the kommerkiarios, 167–8
Glass, 72–3
Glazed pottery
  Amorium, 59
  Anemurium, 53
  Armstrong, Pamela, 58–9
  Butrint, 59–60
  coarse wares, 61–2
  Constantinopolitan Glazed White Ware, 55–7
  Cypriot cooking pot, 64
  early antiquity, 54
  excavations, 55, 57, 59–60
  forms, 60–1
  Günsenin, Nergis, 58–9
  handmade wares, 62–5
  imports, 61
  Impressed White Wares, 57–8
  introduction, 52–3
  James, Liz, 54
  knowledge, 58–9
  manufacture, 55
  mould-made lamps, 61
  origins, 53
  polychrome ware, 58
  reasons for adoption, 54–5
  Slavic Ware, 62–3
  Ward-Perkins, Bryan, 65
  wheel-turned pots, 64
Gortyn, 140–1
Greece
  field surveys, 134–6
  historical overview, 17, 19
Günsenin, Nergis, 58–9
Günsenin type 1 amphorae, 179–80

Haldon, John, 149–50
Handmade wares, 62–5

Hard-to-track goods
  Avar/Albanian Treasure, 168–9
  buckles, 170–1
  Charlemagne, 165–6
  Constantinople, 162, 164–5
  copper objects, 169–70
  Coptic wares, 170
  'elephant' silk, 165
  George the kommerkiarios, 167–8
  holy relics, 163
  imported metal wares, 168–9
  introduction, 161
  jewellery, 171
  Jewish merchants, 167
  prestige goods, 163
  Radhaniyya, 167
  Rotman, Youval, 166
  shipping activity, 163–4
  silk and luxury cloth, 165–6
  Slav slaves, 167–8
  Slavery, 166–8
  Synkellos, John, 163
  Tintagel, 162
  trade, 161–2
  Vrap Treasure, 168–9
  widow Danelis, 164–5
Hellenistic era, 40
Hendy, Michael, 36
Heraclius I, 14–15
Hierapolis
  abandonment, 117
  churches and cathedrals, 116–18
  decline, 119
  earthquakes, 114–15
  evidence, 119–20
  excavations, 114, 119–20
  houses, 116–18
  introduction, 114
  Martyrium of St. Philip, 116
  organization and layout, 114–15
  plan, 115
  settlements, 118–19
Historians, 26–7

Historical overview. *See also*
    Archaeology
    Agrarian Life of the Middle Ages,
        29–30
    Alexandria, 16
    Amorian dynasty, 24
    Andréadès, 29
    Balkans, 9, 16–17
    Brentano, Lujo, 28
    Bulgars, 21, 23
    Bury's Cambridge Medieval
        History, 28
    Byzantine studies, 12–14
    caliphate, 18, 20
    Cambridge Economic History,
        29–30
    Constans II, 18
    Constantine IV, 18–19
    Constantine V, 21
    Constantinople, 10, 20
    cultural relativism, 38–9
    Dark Age research, 28–37
    Dark Ages, 24–5
    'decline and fall' model, 41
    Diocletian, 15
    dust-veil (536–7), 11–12
    economy, 28–9
    Egypt, 16
    eighth century map, 22
    epidemics, 11
    evidence, 26
    Greece, 17, 19
    Hellenistic era, 40
    Heraclius I, 14–15
    historians, 26–7
    historical works, 27–8
    introduction, 7
    Isaurian dynasty, 21
    Justin I, 7
    Justinian II, 20
    Justinianic Plague (542), 11
    language and literacy, 15, 25
    late antiquity, 39
    Leo III, 20–1
    Macedonian dynasty, 25–6
    Macri, 28
    Michael II, 23–4
    Michael III, 24
    Muslim empire, 18, 20
    Nicephorus I, 21
    Ostrogorsky, George, 28–30
    Pirenne, Henri, 28
    Pirenne Thesis, 30
    plagues, 11
    political economy, 28–9
    Roman Empire, 18
    Roman Empire (fall and decline),
        38–42
    Runciman, Steven, 30
    sixth century map, 8
    Slavs, 17
    Syncellus, George, 27
    Theophanes the Confessor, 27
    Theophilus, 24
    Theophylact, 26
    transformation model, 40
    Ward-Perkins, Bryan, 41
Historical works, 27–8
Historiographical and
    anthropological approaches,
    35
Holy relics, 163
Houses
    Hierapolis, 116–18
    Nicopolis ad Istrum, 88, 90

Imports
    glazed pottery, 61
    metal wares, 168–9
Impressed White Wares, 57–8
Isaurian dynasty, 21
Israel, 128
Ivory items, 78

James, Liz, 54
Jewellery, 171
Jewish merchants, 167
Justin I, 7
Justinian II, 20
Justinianic Plague (542), 11

Kaukana, 138–9
Kennedy, Hugh, 85–6
Kos, 176–7

Lamps
   ceramic production, 174
   mould-made lamps, 61
Language and literacy, 15, 25
Late Roman D Ware, 47–8, 51
Leo III, 20–1
Liebeschuetz, Wolf, 84–5
Luxury cloth, 165–6
Lycia, 142–3

Macedonian dynasty, 25–6
Macri, 28
Martyrium of St. Philip, 116
Marxist approaches, 35
Material evidence. *See* Evidence
McCormick, Michael
   economy, 156
   trade and sea travel, 181, 183
Merchant's House, 96
Metalwork
   copper vessels, 75
   Coptic bowls, 74–6
   introduction, 73–4
   summary, 76
   wares, 168–9
Michael II, 23–4
Michael III, 24
Monetization. *See* Coins
Morrisson, Cécile
   archaeology, 35
   economy, 159–60
Mould-made lamps, 61
Muslim empire
   cities, 86
   historical overview, 18, 20

New Archaeology, 36
Nicephorus I, 21
Nicopolis ad Istrum
   churches, 91
   destruction and abandonment, 90
   economy, 91–2
   fifth/sixth century re-founding, 90–1
   fire and invasion, 90
   houses, 88, 90
   introduction, 88
   plan of Nicopolis, 89

Olympia, 135–6
Opus sectile, 77
Orsi, Paolo, 138
Ostrogorsky, George, 28–30
Oxford Companion to Archaeology, 34

Painted pottery, 50
Patlagean, Évelyne, 35
Periodization
   archaeology, 37
   generally, 2–3
Pettigrew, Richard M., 132
Pirenne, Henri, 28
Pirenne Thesis, 30
Pisidia, 144
Plagues, 11
Political economy, 28–9
Pollen analysis, 149–53
PolychRome ware, 58
Popular culture, 187–8
Pottery. *See* Ceramic production; Ceramics; Glazed pottery; Red slip ware
Prestige goods, 163
Production, 185–6
Pyrgouthi, 136–7

Radhaniyya, 167
Red slip ware
   African red slip ware, 45–7
   ceramic production, 174–5
   characteristics and forms, 49–51
   Cypriot red slip ware, 47–8, 51
   generally, 45–52
   Late Roman D Ware, 47–8, 51
   other varieties, 48–9

painted pottery, 50
summary, 51–2
Regional exchange patterns, 179
Regional manufacture, 175–6
Religion. *See also* Churches and cathedrals
  generally, 83
  holy relics, 163
Research. *See* Dark Age research
Resettlement, 113
Roman Empire
  cities, 81–2
  historical overview, 18
Roman Empire (fall and decline)
  cities, 84–5
  cultural relativism, 38–9
  'decline and fall' model, 41
  generally, 38–42
  Hellenistic era, 40
  late antiquity, 39
  transformation model, 40
  Ward-Perkins, Bryan, 41
Rotman, Youval, 166
Runciman, Steven, 30
Rural areas. *See also* Countryside
  Corinth, 106, 108

Sacking
  Amorium (838–42), 112–13
  Corinth (584), 103–4
Sagalassos
  environment, 151–2
  field surveys, 144
Sanders, Guy, 133
Scranton, Robert L., 102–3
Sea travel and trade. *See also* Shipwrecks
  introduction, 180–1
  McCormick, Michael, 181, 183
  production, 185–6
  shipping activity, 163–4
  trade routes, 185–6
Settlements
  field surveys, 130–1
  Hierapolis, 118–19

Shipbuilding, 184–5
Shipping activity, 163–4
Shipwrecks
  introduction, 181, 183
  medieval shipwrecks, 182
  shipbuilding, 184–5
  Theodosian Harbour, 183
  Yassi Ada shipwreck, 181, 183
  Yenikapı, 183–4
  YK 3, 184
  YK 12, 184–5
Sicily, 138
Silk, 165–6
Site classifications, 125–6
Slavery
  hard-to-track goods, 166–8
  Slav slaves, 167–8
Slavs
  historical overview, 17
  slavery, 167–8
  Slavic Ware, 62–3
St. Elias the Younger, 97–8
St. Kodratos Church, 105
Stone items, 76–7
Supersano, 137
Surface finds, 133
Surveys. *See* Environment
Syncellus, George, 27
Synkellos, John, 163

Tabula Imperii Byzantinii, 36
Terra sigillata. *See* Red slip ware
Textiles
  evidence, 78–9
  silk, 165–6
Theodosian Harbour, 183
Theophanes the Confessor, 27
Theophilus, 24
Theophylact, 26
Tintagel, 162
Trade, 161–2
Trade and sea travel. *See also* Shipwrecks
  introduction, 180–1
  McCormick, Michael, 181, 183

production, 185–6
trade routes, 185–6
Transformation model, 40
Triconch Palace, 96
Turkey, 36–7

Urban decline, 84–6
Urbanism, 191–2. *See also* Cities

Vrap Treasure, 168–9
Vrina Plain, 137–8
Vroom, Joanita, 132

Walls
    Amorium, 109
    Butrint, 95

Ward-Perkins, Bryan
    economy, 156
    glazed pottery, 65
    Roman Empire (fall and decline), 41
Water, 112
Wheel-turned pots, 64
White wares. *See* Glazed pottery
Widow Danelis, 164–5
Written evidence. *See* Evidence; Hard-to-track goods

Yassi Ada shipwreck, 181, 183
Yenikapı, 183–4
YK 3, 184
YK 12, 184–5

www.ingramcontent.com/pod-product-compliance
Lightning Source LLC
Chambersburg PA
CBHW050137240426
43673CB00043B/1702